COMING
BACK
TO GOD

Resources by Patrick Morley

Coming Back to God
Coming Back to God audio
The Man in the Mirror
The Rest of Your Life
Devotions for Couples
Second Wind for the Second Half
Second Wind for the Second Half audio
The Seven Seasons of a Man's Life
Ten Secrets for the Man in the Mirror
Ten Secrets for the Man in the Mirror audio
Walking with Christ in the Details of Life
What Husbands Wish Their Wives Knew About Men
What Husbands Wish Their Wives Knew About Men audio

COMING BACK TO GOD

Answers to Men's Honest Questions and Doubts

PATRICK MORLEY

Author of *The Man in the Mirror*

ZondervanPublishingHouse

Grand Rapids, Michigan

A Division of HarperCollinsPublishers

Coming Back to God
Copyright © 2001 by Patrick M. Morley

Requests for information should be addressed to:

📖 ZondervanPublishingHouse
Grand Rapids, Michigan 49530

Library of Congress Cataloging-in-Publication Data

Morley, Patrick, 1948–
    Coming back to God : answers to men's honest questions and doubts /
Patrick Morley.
        p. cm.
    Includes bibliographical references.
    ISBN 0-310-23618-5
    1. Spiritual life—Christianity. 2. Christian life. I. Title.
BV4501.3 .M67 2001
248.8'42—dc21   00-054991

This edition is printed on acid-free paper.

Published in association with the literary agency of Wolgemuth & Associates,
Inc.

Interior design by Nancy Wilson

Printed in the United States of America

---

01 02 03 04 05 06 /❖ DC/ 10 9 8 7 6 5 4 3 2 1

To my brothers,
Pete and Bill

CONTENTS

INTRODUCTION

On my computer I have a library system with hundreds of research books. Sometimes after several complicated searches, the software will freeze up. I think it must be like overloading an electrical circuit with too many strings of Christmas lights or extension cords. Fortunately, the software developer anticipated this and built some grace into the system. There is a reset button I can push that lets me start over. This book is a "reset" button for men who want, or need, some grace to start over.

In business we have the helpful idea *Your system is perfectly designed to produce the result you are getting.* This book may be particularly useful to men who have become jaded about life in general and doubtful about Christianity in particular because of a bad experience or some faith-shaking book, fact, or professor and therefore have lived by a system that has led to a feeling of futility.

In this book I will show you the four systems by which men live. I will help you identify, explain, and correct the problem of futility. I will show you how to resolve the most common honest causes of doubt. Then I will explain how you can progress to a system that will satisfy your deepest yearnings for happiness, meaning, and purpose.

A word to women readers: The principles in a book on this topic, of course, apply to all people equally. While I have contextualized this work for men, I believe you will also find the book helpful, and I encourage you to read it.

PART ONE

SYSTEMS THAT END IN FUTILITY

THE SOUL'S SEARCH FOR REST

"Why Am I Still So Restless?"

Bill Reed heaved a sigh of relief as he left his office to meet his friend Jerry Steele for lunch.

Reed's morning had been filled with too many meetings, too many people, too many opinions, and too many decisions. It was all so exhausting.

The economy had been booming for several years. A strong market had catapulted his real estate development company into a manic state of *grow, grow, grow.* Bill Reed had hit it big, but he was tired.

Jerry Steele sells cars, the kind of cars that men stare at when sitting at a red light. Jerry had sold Bill Reed three of these power cars during the last six years. They first met during a charity golf tournament at their country club and hit it off later after a few more rounds together. Steele recognized Bill Reed as a good prospect for his luxury cars; Reed enjoyed the chance to play with a scratch golfer.

Earlier in the week Jerry had invited Bill to lunch. With all the pressures of the morning, Bill was really looking forward to seeing Jerry. Frankly, Jerry's call about lunch had surprised him. He'd purchased a new car from Jerry a mere six months ago. He figured Jerry must be out raising money for a charity or something like that. Whatever. Bill Reed genuinely liked Jerry Steele.

The waiter served them salads. During lunch they must have greeted a dozen friends who walked by their table. After they finished eating, their waiter brought coffee. Bill asked, "So, what's up, Jerry? Why did you want to get together today?"

For the next few minutes Jerry Steele shocked Bill Reed by sharing personal details about Jerry's own search for happiness. At first, Bill was extremely uncomfortable. *Why's this guy spilling his guts to me?* Bill thought. But Jerry seemed so genuine that Bill soon calmed down. Jerry explained how he had "found God" fifteen years ago, but without much impact. About five years ago, though, things had changed.

Jerry explained, "By the age of thirty-five I'd achieved most of the goals I had set for my life. Yet the more I achieved, the emptier I felt. I couldn't understand why I was still so restless, and I was really getting down about it. My chest was starting to feel like it was imploding—like one of those gas cans crunched up in a high school chemistry experiment.

"For several months I tried to hide my feelings from my wife. One Saturday morning, though, she asked me, 'What's wrong?' The next thing I knew, I had spent over an hour pouring out my frustrations to her. Together we decided to look for some encouragement—for someone to help me sort it out.

"A friend of mine had been after me for some time to have lunch with him. But I had avoided him because I knew what he'd want to talk about. God. I guess it was just my time, though, because the next thing I knew we were sitting together over lunch." Jerry went on to describe their conversation. Bill was drawn into the story. At the same time he was terrified of becoming too interested.

Though surprised and still somewhat uncomfortable about Jerry's revelations, Bill was touched by Jerry's story and genuinely happy for him.

On the drive back to his office, Bill reviewed Jerry's story in his mind. It was a terrific story, and for a brief moment Bill Reed envied Jerry Steele. Bill was more successful than Jerry, but not nearly as happy. All such thoughts were quickly washed away, though. One of his managers was waiting for him as he pulled into his private parking space.

"There's been an accident on the Granada job site." And with that, fate sucked Bill Reed back into "the real world."

For the rest of the day Bill continued privately to replay parts of Jerry's story. Jerry appeared to be at peace. That was the main reason Bill liked Jerry so much. Jerry Steele had something going for himself.

Tending to the Granada accident consumed most of Bill's afternoon. An exterior wall had collapsed during a storm. Fortunately, no one was injured. Then Bill worked late that night on a contract revision that "had" to go out the next day—a pattern he had slipped into over the last several months. On the way home he continued thinking about Jerry. He just couldn't let it rest.

It was 9:00 P.M. when he finally walked from the garage into his kitchen. His wife had left a note, pointing him to dinner in the microwave. She had gone to bed. He realized he had not seen any of his three children for three days. He was already feeling weary. Suddenly he felt bitter, too. The business he owned was starting to own him.

Three days later Bill was sitting in a staff meeting at about 10:00 A.M. His employees were droning on about "this" banal project and "that" trivial problem. He stifled a yawn. He thought, *You know, I need to do something for myself. I need to have some fun.* For about the twentieth time he remembered Jerry— happy Jerry. *I'll bet he's having fun.* Unexpectedly, he lurched forward in his chair. The current "talking head," midway through a sentence, fell silent and obediently waited for another signal from the boss.

"Mary!" Bill yelled to his secretary. "Can you come here for a moment?"

"Yes, Mr. Reed," said Mary, who through efficiency kept his schedule moving and through good looks kept his lenders smiling. Nothing was more important to Bill Reed than his schedule and his lenders.

"Would you give Jerry Steele a call and see if he's open for lunch today?" Maybe Jerry could cheer him up with more of his stories.

Mary returned moments later to say that Mr. Steele would meet him at their club at noon. Bill felt a small wave of joy—ironically, the same way he would feel if he had just closed a big deal. He realized there had not been much of that joy in his life for a long time.

A little before noon Bill got into his car and turned left out of the parking garage onto Central Boulevard. His car could find its own way to the club. He lunched there two or three days a week. His mind wandered. Bill suspected that Jerry Steele, a car salesman he barely knew, had put his finger on the problem he was facing.

Bill grew up believing that happiness and success were the same thing. If you achieve your goals, you get "happy." If you don't, well, then you're unhappy. But that wasn't the way it had worked out for Bill.

While still in college Bill decided that he didn't have to be the richest guy in town, but he still wanted to make a lot of money. That was "success" for him, and so he decided that's what would make him happy.

Bill competed on his college debate team, where he displayed a knack for persuading people. Several people told him he would be natural for a sales career. He found that thought agreeable and decided to look into it. Since he also wanted to make a lot of money, he decided to sell something big. As graduation approached he networked with several of his father's friends. They helped him zero in on commercial real estate.

The owner of the first real estate company where Bill interviewed told him, "You're too young. No one will do business with you until you have some experience." Many lesser men would have absorbed that as a fatal blow. Instead, this comment only motivated Bill to prove the man wrong.

Eventually, Bill was introduced to a top salesman at one of the city's most respected commercial real estate agencies, who told him, "Let's get together sometime." This proved to be easier said than done. After several persistent phone calls, though, Bill finally arranged an appointment.

They had barely seated themselves when Randy Wood, the salesman, said, "You know, I can't keep up with all the deals I've got going. Why don't you come aboard as my assistant? You do some of the background and research work that I'm having a hard time getting done. In exchange, I'll teach you how to sell real estate. What do you say?"

Bill almost leaped on top of the desk, but he restrained himself and said, "Well . . . yes! Of course I'll do it." So began an incredible five-year "partnership" and learning curve. Bill did the grunt work, but in the process he learned the ins and outs of commercial real estate like few others in his city ever had. And the money started to flow too. He loved looking at the growing balance on his monthly bank statement.

After five years of rustling up deals for Randy Wood, Bill hung up his own shingle. First-year sales were astounding. For the second year he set a goal to move 20 percent more property than he did the first year. He worked hard to make it happen. When he ran the final tally, second-year sales were up a whopping 83 percent! A wave of euphoria swept over him. Bill Reed was going to be somebody. He bought himself a new platinum watch as a reward. But two weeks later the novelty wore off. So Bill set a new goal.

This process became his custom. Set a goal. Work hard. Meet the goal. Euphoria. Two weeks go by. Novelty wears off. Have to set a new goal. Each new goal he set, of course, had to be bigger, brighter, and shinier than the previous goal. After a decade of repeating this cycle, the whole success process had become repetitive and boring. The goals reached had become a string of hollow achievements—more frustration than fulfillment. He felt like a hamster spinning in a wheel. He couldn't help but wonder, *Surely there's more to life than this endless repetition of accumulating more and more?*

UNEXPECTED QUESTIONS

One day in Oxford, England, I was walking between two buildings that captured sound like the acoustics of an old European cathedral. This had not gone unnoticed by a street musician who was playing his guitar and singing for pocket change. Chills went up and down my spine as I walked by and heard his lyrics reverberating off the buildings:

> So this is what it feels like to be lonely,
> So this is what it feels like to be small,
> So this is what it feels like to realize,
> my work doesn't matter at all.

His words capture the feelings of a man who has run his experiment—perhaps successfully, perhaps not—and is asking, "Does anybody care?"

Many men feel as though their lives are futile, not because they didn't get what they wanted, but because they did. One man struggling with futility put it this way: "If I had known how empty I would end up feeling, I wouldn't have done it that way."

Here is a common complaint. A man will say, "After all I've been through, after all I've achieved, after surviving several major crises, after all the obstacles I've overcome, after all the work I've put into this life of mine, after enjoying some success, after getting the spouse that I wanted, after getting the children that I assumed would bring me joy, after all of this, why am I still so restless?"

Another man, Warren, at an age when most men are playing with grandchildren, doesn't know where his ex-wife is living, and his son, much to Warren's disappointment, cannot keep a job.

Even when we get what we want, it often doesn't make us happy. As Jerry said, "I got what I wanted, but it's not enough." I think our real estate developer, Bill Reed, would agree.

These few illustrations point to a handful of unexpected questions that many people find themselves struggling to answer:

- Why am I still so restless?
- Why do I feel empty?
- Why do I feel lonely?
- Where can I go for relief?

If the answers were easy, everyone would have them. Diagnosing the disease is no problem, but the cure is elusive. And older doesn't necessarily make wiser. As the Danish philosopher Søren Kierkegaard once wrote, "The wisdom of the years is confusing."[1]

If these are some of the questions you are attempting to answer, then it is for you that I've written this book. I want you to be happy. The great philosopher Blaise Pascal wrote these timeless words: "Despite these afflictions man wants to be happy, only wants to be happy, and cannot help wanting to be happy."[2]

YOUR "SYSTEM"

No one who ends up feeling empty inside would have let it happen if they had seen it coming. So how does it happen?

America is great because our economic system gives us the freedom to pursue our own ideas. This is important, because ideas are more powerful than labor. Ideas set forces into motion that cannot be contained. For example, Bill Gates pronounced his idea of "a computer on every desk and in every home"—an idea that has animated Microsoft since its inception. By thought, more than by sweat, you can achieve nearly anything to which you set your mind.

This is also true in our private lives. The "collection" of ideas we embrace forms a *system* that guides our choices and, hence, shapes the course of our future. Here's the problem: If the "system" you build will not work, you will not know it doesn't work for ten or twenty years. By then the damage is done, and you will have given the best years of your life to a system that has failed you.

However, this failure usually comes at a point when you can ill afford to "drop out" or make sweeping changes. The uncontainable forces your system set in motion have blown you far off course into a sea of stressful obligations. I asked a friend, "How are you doing?" He said, "Friday night I got back into my office at 6:00 P.M. I had 148 e-mails and 45 voice mails. I couldn't go home until I returned the priority voice mails. Now, what was your question?"

Here's the catch: You can get all you want in this world, but only that. And that is not enough to make you happy. What makes it even worse is that you must pretend you are happy.

As tennis superstar Andre Agassi said, "Without the cake the icing sucks." I realize this is indelicate, and I don't mean to offend anyone's sensibilities, but this is the way many people think these days, and it does capture the intangible pain of emptiness many are feeling.

PERFECTLY DESIGNED THAT WAY

In business we have the useful idea, "Your system is perfectly designed to produce the result you are getting."

For example, if you manufacture cars and every third car that rolls off the assembly line is missing a front right fender, you can be certain that your system is perfectly designed to produce that result. Or if you sell insurance and the person in the office next to you consistently sells twice as much as you, his or her system is perfectly designed to produce that result. Unfortunately, your system is perfectly designed to sell the lesser amount.

There are many types of systems: banking systems, solar systems, justice systems, civil defense systems, transportation systems, data processing systems, national defense systems, welfare systems, farming systems, distribution systems, heating and air condition-ing systems, digestive systems, circulatory systems. There are also belief systems.

We can say that we each have a belief system that is perfectly designed to produce the result we are getting.[3] A good synonym for belief system would be *worldview*. So we could also say: We each have a worldview that is perfectly designed to produce the result we are getting. The difference between Adolf Hitler and Mother Teresa comes to mind.

Systems are good. They provide order, efficiency, and predictable results. But once the wrong system is designed, the wrong result is inevitable. Someone who is feeling puny about life—whether that feeling is emptiness or restlessness—has a "systems" problem. Their system is perfectly designed to produce the result they are getting—even though it's not what they want. Their souls are searching for rest.

What is the problem we need to solve? That I will take up in the next chapter.

THE FEELING OF FUTILITY

"There Must Be More"

The first time Sarah saw Bill in class she found herself attracted. They sat next to each other, and from the way Bill answered questions in class, she knew he was a sharp guy with good character.

Character was especially important to Sarah because of her dad. He was a respected banker who lifted up integrity as the highest virtue a person can have. All her life she had dreamed of a marriage like the one her parents had. Besides, her father had doted on her mom, and Sarah wanted a man who would do the same.

When they first began dating, Bill had been so attentive. Sarah's every interest had captivated Bill. Boy, had that changed!

What Sarah didn't understand (Bill either, for that matter) was that Bill viewed courtship in the same way he viewed everything else: It was a mission. He had been a man on a mission—to win Sarah's love and her hand in marriage. Once the mission was accomplished, though, he quickly moved on to the next challenge.

Meanwhile, Sarah was stunned at how quickly Bill had changed his colors. She tried to talk to him about it. She said, "I thought we were going to build a life together." He always assured her that this was the case, but he just needed to get the business on a solid footing.

"Once I get a few important deals done, then I can back off. Just a few more months, baby, I promise. Then we'll concentrate on us. I promise. You'll see."

This went on for three years, Bill always assuring her that he'd be right there—where he promised he'd be. But his deals didn't come together as easily as he hoped they would, and he often worked weekends to keep his growing business on an even keel.

Three years into their marriage everything changed. Sarah became pregnant. Little Brent weighed in at seven pounds three ounces and measured twenty-one inches. For a few weeks Bill was a changed man. He fussed over Brent. He loved that baby so much. Sarah's heart surged with hope that little Brent was, after all, the answer to all her concerns.

About two months later a big deal Bill had been working on for nearly a year started to unravel. The out-of-town buyer wouldn't return his calls. If this deal fell through, Bill didn't know whether or not he could survive. He had nearly bet the whole farm on this one deal. Bill started having trouble sleeping. He'd wake up at 4:00 A.M. and wouldn't be able to get back to sleep. His head would spin as he worried about all the possible disasters, none of which, of course, he could do anything about as he lay there in bed. So, he would get up, chug several cups of coffee, and go into the office early and do more worrying there. Once the phones started ringing and he could at least "do" something, he felt some relief.

Relief. That was it in a nutshell, really. Bill wanted some relief. Over the course of fifteen years this cycle had become Bill's pattern. He worked on big deals, had too much riding on the success of any one project, then endured severe worry, which led in turn to overwork. That, of course, meant neglecting Sarah, Brent, and the next arrivals, Jonathan and Josh.

In his heart Bill always believed he was one deal away from being able to relax and spend more time with his family. He also was addicted to the thrill of the deal. The deals won this tug-of-war, and he never quite got around to spending more time with his wife and kids.

Meanwhile, Sarah had grown tired of Bill's promises. On at least six occasions Sarah had asked Bill when they were going to build the life together they had dreamed about late into the night, when they were enraptured with each other many years ago. Bill continued to fool himself—but not her—as he said, "Baby, I know I promised we'd build a life together, and we will. But it's just taking longer than I thought it would to get myself established. But I can see the light at the end of the tunnel, honey."

In the early years of their marriage Sarah believed Bill, but by the ten-year mark she realized that Bill was more committed to his career than to his family. One day a thought hit her like a ton of bricks: *Bill will never change.*

Sarah felt betrayed. She began to brood on this thought; she turned it over and over in her heart. She stopped talking to Bill about their future. Something inside Sarah had died.

A group of women in Bill and Sarah's neighborhood had been meeting for several years. On many occasions Sarah had been invited to attend. She had gone once, but they had talked about the Bible, and frankly, though she was "religious" and believed in God, she was embarrassed because she couldn't find the passages they were reading.

Still, there was something very attractive about these five women. When Sarah bumped into them at the grocery store, the country club, or the annual block party, she was always taken aback by their apparent joy. This was a mystery to her, because she knew that one woman's husband had had an affair and divorced her, leaving her with four children under the age of eight. Another woman had a child with Down's syndrome. Still another was recovering from breast cancer.

About once a year one of these women would again ask her if she would like to join them. For several weeks she had been secretly wishing they would invite her now. More than anything, Sarah too needed some relief from the pain of her shattered dreams. She was thinking about divorcing Bill.

Jerry Steele's wife, Diane, was part of the group. Actually, Diane was the leader of the group. Sarah had no idea that Bill and Jerry had been talking about spiritual things, but Jerry and Diane talked about everything. Diane had been waiting for an opportunity to get to know Sarah better.

It wasn't too many days later that Sarah and Diane ran into each other at a Little League game. Diane said, "Sarah, I've been thinking about you lately. Would you like to have lunch sometime?" Sarah's heart leaped into her throat, because she felt so attracted to this "together" woman. She said, "I'd love to." The next morning she prayed that Diane would have some secret recipe that would save her marriage. Little did she know.

A few days later Diane and Sarah met at a popular tearoom and took a booth near the back. Sarah started the conversation by dropping a bombshell. "I've decided to leave Bill," she said matter-of-factly.

For the next two hours Diane and Sarah retraced the entire story of Sarah's marriage to Bill and where it had gotten off track, and Sarah's resulting disillusionment and loss of hope. Toward the end of the conversation Diane suggested that Sarah could find the strength to go on by inviting Jesus Christ into her life.

"But I'm already a Christian," Sarah protested. "I've been religious all my life. I even take the kids and go to church when Bill stays home." She resented the suggestion that she might not be a Christian.

Diane continued, "Sarah, I know you have a good heart. I know you are a religious person. But I'm not talking about that. Haven't you ever felt like there must be more?"

"Well, yes, I suppose I have," Sarah conceded.

Diane said, "I know you are committed to a set of Christian values. What I'm talking about is something entirely different from Christian behavior. It's even different from having the correct information about God. What I'm talking about is a commitment to a Person—Jesus Christ."

"What difference does it make whether we are committed to a set of values or to a Person? How could that help my marriage?" Sarah asked.

"Sarah, the plain truth is that your marriage may or may not work out. The only person you can work with, though, is yourself. If you bring your own life into a right relationship with God, then you'll be okay, no matter what happens. The first issue is your own salvation and life."

"I think I'm beginning to see what you mean," said Sarah.

THE THIRD FORCE

What is the problem people like Bill and Sarah are trying to solve? It is the sting of futility. The Christian system claims to solve a number of problems, but perhaps the most sharply felt problem it remedies is the feeling that life is futile.

Suppose a man went fishing, cast his rod, forgot to keep his thumb on the line, and ended up with a big knot of fishing line that took fifteen minutes to unsnarl. This is not a good, but neither is it an evil. It is a futility.

If you had a flat tire, ran out of gas, got stuck in a forty-five-minute traffic delay, or lost a valued customer to a competitor, you would not say, "This is evil." These disappointments are not evil things, but they do seem pretty pointless.

We are all aware that in the world we experience the forces of good and evil. Some things are distinctly good and some things are distinctly evil. There is, however, a *third force* at work in the world—futility, or that which seems like a waste. There are many things which happen to us that are not evil as such, yet leave us wondering, "What was that all about?" They are futile. Synonyms for *futility* include words like *meaninglessness, vanity, frustration,* and *insignificance.*

Other examples are more serious. At the age of thirty-one Alan has twenty-four people reporting to him. Yet he says, "I'm just not happy." He finds it hard to see how his work is important.

Sam has been passed over several times for management—his dream job. At his present age he is too old to be considered again.

Elliot came up to speak to me after a seminar I had taught and said, "You know that plaque you were talking about in your message—the one the salesman worked so hard to get? That's me. Two weeks ago I received a plaque for being the top salesman in my company. But it just doesn't satisfy. There is no purpose. It didn't mean anything. What's the use?" There were tears in his eyes.

Both success and failure can lead to the same result. We can work hard and achieve a goal that leaves us wondering, *What's the point?* Or on another occasion we can fail to achieve a goal that leaves us thinking, *Why bother?*

Futility is life not turning out the way you planned it, not necessarily because some evil befell you but simply because life is so messy. Perhaps one of the most pervasive problems we face is futility.

Our systems are perfectly designed to produce the result we get—and that includes futility. This was certainly the case with King Solomon.

SOLOMON'S PROJECT

Among the talented men of history, few stand in the league of Solomon. He was the richest, most powerful, most respected leader of his era. He was a man able to have whatever he wanted, whenever he wanted it. He lived at a level of luxury unparalleled in his day.

Solomon pursued every possible earthly avenue to find meaning and happiness. It became his passionate mission. He wrote, "I wanted to see what was worthwhile for men to do under heaven during the few days of their lives."[1] He was interested in the question "What does a man gain for all his toil?"[2] Because of his virtually unlimited resources Solomon had opportunities few of us will ever have. He amassed a formidable résumé in business, education, literary achievements, science, massive real estate developments, military power, and wealth accumulation. He also indulged his senses with a wide array of worldly pleasures.

After decades of achievement Solomon still found happiness elusive. Every gift was an empty box. He wrote these stirring words:

I denied myself nothing my eyes desired;
  I refused my heart no pleasure.
My heart took delight in all my work,
  and this was the reward for all my labor.
Yet when I surveyed all that my hands had done
  and what I had toiled to achieve,
everything was meaningless, a chasing after the wind;
  nothing was gained under the sun....
So I hated life....[3]

Solomon's system was perfectly designed to produce futility. We'll come back to Solomon in a later chapter. For now, though, let's ponder why Solomon's system failed him.

WHY SYSTEMS BREAK DOWN

A lot of people are living with a system they built ten or twenty years ago. Their theory is not working out. Their whole paradigm seems to be breaking up. They are not happy campers.

Why do our systems not work out? Let me suggest a reason. Often we form our system when we are young and immature. It seems we have to make many of our most important decisions at an age when we are the least prepared to make them wisely. It can then take many years before we see how empty or useless that system is.

Actor Ben Affleck captured the futility of a young man who realizes his system isn't working when he said, "The reason I'm single is that I wouldn't want to be with anybody right now who would be willing to be with me."[4]

Thomas Kuhn, author of *The Structure of Scientific Revolutions*, is the guru of why systems come and go. He makes a wonderfully transferable insight we can apply to our personal systems. Simply stated, one man develops his system, or paradigm. After a while, anomalies start to appear. A few of these can be explained—or explained away. However, with the passage of time the anomalies keep adding up and become increasingly difficult to fit into the old system. Eventually the whole theory of the system comes under suspicion. Suddenly someone proposes a new system (or theory), which solves the problems of the existing system. Because it seems to be good, it is enthusiastically embraced, until after a while it too has anomalies that begin to appear. And so the cycle repeats.

This is exactly what happens to belief systems, or worldviews. I teach a Bible study to about 150 men on Friday mornings in Orlando. Our single largest category of weekly visitors are men who have made some type of commitment to God at a point in their lives. But for a decade or two they have lived by a different system—a system of their own design (often these men do not stop professing a commitment to God). But after many years the wheels start coming off the wagon, and they realize they need to get to, or back to, a biblically based Christianity (but I'm starting to get ahead of myself).

I always tell our first-time visitors that they could just as easily have attended one of a dozen other meetings taking place around Orlando where interesting philosophies of life are being discussed. The problem is that these philosophies are systems that will soon be replaced by new systems that explain all the anomalies the current systems cannot explain. The current followers will soon be disillusioned to learn they have believed what was not true, and they will be bitterly disappointed as well to have likely given the best years of their lives to an idea that didn't work.

Solomon's system broke down because he still felt empty inside, even after getting everything he ever wanted. It is the same today.

If a man's system is not working, he shouldn't pretend it is. Our first choice would be not to make a mistake at all, but if we do, let's at least not pretend we didn't err. No matter how far one has traveled down a wrong road, the only solution is to turn back.

USELESS OR CONFUSING?

A man thirsty for relief from futility must decide whether his condition is hopeless or merely confusing.

There are two types of futility. *Futility—Type One* ends with the thought *This is all there is.* It expresses the loss of all hope. If God cannot be known or does not exist, then life is hopeless: "Let's feast and get drunk, for tomorrow we die." After looking at the human condition, the French existentialist Jean-Paul Sartre concluded there was no God and that life was hopeless: "Man is an empty bubble with nothing at the center. Man commits himself, draws his portrait, and that's all there is. Life is a useless passion."[5]

Is it true that life is a useless passion—that man is nothing? Indeed, the nature of life can be tragic and futile. Why? Because man has a problem. He is alienated from God. However, man is not nothing. Christian thinker Francis Schaeffer explained it this way:

> The Bible teaches that, though man is lost, he is not nothing. Man is lost because he is separated from God, his true reference point, by true moral guilt. But he will never be nothing. There lies the horror of his lostness. For man to be lost, in all his uniqueness and wonder, is tragic.[6]

Futility—Type Two ends with the thought *There must be more.* A man is confused but feels intuitively that he has been made for a reason—he knows that he is *not* nothing. His futility is that he has not yet discovered what that reason is.

Sartre was correct that life is filled with anguish, abandonment, and despair. Sartre's system does accurately describe the feelings of the human lot but fails to understand the reasons why. As we will see, he was wrong to say that's all there is. There is hope.

In the next chapter I'll begin looking at the different systems by which people live and how they can derail.

THE WORLDLY SYSTEM

"I Can't Take It Anymore"

Bill pulled into the parking lot at the club and went inside. Jerry was already seated, waiting for him.

They plowed through the usual "buddy, buddy" chitchat, but about halfway through their salads Bill said, "Jerry, I really resonated with what you said the other day about meeting goals and then later feeling empty again. I'm also real interested in what you had to say about finding God and all that. I'd like to talk with you about it some more."

"Sure, Bill, I'd love to. But first let me ask you something. Would you mind taking a few minutes and telling me about your own experience with God in the past?"

"Well, okay then," Bill said haltingly, as a wave of second thoughts rushed through his bloodstream.

Bill weighed carefully just how honest he ought to be. He decided to be direct, and so he plunged in. "Jerry, the plain truth is that I'm bored to tears with my life.

"You know, I go to church—the same one I grew up in. But to be honest, I guess I've been hanging around the fringes of church for most of my adult life. Religion just didn't seem to 'take' for me. It sure hasn't done for me what it's done for you or, for that matter, a number of other guys in my church. Sometimes I envy those guys, but mostly I think they're a bit odd—too zealous or something. It's like they're not really in touch with reality.

"I was a lot more active when Sarah and I first married. We met on a blind date when I was a senior in college. One of my fraternity brothers fixed us up."

Bill went on to explain that Sarah had always been a very religious person. But as his business had grown, church involvement had dropped away. Frankly, Sunday mornings were a good time to catch up on sleep. And when he did get up early, he really enjoyed lounging around and reading the Sunday paper. Now, though, his kids were starting to ask questions about God, life, and heaven, and Bill didn't really know how to answer them.

"You know, Jerry, since our lunch the other day I've been thinking. I believe I may have a real problem here. I'm an expert at developing buildings because I've studied it. But I just realized that I've never spent any serious time thinking or studying about God. In fact, I've blamed God for a lot of my problems. Then yesterday I think I had an epiphany. I realized I only know enough about God to be disappointed with him."

Jerry looked into Bill's eyes for so long before speaking that it made Bill feel uncomfortable. Finally, to Bill's relief, Jerry spoke.

"Bill, here's the deal. You've been pursuing happiness, and it has eluded you. Right?"

"Well, basically, yes. That's right."

"There is a good reason why that's happened. Do you want me to tell you what it is?"

Uh oh, thought Bill. *Here it comes. I'm not sure I'm ready for this. But, hey, what have I got to lose. I'm already miserable. How much worse could this make it?* "Yes," he said. "Yes, I do."

"Did you know that I row for exercise?" Jerry asked.

"No, I didn't. What do you mean? Like on a rowing machine? Do they have one here at the club?" Bill responded.

"No, I mean I have a one-man rowing scull, and three days a week I row on our lake for about thirty minutes," Jerry continued.

"That's great," said Bill, not knowing exactly what to say.

"I get started at first light and time it so I get back to my dock just about the time the sun rises," said Jerry. "It's always a beautiful sight.

"So one day I'm feeling like everything seems so futile and meaningless—like I'm on a sinking ship. I decide to go for a row. Just as I pull away from shore I look down and see a chameleon sitting on the deck of my boat staring at me. By then we were already a few hundred feet from shore. My scull is bouncing every which way, and this little guy is really getting jostled around.

"I feel sorry for him. I mean, the night before he obviously thought he had found a nice comfortable place to bed down. Then I come along, flip the boat over, plop it in the water, and the next thing he knows, he's on the sea cruise from hell.

"Anyway, I look at this little guy, and you can tell he's confused and shaken. I'm thinking, *I know how you feel, little fella.* So I decided to try to help him out. I started talking to him—real soft at first, because I didn't want to scare him out of his wits.

"'Hey there, little buddy,' I said. 'I know you must wonder, *What in the world is going on!* I'd be terrified, too, if I were you. Listen, guy, I want you to hang on and not get scared. I don't want you to go and do anything foolish, like jump into the water. Just hang on, and I'll save you. I'll get you safely back to shore, but you've got to trust me. If you don't trust me, if you try to save yourself, you're going to end up as fish food. But you're going to have to be patient because it's going to be a while.'

"You could tell he was nervous. He just kept looking up at me. I didn't know what to do, so every couple of minutes I said something to keep him from doing something stupid. About halfway back to shore the chameleon took a step or two toward the side. I said to him, 'Don't do it, little guy. You're going to make it if you just don't give up. We're almost there. Don't quit now. You've almost survived. Relax, fella. Take deep breaths.'

"That seemed to work. But by then he'd moved away from the middle of the deck—it's only sixteen inches wide anyway—and crawled to within a couple of inches of the side. I could just tell what he was thinking: *Should I trust this guy or should I try to save myself?* I couldn't blame him one bit. On his scale, the boat was bobbing around like a dinghy in a typhoon. He kept glancing back and forth between me and the water. So I stepped up my encouragement.

"'Okay, guy, we are really close now.' Shore was only a few hundred feet away. I tried to reassure him, so I said, 'Listen, little fella, haven't I done what I said I would do? You're almost home. Now is not the time to give up. Hang on for a few more minutes, and I'll be able to put you safely back on solid ground.' I was starting to feel pretty good about myself. I was doing a good deed.

"The chameleon kept looking at me, then glancing over the side of the boat. I kept coaxing him to be patient. He looked up at me one more time—and then disappeared into the water. I felt so deflated. We only had a hundred yards to go.

"Bill, that's the story of my life. Every man at a point finds himself on a confusing journey, unable to explain how or why he ended up where he is, not knowing where he's going or how long it will take, wondering if he will be saved or if he will perish. Make sense?"

Bill reflected on what Jerry was saying. *I can sure identify. Sometimes I'd like to jump ship myself.*

"You know, Jerry," Bill responded after a moment's silence, "I'm starting to get the picture. I was blessed with a great wife, great kids, and a wonderful business. But my wife seems distant, I'm missing it with my kids, and the business, for all its gains, is boring me to death. It *is* confusing. I sure know success has not made me happy. But how does it work? I mean, I believe in God. I'm not the most religious guy in the world, but I believe. I may not be the most faithful churchgoer in the world, but I don't chafe against it. I'm willing, but there must be something I just don't get.

"Jerry," he said. "I want to come back to God. What do I need to do?"

In the weeks that followed, Sarah and Bill became aware that they both had been on a spiritual track that was leading them back to God. They began to encounter God in a way they had never experienced before. Over the next year a lot of tears were shed—the wounds were deep—but with God's help, Sarah began to think that maybe the marriage could work after all. Jerry invited Bill to join a small group of men that met in the locker room at the club once a week. There Bill realized that Christianity claimed to answer the most difficult questions about life, meaning, and purpose. One morning he admitted, "I guess I need a new paradigm."

THE "SYSTEMS" OF THE SOUL

Our lives vacillate between joy and sorrow, sickness and health, success and sadness. Yet no matter how much joy, health, and success a man finds, Solomon's futility always overtakes that man in the end. There are no exceptions; it is an iron law. Men have therefore always devised systems to explain and cope with their futility.

When reading the literature on life and spirituality, a pattern of four different "systems" emerges—*worldly, moral, religious,* and *Christian* (see endnote for additional detail).[1] Each of these systems has "goods," each contains truth, and each has wonderful people as disciples. Nevertheless, there is a ladder of progress as systems break down and are replaced. Since every system has some good to it and contains some truth, it seems natural that after a man has lived by a system for ten or twenty years and it has failed, he would blow away the chaff but carry the remaining kernels of good and truth into his new system. In other words, each new system builds on the strengths of the system it leaves behind. Of course, a man can also lapse and fall backward, for example, from a religious system into a worldly system.

Suppose an ambitious young man who has just completed college wants to "strike it rich" and thus adopts a worldly system. Suppose he leads that worldly life for ten years. He comes to realize that this dog won't hunt. Over the course of ten years, though, he has found joy whenever he helped other people. Then he reads a book like *Tuesdays with Morrie,* written by Morrie Schwartz's disciple, Mitch Albom. He finds that the values of Morrie, an evangelist for the gospel of "try to be a better person and love others," resonates with his spirit. It is an uplifting book with a lot of truth and good in it. It is a book about the *moral* system. So the young man adopts the moral system.

Another fifteen years peel off the calendar, and even though he can say, "I tried to do the right thing by every person I met," he still experiences a vacuum in his soul for peace. One day he is sitting alone on the beach in contemplation. He reviews his life "so far" and recognizes a spiritual void. He watches the sun set and the evening sky turn dark. As the stars appear he is overwhelmed by the grandeur of the heavens. He has a religious experience.

In the weeks ahead he begins attending a church. He finds one that emphasizes the values he still believes to be true. This church preaches a gospel of love and social responsibility. He has always thought that these values were important, so he embraces a *religious* system. Another ten years fly by, and he asks himself, *Why am I still so restless?* It occurs to him that there were elements of truth in each system he tried, and elements of truth in the religious system he has now embraced, but somehow it still doesn't satisfy. He feels as though he has been robbed of the best years of his life.

ALL SYSTEMS HAVE EVANGELISTS

We are attracted to our systems by people we respect—people we might call *evangelists.* All systems have evangelists who are seeking disciples. It makes sense. If you believe in something strongly enough, you seek converts, whether it's Mothers Against Drunk Driving or coin collecting.

Often people are attracted not so much by the truth of the system as by the charisma of the evangelist. Madonna and Hugh Hefner have their followers, just as does the Dalai Lama of Tibet. To their followers they each have the ring of authenticity.

Why is Billy Graham so admired? Even though some people may not necessarily believe what he believes, they are utterly convinced that *he* believes what he believes. There is no falsehood in him. There is a one-to-one correlation between what he says and how he lives. This is authenticity; this is integrity. (On the other hand, people are sometimes turned off by a system because its strongest proponents are polemical and harsh. Certain televangelists come to mind.)

All belief systems are trying to solve the same problem: "At the end of the day, after I got what I wanted (or didn't), what do I do with the futility of it all? Do I anesthetize the pain, give something back to the world, try to be a better person, love more, seek spiritual relief—which is it?"

ALL SYSTEMS HAVE TRUTH

All systems contain traces of truth. No man would adopt a belief system unless he honestly believed it addressed the problem he was trying to solve. The more "true" the system seems, the more followers its evangelists will attract. Which counterfeit bill makes it successfully into circulation? Isn't it the one that looks most like the real thing? We would never intentionally adopt a system that wasn't the real thing, yet just as people unwittingly accept counterfeit bills for the real things, we often adopt systems that don't deliver because they *can't* deliver—they're not true. As one of my professors was fond of saying, "It takes a lot of truth to float an error."

As you read the explanations of these systems in this chapter and the ones that follow, you may want to consider which system best describes the one you've adopted. For the rest of this chapter we will briefly examine the worldly system.

THE WORLDLY SYSTEM

Only a tiny fraction of people wake up in the morning planning to carry out an evil deed; the rest of us are trying to raise families, be good neighbors, show some civic pride, earn a decent living, and enjoy a few pleasures.

As has already been seen in Bill Reed's life, we pursue our lives out of a system, or worldview, that is perfectly designed to produce the result we are getting.

The level where we all start—the "default" system, so to speak—is the worldly system.

The worldly system changes with each generation. Boomers from the 1960s have a different worldly system from Gen Xers. What they share in common, however, is a core value of "getting the most out of life." For some that means leaving the world a better place; for others it means getting the maximum pleasure with the minimum pain. These two approaches are in reality not so different. Writer C. S. Lewis put it this way:

> Every age has its own outlook. . . . All contemporary writers share to some extent the contemporary outlook—even those, like myself, who seem most opposed to it. Nothing strikes me more when I read the controversies of past ages than the fact that both sides were usually assuming without question a good deal which we should now absolutely deny. They thought that they were as completely opposed as two sides could be, but in fact they were all the time secretly united— united *with* each other and *against* earlier and later ages—by a great mass of common assumptions.[2]

Every system has its gods. In the worldly system athletes are our "living" gods, and CEOs have become our high priests. Pleasure, no doubt, is also a favorite god. Money, too.

One day a man was talking to a college student who was about to graduate. "What's your next step?" the man asked.

"Law school," he answered.

"So, then, you're going to change the world!" said the man.

"No, I'm going to make some money," said the young man.

The older man replied, "Ah, you're going to let the world change you."

The worldly person is looking for diversions. Pascal said, "They spend all day chasing a hare that they would not have wanted to buy."[3]

Perhaps a man still thinks pleasure is the highest good. Or perhaps, after realizing it is not, a man wants to anesthetize his futility. These unbelievers' motto is "Let's enjoy life while we can, for tomorrow we die."

Some worldly people are crass pagans who would disgust even radio personality Howard Stern, but most are refined businesspeople who scurry around like industrious ants building empires in the sand. They throw themselves into their work—or get sucked in. Mike, a lawyer, said, "The law is like a jealous woman. It will suck you in. I used to work nights and weekends. Most of [the other lawyers] still do."

The worldly man sees no meaning beyond the physical realm. He is not yet looking for rest for his soul. He is still enamored with the idea of leaving his mark. He is not asking any questions for which Christianity is the answer.

The biblical language is that he is conformed to the pattern of this world,[4] not concerned with doing right, and living according to the desires of the flesh (or sinful nature).[5] He is a slave to his passions.

We all experience seasons of discouragement and futility. There are watersheds, though, when our worldly system no longer works. It has produced too many anomalies. It is a system doomed to fail. When this system crashes, the worldly person is filled with anguish and despair. He asks, "Why is my marriage breaking apart?" and a dozen other questions just like it.

Twenty adult years (or fewer) into the worldly system leave most people weary, confused, and bored. That was what Solomon found after devoting his entire adult life to a search for meaning in the worldly system. He had all the pleasure he could handle but still found no lasting joy in it.

Like Solomon, these people call out, "Meaningless, meaningless, everything is meaningless, a chasing after the wind." They become ashamed of the things that used to make them proud. They cry out and, if they come to their senses, take (per Kierkegaard) "a leap" into the moral system.

The Leap: "I can't take it anymore."

THE MORAL SYSTEM
"I Can't Fake It Anymore"

Mary divorced Don because he was unfaithful, but she had never been unpleasant about it. If anything, she killed him with kindness, which only made him feel that much more rotten.

Don was not a scoundrel. He hadn't set out to fail. He didn't wake up one day and think, *Well, I wonder what I can do to ruin my life today.* Rather, his fall followed on the heels of thousands of small daily choices he made in his private thoughts over the course of several years.

It all started the day after he and Mary moved into their first home, when he fixed the blinds just right so he could watch the woman next door sunning herself in her backyard. What began as a single act of curiosity snowballed into a regular habit of lust. He was also a little too huggy-kissy around the office, where he was the leading salesman year after year. Don was no Brad Pitt, but he could tell that women found him attractive. This flattered his ego, especially since girls had not noticed him at all in high school. He tended to let his eyes fix a moment too long on his female associates. Often Don found himself engaging in sexual fantasies as he crept along down the freeway on the way home after work.

Evelyn was an ambitious young woman who also worked in the

sales department. She was bright, a quick learner, and was already earning more commissions than most of the men in the office. By virtue of her ambition she was eager to learn from Don, and by virtue of her upbringing she was lonely for love. She had not been hugged enough by her daddy. There was a natural sexual attraction between Don and Evelyn. But for Don this was no more than most men felt toward a physically sensuous woman, which Evelyn certainly was—she had "the look." Neither of them ever overtly acted on the physical attraction by flirting, but the chemistry was there.

One of the company's biggest customers was interested in getting a quote for a privately labeled product. If the numbers worked, it would prove to be one of the biggest sales in the history of their company. Four top salespeople were assigned to work out the details, including Evelyn and Don. About two weeks into the project it became clear that the four of them needed to travel to the customer's home office to work out kinks in the pricing.

After checking in at the hotel two of them wanted to hit the downtown entertainment district that night, but Don and Evelyn both declined. Don and Evelyn waved good-bye as their associates' cab pulled away from the curb. As they walked inside, Don's senses were alert. There was a sense of danger in the air, and he welcomed it. He said, "I'm going to get something to eat. Would you like to join me?"

Evelyn simply nodded as her eyes fell to the carpet, and they walked to the dining room. The maître d' seated them in a booth near the back of the restaurant. Don had already made his first mistake, but it wasn't his biggest mistake. His biggest mistake was mixing wine with dinner. But his real mistake had been made thousands of choices earlier. The wine lowered their inhibitions, which led to exploratory questions. The questions became more and more provocative. Each successive answer signaled interest in going further. By the time Don signed the check, he had pulled the noose tight around his own neck. They walked to the elevator and went up to her room—and Don became an adulterer.

Don woke up the next morning laden with guilt, remorse, and shame. The balance of the business trip was extremely awkward. He resolved in his mind that it was a one-shot tryst and that he was going to change a number of his ways. Unfortunately, that thought came several years too late. Don was addicted, and he couldn't walk away from his lusty habits.

Evelyn, his colleague, was equally flustered by the affair, but she was single. Furthermore, she was highly attracted to Don, and that fed his ego. Less than two weeks later Don found himself at Evelyn's apartment during lunch. For the next three months this was to become their regular rendezvous two or three times a week.

Meanwhile, Mary had been frustrated several times because she had been unable to reach Don during lunch, which in days past he had typically eaten at his desk. He explained his absence by lying to her that he had started taking key customers to lunch from time to time. Meanwhile, it didn't take long for Evelyn's and Don's coworkers to add things up. Several of the women in the office felt scandalized. Don naively thought no one had noticed. One day Mary called and reached Susan, one of the scandalized women. Mary asked, "Is my husband there?" Susan, who could be as vicious as a cornered cat, shot back in a villain's voice, "No, and you may want to look into it a little further."

Mary sat with the phone hanging limp in her hand until the phone company's "you-didn't-hang-it-up-right" ringer brought her back to earth. The next day Mary—she couldn't help herself— went to Don's office and followed his car as it pulled away at lunchtime. When she saw him go into an apartment, she didn't want to see any more. She sped away, sobbing hysterically.

As soon as she arrived home, Mary called her mother and spent ten emotional minutes telling her what she had just seen. "Mom, I'm just so scared. I don't know what to do."

"Honey, I am so, so sorry," her mother began, then followed with twenty questions. After talking out every possible explanation and course of action, they agreed that Mary would tell Don that very evening exactly what had happened, step by step, starting with Susan's offhand phone remark.

After the children were in bed, Mary asked Don to come with her into the den. As she shut the door, she began trembling, and tears streamed along the creases of her face. Don knew he had been caught before Mary even said a word. The guilt had been eating away at him. He started crying, too. He made it easy for her by asking, "How did you find out?" For the next two hours they covered every angle. Don, a former altar boy, was defrocked. He confessed how it all got started, including the hundreds of little sins that led up to the big one.

Mary heard more than she thought she could bear. That night Mary set her course, and she never wavered from it. She was a woman of faith—strong faith—but she would not be married to an unfaithful husband.

The divorce process took six months. The awful pain didn't begin to recede for two years. Then she met Sid. Sid was a lot like Don. After all, she had never found anything wrong with Don's personality, just his character. At the end of twelve months of dinners and picnics with Mary's three children, both Sid and Mary started thinking, *This might work.*

Four years after Don took Evelyn to be his unlawful mistress, Sid took Mary to be his lawful wife.

It took another year or so to work out the details of shared parenting. Eventually the children each had two toothbrushes, two beds—two of everything. The children spent every other weekend with Don, and he was permitted to attend all their contests and concerts, which he faithfully did.

One Saturday morning he arrived a few minutes early to pick up the kids for the weekend. Don's children—ages 14, 12, and 9—were sitting at the breakfast table when he knocked on the kitchen door. Mary and new-husband Sid were scurrying around the kitchen, fetching more milk and cooking scrambled eggs. Mary went to the door, swung it open, smiled a genuinely friendly smile, and invited Don to come in for a cup of coffee while the kids finished breakfast.

Don came in, feeling quite awkward—this was the first time they were all together in the same room. He sat down at one end of the kitchen table. The kids were at the other end of the table, with a couple of empty chairs between him and them. The kids didn't greet him right away because they were arguing about who should get the last piece of toast. He felt like he wasn't really even there—like he was a ghost—and he felt like a giant horrible, smelly toad.

Mary intervened and calmed the toast storm. Sid said, "Thanks, honey," gave her a soft kiss on the cheek, then served the kids their eggs and asked if they wanted more milk. Sid tousled Tommy's hair, and Tommy smiled that toothy grin that had always melted Don. But today he was flashing it at Sid. Don was melting anyway, but for a different reason. Then Sid turned to get the milk bottle and brushed his arm across Mary's back, giving her a love pat. He poured the milk into Anna's glass, and she said, "Thank you." Sid said, "You're welcome, sweetie." Sid turned toward Don and exhorted the children, "Okay now, kids, your dad's here. Aren't you going to say hello?"

I cannot believe this is happening to me, Don thought, as he turned numb. *Here is "another man" doing what I'm supposed to do. Here is "another man" calling my wife "honey," kissing her face, cooking for my children, tousling my son's hair, touching my wife's body, calling my daughter "sweetie," and my children can't seem to get enough of him. Meanwhile, it's like they didn't even see me come in. There must be some mistake!*

There had been a mistake, but it was too late to do anything about it now. Don was going to watch another man raise his children and love his wife.

BECOMING A "GOOD BOY"

The decision to leap into a moral system is the decision to be "a good boy." If the god of the worldly person is *pleasure,* the devotion of the moral person is *good deeds*. His aim is a Pelagian salvation by the merit of ethical living: "I can do this on my own."

C. S. Lewis noted that all the human beings history has heard of acknowledge some kind of morality. In other words, they feel toward certain proposed actions a feeling captured by the words "I ought" or "I ought not."[1] To live by this sense of "ought-ness" is the most noble thought of the moral system.

Filled with fresh passion and revived motives, the moralist abandons self in an admirable attempt to leave the world a better place. Full of optimism, the moralist believes the world can be set right. He is a crusader, a motivator, an industrious worker. This is the stage of positive thinking and success seminars. Great communicators help us realize that our potential is greater than what we see. We awaken to the holy idea that we have value and dignity as human creatures. We sense we have been made with a certain nobility, and our task is to discover our destiny among men. We are captivated by the possibility of our potential. We want to leave the world a better place and take our place among men. Joining a church may well be part of this system—Jesus is a wonderful example to follow, after all. It is very important to "look" good. A church membership can't hurt.

Our impulse or instinct is to do something good for ourselves and others. We begin this stage with optimism. Along the way we experience joy and success, we progress through disappointments, we eventually get what we wanted—or we don't—but toward the end of this stage of the soul, optimism in the genius of the human spirit lies mortally wounded, defeated by the "laws" of the jungle.

There is devotion to Solomon's task of finding meaning and happiness. It is a season of exploration, experimentation, and finding one's identity and purpose. We experiment to find out who we are, and in the process we find out who we are not.

This is an exhausting experience because man is not as good as we thought we could make him; what's more, our own nasty secrets keep rearing their ugly heads. As C. S. Lewis noted, all 'moral systems "agree in prescribing a behavior which their adherents fail to practice. All men alike stand condemned, not by alien codes of ethics, but by their own."[2] We are at a loss to explain the gaping inconsistencies, the lack of genuine power, the seeking to be righteous yet the experiencing of constant failure. He who would start strong in humanity ends up anemic.

There may be successes along the way—but not enough to cover up the anomalies, as the following story illustrates.

THE ROGERS KIRVEN STORY

As an investment banker, Rogers Kirven got tired of watching other men take his advice and get rich. So, nine years after he began his career, Rogers started his own company and plunged into the world of accomplishment, accumulation, and recognition.

By the age of forty-four, Rogers had met his goal—a net worth in the top one percent of the United States. "I'm a counter," he confessed.

Then Rogers received an unsolicited offer to sell. "My first impulse," said Rogers, "was to take the money and run. Instead, I called up three friends who had sold their companies, told them I was getting ready to pull the trigger, and asked them to join me for dinner to give me their advice.

"These were good moral men, some of the most successful men in the world of business," said Rogers. "As the four of us sat at dinner, I only asked them two questions. First, what was your planned use of the time you would gain? They all had the same three answers:

- I want to spend more time with my soul and grow personally.
- I want to spend more time with my family.
- I want to do some things (basically toys and travel).

"Then I asked the second question: What is your actual use of time? All three had gone through a divorce since selling their companies. Each had bought a bigger toy. All were in a deep crisis of meaning.

"They stepped into a stream so strong. They had no idea. They want all of life as fast as they can get it in the shortest amount of time possible. As Mike Tyson said, 'They all have a strategy until they get hit.'"

Fortunately for Rogers, when he sold his company he remained as the president and CEO. But the subject continued to fascinate him. Since that dinner meeting Rogers has formally interviewed thirty-nine men who have sold their companies. Here is a summary of what he found:

- None could robustly say their lives were better.
- Money and freedom had made life more fragile.
- Some who didn't have "keel below the water line" had breaches of character.
- Thirty-three were divorced.
- Many took up golf, which lasted, on average, six months.
- Many bought exotic cars, which held their interest, on average, ten months.
- Many bought boats, which lasted, on average, eighteen months.
- All had a crisis of meaning.

Evidence and observation prove that the worldly system and the moral system are insufficient to solve the problem of futility.

WHY THE MORAL SYSTEM FAILS

Why does the moral system fail? Quite simply, because we cannot keep the principles of our own system. We lack the power to do what we "ought" to do, even when we want to. Even the good we do just never seems good enough. This system is a black hole that swallows up everything we give it, then demands more.

Even for all of its wonderful contributions toward making the world a better place, the moral system, in the end, has no power to deliver us from our darkest thoughts and deeds. As we walk to the podium to receive a plaque acknowledging our service to the community, our mind can be lusting for a woman in the front row of the audience.

People are not as bad as they can possibly be, but neither are they as good as they would have to be in order for this system to work. If this system were to work, the nature of man would have to be basically good—an experimental view that has undeniably collapsed in the twentieth century under the weight of two World Wars, the Holocaust, the Korean War, the Vietnam War, the discovery of the Gulag camps in Russia, and countless other examples. My brother came back from Vietnam permanently damaged psychologically by the evils he had seen men do to one another. It eventually took his life at the age of thirty-one. As hard as we try to be good, it is not our basic nature. We can make progress, but at our core we are selfish and sinful.

Eventually the moral system collapses under the weight of a million little lies. You just cannot keep pretending forever. It simply isn't working out. The spirit was willing, but the flesh was weak.

When we finally realize our "bad deeds" are more than a few minor anomalies, the moral system begins to break apart. Perhaps you destroyed the self-confidence of your wife; perhaps you have driven your children away. It begins to dawn on us that we cannot become the men we want to be without "outside" assistance.

Thoughts come to mind . . .

Deep in my soul is a question,
a pain, a thirst, a hunger,
a faint melody growing stronger.
Is it you, God?

Humbled, anxious, we take another "leap"—this time into the religious and spiritual sphere.

The Leap: "I can't fake it anymore."

THE RELIGIOUS SYSTEM

*"Why Do I Feel Robbed of the
Best Years of My Life?"*

The weekend after the sobering kitchen scene Don found himself alone, with no plans. It was Mary's turn to have the kids. On Saturday he watched a little of the NBA play-offs. He surfed the other channels during commercials. *Man, am I bored,* he kept saying to himself. During one commercial he flipped to a religious channel. The station was airing a local church service from the previous Sunday. Don found himself engaged by what the minister had to say. This guy didn't seem to speak in the religious clichés and singsong sound bites Don was used to hearing as he crunched through the channels.

At 10:30 P.M. he crawled into bed, too tired to stay up but too awake to go sleep. He thought for quite a while about what the pastor had said. *I think I'll just drop by his church tomorrow and check him out.* With that settled, he drifted off to sleep.

When he called the church early the next morning, an answering machine said, "Thank you for calling Southlake Community Church. Our single reason for existing is to help you find rest for your soul. Please join us at our service for seekers at 11:00 A.M. Sunday morning. Child care is available for all ages. Just follow the signs to New Visitors parking. Hope to see you then!" *This was not what I expected,* Don thought. *They make you feel wanted but not smothered.*

Don had been walking around in a daze for several years. Right after his divorce was finalized, he had attended his wife's church a couple of times, but he was such a basket case he couldn't bring himself to talk to anyone. He was still weak now but getting stronger. After completing his dressing ritual, he looked in the mirror, straightened his tie, and evaluated his smile. *This is going to be a good day,* he thought.

Don pulled into the church parking lot and followed the directions of the volunteers in orange vests. His palms were sweaty, and he started having second thoughts. He was directed to a special parking area for first-time visitors. He just knew someone was going to latch on to him and try to "save" him.

He pulled into his space, turned off the engine, looked to the right and then the left. He didn't see anyone and thought, *Well, the coast is clear so far.*

When he shut his car door, he noticed signs pointing him in the direction of the sanctuary. As he stepped into the air-conditioned building, he noticed how upscale the finishes were. A friendly man, but not overly so, greeted him and offered him a church bulletin and program for the day. "First time?" he asked in a nonthreatening way.

"Yes," Don replied weakly.

"Well, feel free to sit anywhere. And you're our guest today, so don't feel like you need to put anything in the offering plate."

With that Don kept moving down the aisle, as the usher had already started greeting the people behind him. He sat toward the back in a seat that wouldn't attract much attention. The singing was upbeat, and the people around him seemed very sincere about the words they were singing. *This is very different from what I remember growing up,* thought Don.

After a surprisingly stirring solo, during which time the offering plates were passed, the man he had seen on TV the night before stood and walked to a small Plexiglas lectern—you couldn't really call it a pulpit—and smiled broadly as he looked around the auditorium. He greeted first-time visitors and invited them to join him after the service in a room to which he gave directions.

The pastor told a joke that left everyone howling. Don was feeling more comfortable by the minute. The pastor next asked everyone who had a Bible to open it to a passage in Luke—Don didn't hear exactly where. Then he said, "If you don't have a Bible, why don't you look on with someone who does. And if you see someone around you without a Bible, why don't you let them look on with you. Again, that's the Gospel of Luke, chapter nineteen, verse one."

With that a very nice young couple in their mid-thirties who had been sharing one Bible between them shifted it so Don was able to see it. "Thanks," he whispered. The couple smiled back warmly.

The pastor read directly from the Bible:

> Jesus entered Jericho and was passing through. A man was there by the name of Zacchaeus; he was a chief tax collector and was wealthy. He wanted to see who Jesus was, but being a short man he could not, because of the crowd. So he ran ahead and climbed a sycamore-fig tree to see him, since Jesus was coming that way.
>
> When Jesus reached the spot, he looked up and said to him, "Zacchaeus, come down immediately. I must stay at your house today." So he came down at once and welcomed him gladly.
>
> All the people saw this and began to mutter, "He has gone to be the guest of a 'sinner.'"
>
> But Zacchaeus stood up and said to the Lord, "Look, Lord! Here and now I give half of my possessions to the poor, and if I have cheated anybody out of anything, I will pay back four times the amount."

Jesus said to him, "Today salvation has come to this house, because this man, too, is a son of Abraham. For the Son of Man came to seek and to save what was lost."

Don's heart was warmed by this touching story.

One thing I know for sure, Don thought. *I'm as lost as a golf ball in tall grass. I wish salvation would come to my house today,* although he would have been hard-pressed to explain what "salvation" actually meant. But it sounded good.

Then the pastor said, "Jesus came to seek and save people who are lost. So how do you get found if you're lost? Consider Zacchaeus. Notice that the crowd will often prevent you from seeing the way of salvation. They will block your view and mutter when you finally get to see.

"Notice also that he crawled out on the limb of a tree. Are you willing to go out on a limb to see Jesus? That's it, really. Are you willing to go out on a limb to see Jesus? If you are, he wants to come give you a visit—just like he did Zacchaeus. And exactly why was Zacchaeus willing to go out on a limb? Zacchaeus was sick of himself. He just didn't want to be Zacchaeus anymore. He wanted to make right what he had made wrong."

Wow! Don thought. *I've never heard anyone explain what the Bible actually means like this. This is pretty cool.* He especially liked the way he could sit anonymously in the back of this church and learn about Christianity.

The pastor continued, "Now, Jesus is considered a great teacher and leader in virtually all religions. One sign of greatness would be the truth of a man's words. Notice what Jesus claimed: 'Today salvation has come to this house.' Either this statement is true, or Jesus was deranged. It cannot be both. We are free to believe what we want, but the results are very different. If we choose to believe he was deranged, we reject his salvation. If we choose to accept that he has the authority to offer salvation, then he will open our eyes so that we can believe and be saved."

The man spoke some more, but Don had already heard enough. He was ready to go out on a limb. *After all,* he figured. *What have I got to lose that I haven't already lost. I'm pretty sick of myself—that's for sure. I really don't want to be me anymore. I want to make right what I've made wrong.*

As the service concluded, the pastor reminded the attendees that first-timers could join him in a room just outside the side door to his right. As the young couple next to him stood, they asked, "First time?"

His face flushed a little. He really didn't want to be singled out in any way. But they were nice and didn't seem to attach any expectations to their question, so he said, "Yes, and I really enjoyed it."

Sensing that he was uncomfortable, the couple said, "Well, we hope you'll come back. It's a terrific church." And with that they said good-bye.

Don started making his way to the exit and found himself strangely curious about meeting the pastor. He had every intention of bolting to his car and getting out of there before anyone buttonholed him. But no one tried to block his exit. On the contrary, people smiled and seemed to make way for him. The visitor parking area was also reached by going out the side door to which the pastor had referred. Don passed by an open door with a sign above it that read, "FIRST-TIME VISITORS MEET HERE." No one was guarding the door, and Don found himself stretching his neck a little to see what was going on in there as he walked by. He was nearly to his car when he planted his foot and turned around. In less than a minute he was standing with the pastor and another normal-looking guy, probably a businessman. Don could hardly believe it as he heard himself say, "Listen, I haven't been doing too well for several years now. I think I'm ready to go out on a limb."

Suddenly Don froze up. He didn't know what to expect next. The pastor put him at ease, though, and said, "Why don't we get together sometime this week and talk about it?" After they discovered a mutual love for golf, they made a date to play nine holes together the following Tuesday after work.

RELIGIOUS EXPERIENCES

As the anomalies of the worldly and moral systems reduce those worldviews to piles of rubble, the clock keeps ticking and the inward groan for relief from futility grows louder. The groan is becoming a monster. It wants to be fed. Once we realize this groaning is pointing to a spiritual need, we begin looking to religion for the answer. The leap to a religious system is the decision to seek salvation in the spiritual realm. It is to become a "seeker."

All people have "religious experiences" at critical points in their lives. (Whether they do anything about it is, of course, a different matter.) Rudolph Otto, in his book *The Idea of the Holy,* called them *numinous* experiences. Otto said we notice that religion doesn't exclusively consist of "rational" assertions. We sometimes experience the holiness of God in a "moment," in ways that remain inexpressible and elude description. During these encounters with God, we become profoundly aware of our creatureliness and, simultaneously, sense the presence of an overpowering, absolute might. Otto goes on to describe these encounters:

> The feeling of it may at times come sweeping like a gentle tide, pervading the mind with a tranquil mood of deepest worship. It may pass over into a more set and lasting attitude of the soul, continuing, as it were, thrillingly vibrant and resonant, until at last it dies away and the soul resumes its 'profane,' non-religious mood of everyday experience. It may burst in sudden eruption up from the depths of the soul with spasms and convulsions, or lead to the strangest excitements, to intoxicated frenzy, to transport, and to ecstasy. . . . It may become the hushed, trembling, and speechless humility of the creature in the presence of—whom or what? In the presence of that which is a *mystery* inexpressible and above all creatures.[1]

Down through the centuries this "feeling" of the holiness of the Divine Being has been described by various names: *the religious instinct, the seed of religion, the sense of divinity, the numinous,* or *the sense of God.* Elsewhere I have called it *the moment of humility.*

In these moments we palpably sense the presence of a Power. It is a feeling of awe, a sense of majesty, a weightiness, a feeling of gravity, or a sense of the holy. It may come by contemplating our own mortality or the greatness of God. (I will explore these contemplations in later chapters.)

Men become religious when they identify this Divine Power for which they feel awe as the guardian of the morality to which they feel obligation.[2] If the devotion of the worldly person is *pleasure* and the devotion of the moral person is *good deeds,* then the devotion of the religious person is *good deeds to please God.*

PERFORMANCE FOR GOD

Instead of doing good deeds to earn favor with *men,* the spiritual person does good deeds to earn favor with *God.* Or perhaps to avoid his wrath. The religious person thinks, "If I can just be good enough and do enough good deeds, then God will accept me, or at least not punish me." It's performance-based religion. How well you do is up to you. The focus is on *outward* behavior and performance rather than on *inward* change of heart.

Unfortunately, the religious system is perfectly designed to produce despair, because no matter how much this person does, it is never enough. Mike, a father of four kids, said, "I put everything into it. I ushered and served on a committee in my church but then got tired of that. Religion wore me out, so I said to myself, 'I'll just put that effort in at work.' Now it's ten years later, and I'm nowhere." In the end, religious systems are "attempted" salvation by works that never seem to be enough or have any real power to overcome ungodly behavior.

The religious person stands on the fringe of the church. He is present but unaccounted for. Or absent. This person has tried to be a good boy and has tried to obey God—but without power. Ironically, the spirit was still willing, but the flesh was *still* weak.

Still perplexed by secret sins, these folks have yet to feel like a beggar before a holy God. They have tried to "deserve" that which can only be had as a gift. They don't know enough to know what they need, but they do know enough to know that this isn't it.

It's frequently easier to know what won't work than what will, as this story illustrates. One day after using a bar of soap I asked my wife to buy some deodorant soap. "What kind do you want?" she asked. "I don't know," I answered. "All I know is that *this* is not it."

Every worldview can be identified as either a worldly, moral, religious, or Christian system. Philosophies of pleasure and self-fulfillment are worldly; philosophies of love and acceptance are moral; philosophies of self-actualization and sin management are religious.

IS THIS HOW YOU FEEL?

Dear God:

If there is a God. Oh, I don't actually doubt the existence of God—not really. True enough, I would like to see, even feel, the weight of the evidence for his existence. But I don't really doubt there is a God. My problem is more practical. I'm lonely. I feel isolated. Empty. Disillusioned.

I don't know the state of my soul. It concerns me. I've done some things I regret, but I don't want to die because of them. But even more, I don't want to live—at least not the way I've been living. Something needs to change. Something's got to give.

I've tried to live a good life—a moral life, but it's not working out. I don't seem to be able to control my destructive emotions. Ironically, the more I care for someone, the more I seem to hurt them. Some of the things I say to those I love the most baffle me—I can be so negative.

To be honest, I'm proud. My pride is killing me. I pretend to know things I don't. I've been religious, but it just seemed like another way of saying "Do this" and "Don't do that." I've been judgmental of people who use Christianity as a crutch. I've ridiculed my Christian friends and associates for being weak. But, hey, I'm feeling pretty weak right now myself. Frankly, I could use a crutch.

Sometimes I feel like I'm nothing but a piece of meat. I feel like a product that people use, then discard. Is there anyone who cares about "me"—just me, not what I can do for them? God, I think that would be you.

I've picked up this book because, if you're really there and if you will have me back, I really need you in my life. I want to come home. My simple, honest prayer is this: I confess that I have been living by my own ideas. It hasn't worked out. I am ready, even eager, to come back to you. But in all honesty, I do not know who you are—not really. But I've created the illusion that I do. So, it's going to take some courage on my part to admit that I've been wrong—courage I'm not sure I have. I'm asking you to give me the courage I need in order to take this step.

I want to know you as you are, not as a figment of my imagination. Not like the caricatures I see on television. Not in a "man-made" way, but as you really are. I open my mind to you, and I ask that you open your heart to me. With this prayer I ask you to reveal the truth to me. Amen.

In the next chapter I'll begin to explain how the Christian system is the most developed form of religion, and how it offers grace where "merit" inevitably fails.

PART TWO

BARRIERS TO RECOVERING BELIEF IN GOD

GIVING THE CHRISTIAN SYSTEM ANOTHER LOOK

Don's divorce was too much for his company to handle. When it became obvious that Evelyn was going to stay, Don realized the brass had decided she was the victim and Don was the perpetrator. They never *asked* him to leave, but it was clear enough that the time had come to move on.

He was too tired to be bitter about it, so he started shopping the job market. Unfortunately, he was so depressed that he wasn't a very good interviewee. After three months he landed a job selling used office equipment. In a good year he might make two-thirds of what he had made before, but he was too weary to care. It all seemed so pointless anyway.

After joining his new company Don's sales steadily increased during his first two years. When it finally dawned on his new employer what a diamond in the rough they had found, they promoted Don to sales manager. His professional progress paralleled his emotional healing. Don had worked through a lot of the grief of his divorce but still had a long way to go. What he really wanted to do was rewind the tape and start over. He knew, of course, that this was impossible. Sensing no future to look forward to, he dwelled on the past. Don realized he had probably gone about as far down the road to recovery as he could on his own. If he was ever going to become a whole person again, he knew instinctively that he would have to come to terms with God and find some spiritual reality. The guilt was eating him alive. The futility was feasting on his remains.

The Monday morning after Don had attended his first church service since his youth, he had a full-fledged anxiety attack as he drove to work. *What have I done?* he wondered. *I've made a golfing date with a preacher. I must be nuts.*

Don arrived at his office Monday morning fully intending to cancel his golf outing. At 9:00 A.M. he picked up the phone to call the pastor's secretary, but instead of a dial tone he discovered that he had picked up the receiver just as a customer was calling in. "Hello?" he said, and then he spent twenty minutes handling a complaint.

For the rest of the day, every time Don made a move toward canceling the golf date, something interrupted. Once his boss walked into his cubicle. Another time a coworker asked him to help put a quote together. He had to spend an hour with a walk-in customer—something that rarely happened. By the time he actually placed the call at 5:30 P.M. the church office was closed. He vowed he would call again first thing Tuesday morning.

Tuesday morning he never stood a chance. His sales meeting started at 7:30 A.M., and people lined up outside his office for the next several hours to get his approval for special prices or for his help in putting together a complex quote. By noon he hadn't yet canceled; he realized it would be bad manners to pull out now. He laughed at the pickle he had put himself into and thought, *I wonder if this is the work of angels or devils.*

At 4:00 P.M. Don hastily left his office to make their tee time. The aroma of freshly mowed grass calmed him like a tonic. By the time he and Hal Dawson, the pastor, found each other, Don was not nearly as fearful as he expected. "Please call me Hal," said the pastor.

Hal teed up his first shot and whacked it a good 225 yards down the center of the fairway. Don's first shot hooked 150 yards into the tall grass on the right side of the fairway. *Figures,* he thought. *I'm not sure that's where I belong, but that's where I always end up.*

Dawson let Don carry and lead the conversation. No pressure. When they climbed into the golf cart after hitting their tee shots on the fourth hole, Don could no longer take the chitchat he was generating and said, "Hal, I've ruined my life. My current existence is only a shadow of my former life. I don't feel like I'll ever get back to that level again. I've pretty much recovered emotionally, but I just have this sick feeling that won't go away. My divorce counselor keeps telling me that I'm not a bad person, I need to forgive myself, and I need to move on.

"But I've got this nagging feeling that what he says doesn't add up. I don't like to think of myself as a bad person, but I really did do something terribly wrong." Don spent the next two holes rehearsing the painful details of his adultery and divorce.

"You know, Hal," continued Don, "I can't move on. I just have this sense that I've got some unfinished business. I keep having this sense that I have offended and let down a higher power. I feel guilty and dirty and unlovable. I can't forgive myself. Maybe I *am* a bad person. Have you ever had to deal with anyone like me before?"

Hal had listened carefully and felt full of pity for Don. Hal didn't let it show, but he was angered by the counseling Don had been given. He was irritated by a therapeutic approach that tried to tell people they were merely victims. People know they really have done sinful things. How can a man accept forgiveness, though, if he's been taught that he hasn't done anything that deserves punishment? How frustrating it must be to hear that everything's all right when you know it's all wrong.

"Don, around this city tonight dozens of groups will be meeting to discuss different philosophies about life—New Age, self-help, twelve-step programs, meditation, Scientology, Hinduism, and all sorts of Eastern religions. Some of them will be quite novel. I know. Before I committed myself to the Christian faith, I explored many of these ideas.

"Many of these ideas will be disguised as Christianity. The problem today is that the true meaning of Christianity has been so watered-down and caricatured that many people think they have understood and rejected Christianity when in actuality they have yet to understand it at all."

"That's me," interjected Don.

"In my own faith search what I discovered is that Christianity is the only religion that offers a coherent, satisfying explanation for why the universe operates as it does. God has given ample proof of his existence. He also has a plan to deal with the true guilt we feel for the truly sinful things we have done. Would you like me to explain how Christianity can get you over this hump?"

Don didn't hesitate. "I sure would. Like I said Sunday, I'm ready to go out on a limb."

THE CLAIM

The Christian system makes the claim that it will get us over the "hump" and solve the problem of futility. That in itself is not unusual, since all systems justify their existence by making the same claim. If your system has been worldly, moral, or religious, you have quite likely already concluded that the anomalies just don't add up to a solution. Can the Christian system, though, really solve the problem of futility—a problem the worldly, moral, and religious systems fail to solve?

In the movie *The Hurricane,* Denzel Washington portrays Rubin "Hurricane" Carter, a real-life boxing champion wrongfully imprisoned for nineteen years in the aftermath of the 1966 slayings of three people in a New Jersey bar.

A group of people believed in his innocence and began to champion his cause. They met repeated disappointments in their legal challenges, which was psychologically tough on Carter. He would get his hopes up only to have them dashed. One day Carter sat down and wrote a letter, telling his friends that while he appreciated their efforts, he wanted them to stop visiting him. He wrote, "Please find it in your hearts not to weaken me with your love."

Carter believed he would never be set free. He believed he needed to toughen himself up in order to survive the cold, harsh, jaded "system" of which he had become part. He thought that to survive the system, he needed to reject the love that was being freely offered—that it would somehow make him weak. He just didn't think he would ever get to be part of any new system. He didn't want to get burned again.

Maybe you have considered the Christian system, or are willing to, but, to be honest, you don't want to get burned again. No doubt many men today feel that if they are going to survive the cold, harsh realities of their systems, they need to become hardened, tougher, even mean. Like Carter, they may not think there is any way out. So they become cynical and jaded in an attempt to anesthetize the pain of their futility. They don't want to make another mistake. They don't want to give the next ten years to a system that will let them down.

I will confess this to you now: The Christian system claims to be rooted in the love God has for you. If you proceed, God will weaken you with his love. By this, I mean he will lovingly pry your hands off the system that has failed or is failing you. It will be easier for you if you decide now to open yourself up to this love.

GETTING A FAIR TRIAL

A professor of mine once told the story of a man out hiking on a cold winter day. He came to a river that appeared to be frozen over. Since he was unfamiliar with the area, he didn't know how thick the ice was. Naturally, he was afraid of walking out and falling through. So he got down on his stomach and slowly began to inch his way out onto the ice.

When he had crawled near the middle of the river, the air began to tremble as he heard a rumbling sound drawing closer and closer. Suddenly a wagon with four horses at a full gallop shot over the crest of the riverbank, thundered across the river, then disappeared over the crest on the other side. And there he was, lying on the ice, feeling foolish.

It's difficult to trust something we don't know much about. The man lying on the ice had difficulty trusting the ice because he didn't know much about the river. But it isn't odd that he would do so. What would be odd is to see a man walk up to an unfamiliar frozen river and confidently walk out on it. In the same way, it would be odd to trust an unfamiliar God we have not properly understood.

People are often opposed to things they have never properly understood. Christianity is no exception. C. S. Lewis once said of the atheists and agnostics he debated, "Our opponents had to correct what seemed to us their almost bottomless ignorance of the faith they supposed themselves to be rejecting."[1] Pascal made a similar observation: "Let them at least learn what this religion is which they are attacking before attacking it."[2]

It would be intellectually dishonest to never give Christianity a fair trial, then claim it doesn't work. If you became a true Christian, accepted the gift of faith, and *then* it didn't work, *then* you would have a basis for honestly rejecting it. No jury ever gave their verdict until they first heard the evidence.

I have no problem with a man who, after making a thorough and honest investigation, correctly understands Christianity and decides to reject it. That passes every test of honesty I can think of. The person I feel pity for, and would like to challenge, is the one who rejects Christianity without ever understanding it.

In any event, in this book I will explain the Christian system so that one can at least reject the right thing. Let's at least make sure that if a man rejects Christianity, he is rejecting what Christianity actually is and not what it is not.

CONFUSING A LITTLE KNOWLEDGE FOR A LOT

Each summer I study a subject completely unrelated to my vocation. In recent years, for example, I've studied sailing, sculling, interior design, container gardening, and cigars. It's a nice diversion.

In the process I usually end up knowing more than most people about the subject under my microscope—at least until the forgetfulness of age sets in. However, I usually fall prey to a common mistake. The tendency is to confuse knowing a little with knowing a lot.

Because I do know more about certain things than some other people do, it's easy to get mixed up and think I know more about the subject than I really do. Can you remember how embarrassing it is to act like a know-it-all around someone, and then you discover you're talking to a person who really knows what they're talking about? I can. I remember confidently telling my sister-in-law about one of the Miami Dolphins' football players—something I'd read in the paper. I was feeling pretty smug . . . until she quoted his college record, year-to-date performance, and family information. A real fan can make a pretender feel like a fool.

It's the same with God. Our tendency, if we're not careful, is to think that because we know a little about God, we know more than we actually do.

PSEUDO-CHRISTIANITY: INOCULATION

Some commentators suggest that America has become a *post-*Christian culture, a *formerly* Christian nation. However, most Americans still consider themselves Christians—one poll revealed 88 percent are sure they are going to heaven (ironically, in the same poll only 67 percent are sure there is a heaven, so 21 percent of Americans are sure they are going to a place they are not sure exists).

For this reason I think it would be better to say that we live in a *pseudo*-Christian culture. A pseudo-Christian culture is a non-Christian culture that thinks it is Christian. A pseudo-Christian is someone who is Christian by *custom* rather than *conviction*.

I know from my ministry work that many men become closely associated with their Christian churches but don't really know what's going on. Although they are often regulars at church—and sometimes even pillars—they are too embarrassed to admit they don't really get it. They know enough of the lingo to make it seem like they know what they don't really know.

Many men *think* they have heard the true gospel, found it wanting, and have rejected it, when in fact they have yet to hear it. What they have heard instead are enough sound bites and clichés to inoculate them against the real thing. An inoculation is a small dose of the real thing.

AN AGE OF SPIRITUAL NOVELTY

Another barrier to authentic Christianity is that we live in an age flooded with spiritual novelty. Every year new movements pop up. Perhaps the digital speed and ease with which these new ideas can be disseminated has caused, or at least is contributing to, this phenomenon.

Creativity and novelty are different. Creativity finds fresh ways to express time-tested truth; novelty attempts to "rewrite" truth. Creativity is grounded in orthodoxy; novelty is running loose. It is no easy task to tell the difference.

Most of these movements will collapse in ten or twenty years—just after you've given them the best years of your life. I don't want that to happen to you. Here is the risk: Do you really want to stake your present contentment and eternal destiny on an idea that didn't even exist forty years ago—especially when it contradicts orthodox ideas that have stood the test of centuries?

While I'm writing in reaction to all of the spiritual novelties of our time, I'm offering nothing new. It comes directly out of the tradition of classic, historic, orthodox Christianity. It is intended to give you the feeling of a solid mass across which you can safely walk—not thin ice.

THE PROBLEM WITH BUSY

As a salesman Joe was without peer, which eventually resulted in him becoming the sales manager for his company. One day he flew into Texas to help a new salesman, Mike, make an important presentation. Over the course of that twenty-four hours they talked about their lives and became friends.

When Mike dropped his boss, Joe, off at the airport, he said, "Joe, you're amazing the way you present our product. You're brilliant. As smart as you are, though, you baffle me. You don't have a clue about where you came from. You don't have a clue about where you're going. And you don't have a clue about your purpose in life." With that out of the way, Mike said good-bye, and Joe got on the airplane and flew home.

Several months later Joe attended a prayer breakfast, sponsored by local businessmen, where he heard how Christianity answers those deeper questions about life posed by Mike. He listened and made some changes. A month later he suffered a mild heart attack (at the age of forty-four) and needed bypass surgery.

The night before his surgery he took his Ph.D.-educated wife out to dinner. She was a basket case and could not understand his incredible calm in the face of this trial. He said, "You know. I love you very much. You're brilliant. But you baffle me. As smart as you are, you don't have a clue about where you came from. You don't have a clue about where you're going. And you don't have a clue about your purpose in life."

PERSONAL REFLECTION

Pascal once said, "The sole cause of man's unhappiness is that he does not know how to stay quietly in his room."[3]

Picture your life recorded on a single sheet of paper. Suppose the front side is the first half of your life, and the back is the second half. Some percentage of your "life script" has already been written—whether a quarter, a third, half, or more. The rest is blank—waiting to be written. Ask yourself, "Where did I come from? Where am I going? What is the purpose of my life?"

What else can we learn from this sheet of paper? First, think for a moment about the past. Are you surprised by the path your life has taken? Was it the script you set out to write, and why or why not? Perhaps you lived for yourself or someone else. If for someone else, do you appreciate or resent them now? Did you "consume" and discard them? Second, think about the present. Are you happy with the way the script has turned out so far? Or would you like to change?

To change you have to become uncomfortable with something.

CONCLUSION

In the next chapters I would like to introduce, or reintroduce, you to the Christian system by proving to you that it is not unreasonable to believe Christianity.

There are many things about the Christian system that are matters of faith, but you may be surprised to learn that many things are also matters of fact. Factual evidences of the Christian God are found in creation, science, history, and suffering.

IS THE IDEA
OF GOD LOGICAL?

It happened so fast. Peter's cell phone rang. His brother, Paul, was talking hysterically on the other end. Paul wasn't making any sense, so it took a few seconds for Peter to figure out that something was wrong with their father, who had a history of heart disease.

"Slow down, Paul, and start at the beginning."

Paul said, "I just called Dad a minute ago, and when he answered, all I could hear was the television in the background. I called back, and the same thing happened. What do we do?" Peter had always been the one the family depended on to know what to do. He always did know—and this would be no exception.

"Paul, hang up the phone. I'm going to call 911." Peter didn't wait for an answer. He pressed end and punched in 911.

"Is this for fire, police, or ambulance service?" said the voice.

"I need an ambulance."

"What's the address?"

"I think my father may be having a heart attack."

"Yes, sir, may I have the address?"

"3601 Beverly Lane."

"Okay, now what's the problem, sir?"

"Well, I just tried to call my dad . . . well, actually it was my brother who called him. Anyway, he has a history of heart trouble, and when he picked up the phone he couldn't talk. So my brother called him back. Same thing. All he could hear was the TV blaring in the background."

"Okay, sir, we're already rolling. We'll be there in just a few minutes. I have your number here, and I'll call you back just as soon as we have some word."

"Please ask them to hurry."

"Yes, sir, I will. I'll call you back as soon as I have word."

"Thank you," Peter said, and he hung up.

He pressed the speed-dial number for Paul. "Hello?"

"Yeah, Paul, an ambulance is on the way. How far are you from Dad's house?"

"Peter, I'm way down on the south side of town delivering some lumber. It would take me forty-five minutes to get there."

"Okay, Paul. I'm going to leave my job site and run over there. I'll be there in about fifteen. I'll call you from there as soon as I know something." Peter was a self-employed carpenter. He usually had a couple of apprentices working for him. He jogged to his truck without speaking to either of them and sped away.

Peter and his dad had rarely seen things eye to eye, but below the veneer of friction he still loved his father. He made the drive in twelve minutes, but it seemed like an hour.

The ambulance was already in the driveway. The lights were still flashing. One man had just rushed out of the front door. He motioned, and two paramedics ran inside with their equipment. A small crowd of neighbors had started to gather on the sidewalk. Peter raced up the street at nearly fifty miles per hour and skidded to a stop in the middle of the street. He jumped out of his truck and ran toward the house. The door to the truck was still open.

As Peter entered the house, he saw that the paramedics had removed his father's shirt and were preparing to hit him with two shock pads.

"Sir, I think it would be best if you waited outside." The directive was intended as an act of mercy.

"I'm not going anywhere," said Peter in a stern voice the paramedics had heard before. Nothing else was said as they went back to their work. They hit Peter's dad with a shock. His body jolted. The monitor showed no response. They hit him again. Still the monitor showed no response.

After the third shock the woman looking at the displays said, "Still nothing. We've got nothing here."

Peter could not believe what he was hearing. This was no movie set. This was his father, and he was watching him die.

The one holding the pads said, "Let's try it one more time."

Still nothing.

"We've lost him," the paramedic said.

Peter was speechless. A feeling of numbness began to overtake his arms and legs. For the next several minutes he watched in disbelief as the paramedics loaded the body of his father onto a gurney, pulled a sheet over his face, and carried him to the ambulance.

Peter stood in the front doorway and dialed his brother. "Hello?"

"Yeah, Paul, this is Peter. Paul, Dad didn't make it. He's gone."

THE IDEA OF NO GOD: WHAT IF WE ARE ALONE?

Once I saw a poster of outer space taped up in a hallway leading to a high school cafeteria. The poster read:

> Either we are alone in the universe or we are not.
> Both ideas are overwhelming.

In the movie *Contact,* a scientist, portrayed by Jodie Foster, asks a troubled priest, "What makes more sense: That an all-powerful, mysterious God created the universe and then decided not to give any proof of his existence? Or that he simply doesn't exist at all, and we created him so we wouldn't have to feel so small and alone?"

"I don't know," the priest responds. "I couldn't imagine living in a world where God didn't exist. I wouldn't want to." The ultimate futility would be that we are alone.

Are we alone? Is it true that God has given no proof of his existence? Is God just something we have created to take care of a psychological need?

Most philosophers, scientists, and theologians did not debate the question of God's existence until the last few centuries, as scientific knowledge gained stature and philosophy engendered a climate of skepticism. It seems the more we know the more confused we become. These debates over God's existence leave a lot of good people doubtful, especially now that new ideas streak across the globe at digital speed. There are, of course, skeptics who will never accept what's been proved, much less what's probable. But what can we do for the many people who are open to considering a reasonable explanation but have sincere, honest doubts. What constitutes "reasonable proof"?

WHAT IS REASONABLE PROOF?

In a court of law there are two different standards of proof, depending on whether the case is criminal or civil. The lowest burden of proof is for a civil case, like a contract dispute. In a civil case the plaintiff must only prove "a preponderance of the evidence," so a jury can render a guilty verdict even though doubt remains.

In criminal cases, however, the prosecutor must prove his or her case "beyond and to the exclusion of every reasonable doubt." The most brutal judgment our judicial system can render is capital punishment; you cannot punish a person more severely than taking his life. It is interesting that even for the most severe form of punishment, the standard is not *absolute* proof, but the exclusion of reasonable doubt. (This explains why O.J. Simpson could be found innocent in his criminal case but guilty in his civil wrongful death case with the same evidence.)

It is worth mentioning that neither of these two standards of proof requires the 100-percent elimination of all doubt. Instead, the jury or judge must apply wisdom to the evidence they are given, then make a reasoned decision.

For our purposes we will hold to the higher standard of proof. Our goal will be to eliminate every reasonable doubt.[1] Christianity teaches that faith is a gift, but addressing honest doubts with known proofs will make any seeker more confident to move forward.

Some of the most brilliant skeptics in history, once they decided to make an intellectually honest investigation of Christianity, have found reasonable proof for the existence of God and the deity of Jesus Christ. Christianity offers a satisfying antidote to futility. Let's turn our attention to some of the proofs.

THE IDEA OF GOD

I'm going to ask you to do some "heavy lifting" in this section. I would like to ask you to picture "the world" in your mind. You may want to picture the earth, the United States, your community, our solar system, or the universe. You may choose to picture the world of your relationships. Any of these will work. Whatever comes to your mind, focus on that picture for a few seconds until you "see" it clearly.

Next I'd like to ask you a question, one you have no doubt already considered many times: Where did this world come from? Ponder this for a moment.

When we picture the world, we are *not* forced to conclude that the world is *necessary*. There is no necessary reason why there is "something" instead of "nothing." Nonetheless, there is "something," so when we ask "Where did it come from?" it is natural to be struck with the idea that it had to come from "somewhere." This leads us by *intuition*[2] to the idea of a *Necessary Being*, which most people call God. For example, if you were to come into your kitchen and see a cake on the counter, you would immediately conclude that someone had put it there. You may be surprised that there is a cake rather than no cake, but once you have seen it, you would never think it got there by itself. You would know that it was *necessary* for someone to have been in your kitchen.[3]

I clearly remember the first time this epiphany dawned on me. It happened in college. I was lying in the grass on my back, looking into the night sky. My eyes were feasting on a dazzling display of stars. Suddenly the mystery of it all became overwhelming. I felt like such an ant. I felt so small and "contingent." It was at that moment that the idea of a Necessary Being hit me.[4] Since I was raised in a Protestant church, my exact thought was *For this to exist it is necessary for God to exist.*

Though I grew up in the church, and so had been taught to believe in God, this was the first time it occurred to me that it was impossible for a Necessary Being *not* to exist. And so, as nearly all people do, I chose to accept the inescapable deduction that there exists a Necessary Being.

I'm not yet suggesting whether this Necessary Being is a machine, a spirit, or a personal being. For Aristotle it was the Uncaused Cause (or sometimes the Unmoved Mover). Some people think of this Necessary Being as a great watchmaker. A few people think of it as a mechanistic, impersonal "Star Wars–like" force ("May the Force be with you"). A few people don't believe it at all. Since most people refer to this Necessary Being by the name *God*, we will use the term *God* from this point forward.

I'm only trying to make this one point: Because the world exists, all people through intuition can have the idea that "God must exist necessarily."

When Mikhail Gorbachev led Russia away from seventy years of Communism, one high-ranking official said, "All these years they have told us there is no God. But we have always known that was not true. Even though they erased the memory of God from our schoolbooks, they could not erase him from our genetic memory."

If you have accepted the idea of a Necessary Being—that "God must exist necessarily"—that is all I'm asking you to presuppose. This, however, is a huge step, a step based on certain and indisputable reason. Unfortunately, for skeptics who cannot accept this starting point, I must regretfully say that I have nothing further to offer here.

On the other hand, if you already believe *more* than "the idea of a Necessary Being," that may or may not be an advantage. I say this because Christianity is just as likely to be misunderstood as understood. So there may be times when you will need to reconsider some things you thought you had already settled.

Once you are struck by this intuition, you may choose to believe it or not—but it is still true. As English essayist Aldous Huxley once said, "Facts do not cease to exist because they are ignored." God is who he is, and whether we believe it or not is immaterial to whether or not he exists, or to what he is like.

What kind of Entity or Being could create this universe?

WHAT CAN BE KNOWN ABOUT GOD THROUGH OBSERVATION

Rational contemplation is not always rational, but what God is like can be deduced by contemplating the work he has done in Creation. Consider these examples.

The naked cosmos would be much too harsh for life—the vast freezing-cold vacuum of space, the desolate asteroids and planets, the extreme heat and unfiltered harmful rays of billions of suns. Yet the earth has air, rain, crops, food, and many joyful hearts. We don't have to gasp for air, or always be thirsty, or waste away from hunger. Whether gazing into the evening sky, appreciating the intricacies of the human organism, marveling over the miracle of human birth, or observing the delicate balance of the environment, we, by intuition, conclude there must be a purpose to it all.

As a painting reveals something about its painter or a poem reveals something about its poet, so the Creation reveals something about its Creator. We would always assume that the character of any creator is in some way revealed in his creation. A building reflects something of what the architect is like. This hospitable environment in a hostile cosmos suggests a God who cares for his creatures.

In chapter 4 we looked at the moral system. We noted that all men history has known have acknowledged some kind of morality, captured by the phrases *I ought* and *I ought not.* Suppose a man got on a plane, opened the overhead bin, and removed someone else's suitcase to make room for his own. All people would feel the injustice—the "ought not"—of such an action. Through contemplation we can ask, "Where did this sense of 'ought-ness' come from?" The immediate intuition is that the attributes of the creature must be attributable to its Creator, who is, therefore, moral and righteous.

Thoughts of eternity lead us rationally to a Supreme Being without beginning or end. Thoughts of infinity lead us rationally to conclude that however large Creation is, it is "contained" within a larger context where God exists. Julian of Norwich, a fourteenth-century English Christian mystic, once pictured something in the palm of her hand the size of a hazelnut. When she asked, "Lord, what is it?" God replied, "This is all that ever has been created." The earth is a pebble in the palm of God's hand. We are struck by the intuition that God must be indescribably powerful.

All of us have moments when we are overwhelmed with a sense of gratitude for our blessings, however magnificent or meager they might be. Feeling grateful is linked to an intuition that we have received something beyond what we deserve—a gift that must come from a Giver.

We have all experienced the joy of love, parenting, doing useful work, providing for a family, or enjoying relaxing days—an accumulation of experiences that seem to say there is something intrinsically valuable about the human experience, and that the Giver of such life must be good. This thought can come suddenly, like being jolted awake by an intense dream, or more gradually, like a gentle whisper that comes softly but repeatedly and finally grows louder and comes more often.

Ockham's razor is the theory that the simplest logical explanation tends to be correct. The simplest logical explanation for the existence of a Creation is that there is somewhere a Creator. Where there is a Design there must be a Designer. Where there is Purpose there must be a Reason. There is somewhere an Architect, a Painter, a Sculptor, a Poet, whose imagination and ability infinitely exceed the limits of human comprehension.

Which seems more reasonable to you—to require proof that there is a Creator, or proof that there is not? Creation exists. Creatures exist. If there were no cake, I would say there was no baker. But since there is a cake, there must necessarily be a baker. It is more than reasonable to suggest that someone claiming that Creation made itself has the burden to prove how that could be.

When we gaze into the bejeweled evening sky, what is it that the twinkling stars are trying to say? They utter, "There is so much more you do not know. The cosmos is so big, and you are so small. Yet look at how magnificently you have been made. We stars didn't appear from nowhere. Where do you think we came from?" Where, indeed?

SHOULDN'T SCIENCE RULE OVER THEOLOGY?

In high school Peter had been the coolest guy on campus. The other students mistook his bravado for self-confidence. They looked to him for leadership. Peter, for his part, was very outgoing but had no sense of direction in life. So he led a crowd of other sharp but aimless youths into a party life of excess and wastefulness.

Peter lived a double life. He was the party animal of Roosevelt High—the kid everyone wanted to impress. Girls swooned over him, and guys nearly genuflected. At home Peter was a model son. His parents were active in their church, and Peter could vividly remember sticking Noah's ark figures onto a green felt board. By the time he entered high school he was commissioned to lead the youth fellowship that met on Sunday nights.

Most days Peter was a nervous wreck that kids from school and kids from church would get together and expose his little lie. Peter picked up his knack for duplicity from his dad. While his father was charming at church, he made their home into hell. He was extremely strict—one reason Peter was so "religious"—and demanded unquestioning obedience. Any deviation from the rules meant swift and angry punishment.

One day, when he was ten years old, Peter rode his bicycle from their house to the ice cream store about three-quarters of a mile up a busy boulevard. When his dad found out, he spanked him so hard he had welts for a week—and his dad sold his bicycle. The welts went down in time, but Peter withdrew from his father after that incident.

Peter had two brothers and a sister. His sister, Penny, had married a man just like their father. Her husband had beaten her severely on several occasions—the last time she had him arrested. Peter, the oldest of the four children, had the "caretaker" personality, so he spent a lot of time trying to advise his sister about what to do.

One of Peter's brothers, Paul, was an alcoholic. The youngest brother, John, had left home at the age of eighteen, and no one had heard from him since. That was ten years ago. Peter had reason to believe he wasn't even alive anymore—though he never mentioned this possibility to their mother. Still, through it all, his father tried to maintain the facade of a happy family.

Peter married his high school sweetheart and became a carpenter. It was a job he loved. He was quite adept at the intricate detail work involved in trim carpentry. His first boss, Ed, recognized Peter's potential immediately and took him under his wing. For several years Peter worked by his side, and Ed taught him all the ins and outs of being a skilled craftsman. Peter found a great deal of satisfaction in doing his work well. That work ethic was the one legacy from his father for which he could be thankful.

Three months after his brother, John, graduated from high school and left town Peter's mother filed for divorce. It slowly came out that his father had been abusing his mother for almost all of their twenty-six married years.

Peter's first and only love had begun the moment he saw Rhonda walk into their ninth grade geometry class. She shook her long blonde hair to the side as she sat in the desk in front of him. By the time her scent arrived a split second later Peter was madly in love. Rhonda, for her part, also came from a religious family. Peter and Rhonda adored each other and couldn't wait to get married. They had three children within four years of their high school graduation date.

Peter wanted to be everything to his kids that his dad had never been to him. He showered them with the affection he had never received when he was a boy. His father had been so aloof when calm, and so dogmatic when upset, that he was like a stranger, and Peter never quite felt like he actually "knew" his father. Instead, to Peter he seemed more like a military commander. You don't ask questions—you just do what you're told.

When Peter's kids—boy, girl, boy—qualified to play T-ball, Peter jumped right in and began coaching his kids' teams. Usually two of his kids would be on the same team, but once Peter found himself coaching three different teams—an almost impossible scheduling challenge. But he loved it. He did the same with soccer. He was going to be the "hands-on" father his own father never was. Every day he made it a point to tell each child, "Brent, I love you," or "Brittany, I am so proud of you." He'd flash his trademark smile and watch his children be transformed into kids who really thought they were special.

If Peter was sunshine, Brian was rain. Brian, a computer technician, was extremely quiet and rarely smiled, but he hadn't missed a single one of his son's soccer games and made it to nearly all the practices, too. Peter coached Brian's son. Peter, as usual, struck up a cordial relationship with Brian. He made it a personal goal to get him to smile at least once whenever he saw him.

Brian, it turns out, knew more about soccer than just about anyone in town. He played the game himself long ago, but, more than that, he was just one of those guys who knows how everything works. It was only a matter of time until Peter realized that Brian could be a big help.

"Brian, you're here every time I am—what would you think of becoming my assistant coach? You know stuff about soccer I'll never know. I could really use your help. Whadda ya say?" Peter asked.

I've always wanted to coach, Brian thought. "Oh, I don't know," he responded dolefully. He couldn't help responding that way—it was such an ingrained habit.

"I could really use you, man. You know this game inside out," said Peter.

Brian, at thirty-two years of age, had never had a close friend his entire life. He spent his high school career building computers after class. His personality didn't exactly attract people either.

"Okay, I'll do it," said Brian.

During two years of coaching together Peter and Brian confided a number of private matters to each other. Brian, though, had one rock in his pack that he had never mentioned to anyone— yet, it forever troubled him. It was an intangible pain that hummed continuously in the background, drowning out all but the loudest joys in life. After practice one day, as they were stuffing equipment into the bags, they got on the subject of their dads. Peter told Brian about how stern his father had been. Peter was surprised by how much emotion Brian showed—he was actually quivering.

"No matter what I did," confided Brian, "I could never please my father. Just once I'd like to hear him say, 'You know, son, I'm really proud of you.' But who am I kidding? I know it will never happen."

Brian's comment struck a raw nerve with Peter. He had never heard it put that way before. For the first time he saw how much a father can cripple a son. For the first time he realized that this was exactly what had happened to him. Maybe that's why they liked each other so much. In any event, they now had a bond built on common pain. After Brian drove away from the practice field, Peter, who by then was alone in the dusk, looked up as the vast evening sky came to life, and he broke down.

So far Peter had managed to control publicly the volcano of inarticulate rage that had plagued him all his adult life. Sometimes, though, life was too much. That day was such a day. Even though his father had been dead for three years, Peter finally understood that, like Brian, he was still living under his father's spell. He drove home, pulled into his garage, walked over to his Peg-Board, picked up a sledgehammer, and in less than five minutes destroyed his workbench. Peter stiffened, gathered himself, and walked into his house as though nothing had happened.

THE VASTNESS OF CREATION

When the vast size of the cosmos is considered, man is either very insignificant or very special.

Our solar system is located 26,000 light years from the center of the pinwheel-shaped galaxy we call the *Milky Way*. One light year is six trillion miles. Our sun is one of 100 billion stars in our galaxy, one galaxy among billions of other galaxies. It takes 226 million years for our sun to circle our home galaxy, traveling at the speed of 135 miles per second.[1] Our bodies are hurtling through space at 135 miles every second.

Our small planet is teeming with life—humans, plants, animals, reptiles, fish, birds, and insects. The conditions for life as we know it to exist fall within an amazingly narrow range of values. Leading scientists now believe that the universe is so delicately balanced that it could not have happened by chance.

Stephen Hawking, the most famous physicist since Albert Einstein, notes, "The odds against a universe that has produced life like ours are immense." For example, Hawking points out that if the electric charge of the electron had been even slightly different, stars wouldn't burn. If gravity were less powerful, matter couldn't have congealed into stars and galaxies. These forces seem minutely adjusted to make life possible. One astronomer calls it "a put-up job." A great conspiracy to make intelligent life possible.[2]

Hawking asks, "Why does the universe go to all the bother of existing?"[3] He concludes, "It would be very difficult to explain why the universe should have begun in just this way, except as the act of a God who intended to create beings like us."[4]

Consider the remarkable efficiency of food chains, insect kingdoms, photosynthesis, animal life, the bird and fish worlds. Not only are these elements of creation remarkably interesting, but they also have beauty and purpose.

To appreciate how delicately conditions for life are balanced, we need only to consider the devastation caused by a flood, famine, or fire. When one considers the precision required of atoms, neutrons, electrons, quarks, and the force of gravity, and how volatile conditions *could* be, the question isn't "Why are there so many natural disasters?" but "Why are there so few?"

NOT ONLY BIG, BUT SMALL

If for the last 15 billion years you had removed one molecule per second from a glass of water, you would not be able to notice any change in the water level. And a molecule may be like an entire universe of its own. You are for all practical purposes "infinitely" larger than a molecule. You are as much larger than a molecule as the known universe is larger than you. Cosmology, the study of the very large, may in the end be eclipsed by quantum mechanics and string theory, the study of the very small.

THE ORDERLINESS OF CREATION

Consider the regularity of sunrise and sunset, moon phases, seasons, tides, crops, forests, ecosystems, air, water, digestion, and procreation. I am profoundly encouraged by every sunrise—its predictability is a powerful symbol, especially when things aren't going so well. Imagine the chaos if we couldn't predict the boundaries of day and night, river and land, or winter and spring. We couldn't leave the house for a walk without a flashlight, build a house near water, or know when to plant a crop.

A man who watches a lot of news will likely wonder *Why is there so much chaos in the world?* The nightly newscast draws our attention to the anomalies, but what goes wrong is infinitesimally small compared to what goes right. What is extraordinary is not that we have so much chaos but so little. Why is there not more chaos? A man who ponders the whole of creation will wonder *Why is there so much order in the world?*

Christianity teaches that God provides order for Creation. Acts 14:17 declares, "Yet he has not left himself without testimony: He has shown kindness by giving you rain from heaven and crops in their seasons; he provides you with plenty of food and fills your hearts with joy."

SCIENCE AND THEOLOGY

People want to know "What is the universe all about? What is reality? What is the stuff the universe is made of?" The task of science is to explain how nature works. To do this, scientists observe nature and then form what at the time seem to be reasonable paradigms (systems) to explain the realities they see.

As I mentioned in an earlier chapter, when too many anomalies show up, a new system emerges to replace the one that doesn't hold water anymore. There have been four major scientific paradigms in the last two thousand years—Ptolemaic, Copernican, Newtonian, and Einsteinian. In about A.D. 150 Ptolemy said, "The earth is round and stationary, the center of the universe"—a geocentric universe. C. S. Lewis was fond of pointing out that, according to Book I, Chapter 5 of Ptolemy's *Almagest,* scientists already knew the universe was very large. The passage says that in relation to the stars, "earth has no appreciable size and must be treated as a mathematical point!"

Ptolemy's system prevailed for fourteen hundred years. But in 1543 Nicolas Copernicus said, "The earth is moving, and the sun is the center of the universe"—a heliocentric universe—and the Ptolemaic system collapsed. Isaac Newton built his science on the foundation of Copernicus.

The "absolute" Newtonian paradigm of gravitation, motion, time, and space lasted for two hundred years. Then in the early twentieth century Albert Einstein observed "relativity" in time, space, mass, motion, and gravitation. He noticed, for example, that starlight bent as it passed near the sun, which led him to postulate a universe of curved space. Suddenly a virtually infinite number of dimensions became possible. His discoveries led to a breakup of the Newtonian paradigm.

You may be surprised to learn that science and Christianity were on friendly terms until the twentieth century. The hostility of science toward Christianity was popularized by the writings of Cornell University president Andrew White (1832–1918). Even in the nineteenth century, when hostilities were just beginning to brew, the vast majority of scientists were adherents of Christianity.

Many twentieth-century scientists and mathematicians (A. W. Whitehead, for instance) said that Christianity and Greek thought provide the soil that enables science to grow. Their argument has much to recommend it. First, the Christian system asserts order and design in nature.[5] Second, Christianity creates a sense of wonder, awe, contingency, and dependency on something bigger than ourselves. Third, the Christian system asserts an open rather than a closed universe, and it is responsive to explanations from beyond nature.[6] Fourth, Christianity, unlike many Eastern religions, believes that nature is real. There is a reality out there, and we can deal with it.

In the middle of the twentieth century, at the encouragement of Albert Einstein and C. F. Weizsacker, leading European physicists invited scientists and theologians to meet together and share their special insights into reality. The annual "Gottinger" meetings took place from 1949–1961 and were succeeded by a younger group of scientists and theologians from 1963–1968. They viewed science and theology as complementary. Science deals with questions about "How does the cosmos work?" while theology focuses on the questions of "Why?" Both groups affirmed the importance of finding answers to both questions.[7]

Science looks at nature and asks, "How does this work?" Theology looks at the same truth and asks, "Why is this important?"

Science is, or should be, the friend of Christianity, and Christianity the friend of science. Christianity has nothing to fear from science; science has nothing to fear from Christianity. Science is exciting because it helps us discover more about God and his ordering of the universe. The problems come when scientists try to do theology, or theologians try to do science. Once the scientist begins asking "Why?" he moves from science to theology.

SUPERNATURAL AND NATURAL

One day Ted, a scientist, said to his friend Roy, a pastor, "The problem I have with Christianity is that it depends on the Virgin Birth and the Resurrection. Now, as a scientist, I believe that natural phenomena can only be explained by natural causes."

"But, just a minute, Ted," Roy interrupted. "I also believe that natural phenomena can only be explained by natural causes."

"Well, then, what about the Virgin Birth and the Resurrection?" asked Ted.

"Oh," said Roy, "I was only trying to agree with you about natural phenomena. I also believe there are *supernatural* phenomena that can only be explained by supernatural causes. But if I get your drift, are you wanting to say that *everything* must be explained by natural causes?"

"Exactly. As a scientist, I observe nature, and I believe everything that happens must be explained by natural laws," said Ted.

"Let me ask you a question," said Roy. "Do you believe it's possible for something to exist beyond or outside of nature? Now, before you answer please understand my question. I'm not asking if something *does* exist, merely if it is *possible* for it to exist. Does anything *necessarily* exclude it?"

"Well, since you put it *exactly* that way," Ted said hesitantly, "I guess to be intellectually honest I would have to say that nothing can disprove the possibility. But it doesn't seem very likely."

"All right, then, but it's possible," continued Roy. "Suppose for a moment that something beyond nature did exist—let's call it *supernatural* for debating purposes. I'm not yet saying it *does* exist, but *if* it did, could it be possible that some of the hard-to-explain phenomena we observe are actually not caused naturally at all, but supernaturally? Again, don't misunderstand me. I'm not asking if you believe it, only if you can exclude it?"

"Roy, you're trying to box me in," said Ted.

"No, Ted, I'm only asking you, 'Is it possible? Does anything necessarily exclude it?'"

"Well, I feel like you're trying to trap me," said Ted. "Anyway, the answer is *no,* I cannot logically exclude the possibility."

"Well, Ted, we've made a lot of progress. You started out two minutes ago by saying that nature is a closed system. Now you have at least agreed that we know of no necessary reason why it *must* be a closed system. At least it is possible that something exists *beyond,* and, whatever it is, it could possibly act *within* the world alongside natural causes. So, I agree with you. Natural phenomena need to be explained by natural causes, but, as you've now agreed, perhaps not all phenomena are natural. If supernatural phenomena do occur, like the Virgin Birth and the Resurrection, then they could be explained by supernatural causes."

A little black cloud lingered over Ted. He looked as though he had just been bushwhacked.

"Ted, do you know why you feel like I've boxed you in? It's because you've been caught practicing theology without a license. You would dismiss me as a quack if I started drawing scientific conclusions. I would be practicing science without a license. It cuts both ways. I'll make a deal with you. I won't try to explain the natural world of science with theology if you won't try to explain the supernatural world of theology with science."

Ted muttered an answer Roy couldn't understand.

MIRACLES

Miracles like turning water into wine, raising the dead, and multiplying fish and bread are impossible naturally. They cannot happen by natural causes. Christianity does not claim that they do. Everyone should understand this point. What Christianity does claim is that "other than natural" causes also exist.

Because things do happen that cannot be explained by natural causes, an "other than natural" explanation is required. The Christian system calls this "other than natural" force a miracle.

Hard-to-believe miracles can be made much easier to accept if we would think for a moment of all the "regular" miracles that take place all around us, which we take for granted. For example, a seed of corn smaller than a fingernail is buried in early spring, then watered and fertilized; life appears, the corn grows knee-high by the Fourth of July, and three weeks later there stands a six-foot-tall plant.

Though a common occurrence, doesn't the fact that the full plant resided in a small kernel have its own reality of miraculous proportions? What is the Intelligence that informs the corn plant to escape from the seed? If this act only happened once, or occasionally, would we not call it a miracle? Such as it is, it is a "regular" miracle. All things considered, the biblical miracles are no more outrageous or amazing than the life of a single corn plant.

THE RELIABILITY OF SCIENCE

It is no small matter that since the time Jesus established the Christian paradigm, at least four major scientific paradigms have found prominence. Science has changed dramatically across the years. Scientists understand that they may have the rug pulled out from under their theories at any time. Science is a "partial" explanation of the "whole" of nature. Does it make sense to have the partial explain the whole?

Science and theology are both trying to help regular guys like Peter, Paul, and Brian. Science, for example, tried to save the life of the father of Peter and Paul. Science could tell them *how* their father died, but only theology could tell them *why*.

Science *discovers* truth in nature, but science doesn't *create* truth—and has never claimed to. Christianity, on the other hand, claims that God is the Creator of all that is, and therefore of all that is true.

Christianity teaches that God created and sustains the universe. Science is limited to discovering what God has already made possible. While scientists keep building bigger telescopes and more powerful microscopes (that lead to still more paradigm changes), the Creator of the scientists offers supernatural stability. Science needs the cosmic glue of Christianity. Science changes, but basic Christianity remains the same.

Notice also that the "useful life" of scientific paradigms has become shorter—the Ptolemaic system lasted 1,400 years, the Copernican system 150 years, the Newtonian system 200 years, and the Einsteinian system has been around for fewer than 100 years. Some prominent theoretical physicists believe that in the first half of the twenty-first century the two great theories of the twentieth century—*general relativity* and *quantum mechanics*—will be fused into a new paradigm, perhaps using *string theory*. As scientific knowledge increases faster and faster, will paradigms fall faster and faster? Christianity has a track record for durability in its essential beliefs. Would it not make sense to explain the "changing" by the "changeless," instead of the other way around?

When we use science to explain theology, we are using the finite to explain the infinite. The truth of archaeology, for example, is limited by what has not yet been found. It is worth mentioning that every major archaeological discovery ever found has increased the confidence of scholars in the authenticity of the Bible.

Much more so than Christianity, science has a lot of unanswered questions. For example, "Does light travel in waves or bundles?" Another is "If the universe is moving from order to disorder (entropy), then how at the same time can evolution move from disorder to increasing levels of order?" Or "If the universe is expanding in every direction and everything is moving farther away from everything else, then where is the point from which everything is moving away—the point where Creation (a.k.a. the Big Bang) began?"

Christianity is a chest full of tools, one of which is science. To be fair, science has never claimed to answer the ultimate questions. Perhaps we should fit the "partial" views of reality given by science into the more "comprehensive" view given by Christianity. As psychologist Abraham Maslow said, "If the only tool you have is a hammer, you tend to view every problem as a nail."

Some may argue, "What a waste of space," but another can argue with equal plausibility, "Man must be very special. All of this so that I might have life." I heard that in the 1990s physicist Stephen Hawking was attending a small Baptist church on the outskirts of Cambridge, England, where he resides. In the end, science can still offer no bread for the deepest hungers of the soul.

SINCE LIFE IS SO FUTILE, WHY SHOULD I BELIEVE GOD CARES ABOUT ME PERSONALLY?

During his first several years of working for himself Peter free-lanced his carpentry skills to a dozen different residential contractors. Over the last year, however, he started working exclusively for one builder whose designs required some ingenuity—something Peter enjoyed.

Ben Silversmith may have built great designs, but he was a ruthless cutthroat. He had a reputation for squeezing his subcontractors. Peter was not unaware of Silversmith's reputation, so he had a candid conversation about working for him before he drove the first nail. For the better part of a year things worked out fine.

On a monthly basis Peter submitted draws for payment. He had to pay his helpers weekly, so this all required a modicum of management on Peter's part. One day Peter opened his monthly pay envelope and immediately saw that Silversmith had deducted ten percent of the requested draw and labeled it "retainage." Peter's blood boiled over. This was exactly the kind of thing he'd heard about. With the check in one hand and the envelope still in the other, Peter stormed up to Silversmith, who was standing next to his truck talking to his superintendent.

"This stinks!" he yelled. "What are you trying to pull here? I thought we had an understanding."

Somehow Silversmith was able to calm Peter down and turn him around. Ten minutes later Peter walked away thinking that the mistake had been his. Silversmith was smooth. He had successfully completed "step one" in the standard scheme he had used to get his hooks into other subs. He smiled at Peter's backside as he walked away.

Silversmith's son was on the soccer team Peter coached. Through this sports involvement Peter had seen a side of Silversmith that most people had never seen. The man did love his family. That meant a lot to Peter, so he cut Silversmith a little extra slack.

For each of the next two months Silversmith again held back ten percent. He convinced Peter that he couldn't give what he didn't get himself, because the owner was retaining ten percent until the job was finished to the owner's and bank's satisfaction. Silversmith was pretty convincing. Peter didn't like it one bit, but there didn't seem to be much he could do about it.

For three months Peter's household finances had been under a strain. He was thirty days late with his mortgage payment, and the bank was calling on his credit card payments. His wife was a jewel and put her full confidence in Peter, counting on him to take care of the bills. He had to carry the weight of the whole thing alone, but at least he wasn't squabbling with Rhonda.

Meanwhile, the work on the house was wrapped up, and the owner moved in on a Tuesday. The next morning Peter went by Silversmith's construction office to pick up his check. The secretary told him that they only cut checks on Friday. At this point Peter was steamed. He had to stifle the urge to put a chair through the front window. He said, "That check had better be waiting for me when I come by late Friday morning," and he stomped out of the office.

On Friday Peter intentionally waited until after lunch to stop by Silversmith's office. The secretary lied and said, "Mr. Silversmith has left for the day. There was a mix-up on the bank's paperwork, and they won't be releasing the final draw until next week, so we won't be able to cut your check until next Friday." She swallowed hard, knowing she could only take telling lies like this a few more times before she would quit.

Peter didn't say anything. He gave her a disgusted look, turned around, and left. Peter knew that Silversmith would be at the soccer game Saturday morning, and he started plotting what he wanted to do.

On Saturday morning Peter was surly. He barked at the kids for not executing plays well, but, of course, ten-year-olds *never* executed them well. Several of the parents noticed that Peter was in a foul mood. When the game was over, Peter asked Brian to give the kids their postgame talk. He then made a beeline to Silversmith. "I don't know what you're trying to pull, but it ain't gonna work, mister," Peter said. The veins in his neck bulged out, and his contorted face was bright red.

Peter sincerely thought he was going to embarrass Silversmith into paying him right there on the spot. Silversmith didn't back up an inch, though, and it was clear to a couple of fathers that a fight was about to start. The women backed away. The young children hid behind their mothers. The yelling escalated. Everyone was watching to see what would happen next.

No one could remember when Dick Mason had not been the president and chief referee of this soccer league. Nothing ruffled Dick. He always brought sanity and wisdom to the Saturday soccer rituals. Well, Dick heard the commotion and jogged toward Peter and Silversmith, not stopping until he was literally standing between them. "Hey, fellas. What's going on?" he said. He pulled Peter aside and said, "Listen, Coach, I don't know what's going on here, but you can't act like this. It's behavior unbecoming to a coach. You want to tell me what's going on?"

"No, I don't," said Peter. He rushed back to where his team was finishing up, gathered up his son, asked Brian to take care of the equipment, and left the field in a huff.

Some of the men had picked up the gist of what was going on. Two of them were in a Bible study group that Dick led on Tuesday mornings at his insurance office. These two guys gave their hypotheses to Dick Mason. Dick thought about the situation and decided to stop by Peter's house after lunch.

He knocked on the door, and Peter answered, looking sheepish. He realized that what he had done was foolish. And now everyone knew what a terrible temper he had. Doubly embarrassing was that he respected Dick Mason more than any other man he could think of. He figured Dick had dropped by to fire him from his coaching job.

"Can I come in for a minute?" asked Dick.

"Yeah, sure, of course. Come on in."

They sat down, and Dick, twenty years Peter's senior, speaking like a father figure, said, "You know, Peter, I've always liked you. You have such a gentle, caring way with your players. And you have a keen sense of what's fair, too. You strike a good balance between trying to win and yet making sure you play all your kids.

"After you left, a couple of men I know from a Bible study I teach told me what they thought happened. They surmised Ben Silversmith hadn't paid you for quite some time, that you were under a lot of financial pressure, and that Silversmith had been repeatedly putting you off. Is that about right?"

Peter couldn't believe how real it sounded to hear someone else actually describe the situation out loud. A wave of emotion engulfed him, and he began heaving. Half of it was the deep encouragement he felt for the kind things Dick was saying; the other half was hearing from someone else's lips how desperate his situation sounded.

"Take your time," Dick encouraged him.

It took nearly five minutes for Peter to gather himself. Quietly he said, "I guess you'll want my resignation."

"Not at all," said Dick. "I came by because I thought you might need a friend to talk to."

Peter had never encountered a man like Dick Mason. They talked for an hour. At the end of their meeting Dick said, "Peter, I want you to know I'm here for you. First off, I want you to call my lawyer right away on Monday morning. I think we can get this problem resolved quickly with a little legal muscle. Secondly, I have a home builder for a client who does upscale custom homes— beautiful homes—and he's as honest as they come. He's been my client for over twenty years. I'd like to get you two together. Finally," he said as he pulled out his checkbook and began writing, "I'd like to loan you enough money to get your bills caught up and then to cover the next couple of weeks."

Peter protested, but Dick wouldn't hear of it. Dick was the father Peter had never had.

"There is one thing I'd like you to do for me, though," Dick said.

"Sure, anything. You name it," said Peter.

"Our Bible study is having a special meeting with Joe Gibbs as our guest speaker. He's going to tell about his own struggles to make sense out of life. Do you know who I'm talking about?"

"Well, of course. He won the Super Bowl when he coached the Redskins, and now he's a top NASCAR race-car owner."

"That's right. He's in town for a race, and he agreed to speak to our group. Would you like to hear him? You'd also get to meet him personally, since you'd be my guest and he'll be sitting at my breakfast table."

"I'd really like that."

"Then it's settled. And you can bring a friend if you want to."

"Really?"

"Yep."

"Well, I know Brian, my assistant coach, loves NASCAR racing. I'm sure he'd like to come."

"Why don't you ask him, and you can give me a call to let me know."

Two weeks later Peter and Brian listened spellbound as Joe Gibbs talked openly about his struggles, failures, and search for meaning in life.

One day later that week, after practice had ended, Brian said to Peter, "You know, that Gibbs meeting meant a lot to me—it got me thinking. I think he's right. I don't think a man can ever have any lasting happiness unless he has God in his life. Peter, I'm going to tell you something that not even my wife knows. You're talking to the loneliest man in the world. I need God in my life. I think I know what I need to do."

For his part, Peter was also interested, though he didn't want to discuss it. Peter had grown up in a "Christian" home, and he was still mad about it. When a few days later Dick Mason asked if Peter would like to go out for breakfast and chat awhile, he reluctantly agreed. After a surprisingly stimulating conversation at breakfast, Peter looked him in the eye and said, "You're going to make a Christian out of me yet, Dick. I'm close, real close."

Peter and Brian started hanging around later and later after practice to discuss their growing interest in God. One day Peter said, "You know what, Brian? I can't manage my life. I'm just so sorry. It would be nice if Christianity was true. I just don't want to be Peter anymore." Together they discussed this until the darkness around them was complete.

Through the course of several breakfast meetings with Dick Mason, Peter began to realize that the Jesus he had heard about—and rejected—early in life, and the Jesus revealed in the Bible—the Jesus that Mason was showing him—were not the same Jesus.

He and Brian discussed these things, and they both decided it was time to give Christianity another shot. Both were simply tired of fighting it—tired of being themselves, really.

THE EMBARRASSING CLAIM OF CHRISTIANITY

It is best to call things plainly, to call them as they are. Many of the basic claims of Christianity are not only the most difficult to explain but also the most embarrassing. A Christian writer, however, has the duty to explain Christianity, not explain it away. There is one claim in particular that many Christians find terribly embarrassing: Christianity makes the remarkable claim to not only solve the problem of futility but also to cause it.

Christianity teaches that the whole world has been subjected to futility (synonyms: frustration, vanity, and meaninglessness) by God. He has done this with the hope of liberating us from our bondage to decay and bringing us into the fold of God's children.[1]

It is the Christian view that if man could find even a trace of meaning in any earthly pursuit apart from God, he would take it. In an earlier chapter we saw how Solomon pursued every conceivable earthly avenue to find meaning and happiness independent of God, and he came up empty.

Christianity teaches that God causes every system that seeks meaning and happiness apart from him to end in futility, while at the same time teaching that this futility is considered a "grace" or kindness from God. In other words, failing was for Solomon's benefit. Christianity teaches that God makes us feel the weight of futility in every worldly pursuit—getting the big promotion, making the big bucks, living in the big house, or getting none of those things. He makes us so miserable through futility that we choose him of our own free will. He sovereignly removes any possibility of finding meaning except in him. We might put it this way: Futility is the chief tool by which God sovereignly draws us to himself of our own free will.

God will not force a man to revere him, but he will make it impossible for a man to be happy unless he does. Solomon said it this way: "I know that everything God does will endure forever; nothing can be added to it and nothing taken from it. God does it so that men will revere him."[2] So even if we get exactly what we want, we will still not be happy apart from God. Apart from God, life has no meaning. That's the deal. I am just reporting it; don't shoot me.

FUTILITY IS PROTECTION

Christianity goes yet one step further and states that if you were to get what you think you want, you would destroy yourself, and your failure to get it is an expression of God's grace and kindness. I personally spent my twenties and thirties working and praying to achieve a type of success that I now realize would have destroyed me, and then I was disappointed when I was spared.

Ken worked for a Fortune 100 company for eleven years. A star, he wanted the brass ring, and he was putting in the seventy hours a week required to get it. What's more, he was a deacon in his church. Ken met once a week with another man in an accountability group. In his hunger for worldly success, Ken became so busy that his accountability partner was driving Ken's son to Little League games. One day he told Ken, "You need to do something about your life. Your son is starting to be closer to me than to you." It woke him up.

Men are interested in *goal* success; God is interested in *soul* success. Would we really want to get what we think we want if we knew it would be our undoing? Of course not. Christianity declares that an all-knowing, all-wise, all-good God actually protects us from greater disasters than the ones we bring on ourselves.

The Bible contains several passages that further explain why *bad* may not be so bad after all:

- But by means of their suffering, he rescues those who suffer. For he gets their attention through adversity. . . . Be on guard! Turn back from evil, for it was to prevent you from getting into a life of evil that God sent this suffering (Job 36:15, 21 NLT).

- When times are good, be happy;
    but when times are bad, consider:
  God has made the one
    as well as the other (Ecclesiastes 7:14).
- For the creation was subjected to frustration [futility, vanity, meaninglessness], not by its own choice, but by the will of the one who subjected it, in hope that the creation itself will be liberated from its bondage to decay and brought into the glorious freedom of the children of God (Romans 8:20–21).
- It was good for me to be afflicted
    so that I might learn your decrees. . . .
  I know, O LORD, that your laws are righteous,
    and in faithfulness you have afflicted me
    (Psalm 119: 71, 75).

The Christian God is the God of love. Christianity explains that while *we* work and pray for things that would destroy us, a loving God—like a loving parent—graciously slows us down. We may wish he would just leave us alone, but as C. S. Lewis noted, that would not be asking for *more* love, but less.[3]

WE ARE EASILY DECEIVED

We are made in such a way that we want to lead comfortable, happy, meaningful lives. We also are made in such a way that we think we know the best way to pull this off. Sin deceives us, and we leave God out of our systems. Commenting on sin's deceitfulness, sixteenth-century Reformer Martin Luther once said:

It is rightly called the deceitfulness of sin because it deceives under the appearance of good. This phrase "deceitfulness of sin" ought to be understood in a much wider sense, so that the term includes even one's own righteousness and wisdom. For more than anything else one's own righteousness and wisdom deceive one and work against faith in Christ, since we love the flesh and the sensations of the flesh and also riches and possessions, but we love nothing more ardently than our own feelings, judgment, purpose, and will, especially when they seem to be good.[4]

In order to change we have to become uncomfortable with something. Christianity states that God loves us so much that he will never let us become comfortable in the world. He does this by removing the possibility of finding any meaning apart from him.

So what's the bottom line? If God does not introduce futility into our lives and make us uncomfortable, nothing will ever change. Christianity never claims that futility is good, but that God uses it for good. Futility sets in when our system fails. It leads us to despair. Despair leads us to the leap. Futility is the grace of God that allows us to be disturbed out of complacency and error.

What we would be willing to accept in life is so inferior to the abundant life God would like us to have.

THE GRACE OF AN UNTAMABLE GOD

By this point you may be thinking *Isn't this a rather brutal system to get men to become Christians?* I suppose it is in one sense. It is brutal for a surgeon to amputate a gangrenous leg, but he does so in order to save the rest of the body. In the same way, Christianity is a gracious system designed to save us from ourselves.

When I was a teenager, I tried to tame my parents. I couldn't. Then I tried to tame my brothers, and I failed there, too. Next I tried to tame my teachers. No dice. I quit high school. My dad escorted me down to the Army enlistment office. I couldn't tame my dad.

Then I got married and tried to tame my wife. I couldn't tame my wife either. Next we had children, and I tried to tame them too, but I couldn't. Then I became a Christian, and, following the pattern, I tried to tame God.

And God is an untamable God. He just will not allow himself to be tamed. The truth is, if we didn't try to tame God, he wouldn't have to tame us.

Is there any doubt that men think they can tame God? Is there any doubt that they will fail? We are being sought by an untamable God. He is the immovable rock dropped in your path. He loves you so much that he will brutalize you, if he must, so that you will choose him of your own free will. It is precisely because of this fierce love of God that worldly, moral, and religious systems don't work. Life becomes futile when we try to tame God.

ABUNDANCE, NOT COMFORT

In the Christian system, God desires men to lead an abundant life. Yet, sadly, men often mistake abundant for *comfortable*.

Someone has told the story about a farmer and his son who cleared a field together over a couple of weeks. They placed the brush in a pile, and after a few days birds came and started to build nests. When the farmer chased the birds away, his son thought he was being extremely cruel.

At the end of the two weeks the field was cleared, and the farmer proceeded to set the pile of brush on fire. Only then did his son see that what he had at first thought was an act of cruelty was actually an act of kindness. This world is not our home. Someday the world will come to an end. God doesn't want us to get too comfortable here.

Everyone experiences futility. That's why Solomon said, in essence, "I'm writing Ecclesiastes because I want to spare my readers the grief I went through. Here are my conclusions: Everything apart from God ends in futility. So revere God and obey his commands."

Futility is the love of God that restrains a man from ruining his life of his own free will.

How Can a Man Stake His Entire Life on Believing the Bible Is True?

Cliff Jackson sat across the mahogany conference table from three smirking lawyers, all ten years younger and impeccably dressed, sporting power ties in a rainbow of yellow, red, and purple—even the female lawyer wore one. They smelled like ambition, greed, and power. Cliff was unimpressed.

After the perfunctory five-minute exchange of social amenities, the hotshot in the dark blue suit briefly reviewed the facts, then threw the first punch. "Will your client return the deposit money by Friday or not? If not, our client has instructed us to file suit for recovery and damages," said blue.

This guy thinks he's pretty tough, thought Cliff, stifling a smile. Far more experienced, he stared at Mr. Tough for a long minute. Hotshot or not, blue's hands started to sweat. Cliff was one of those lawyers who could make you wish you had never been born.

Gifted with an incisive mind, he could cut through the blather and get straight to the meat of the coconut.

Cliff said, "If you will look at paragraph 14.c.1 of the contract between our clients—you did reread the contract for this meeting, didn't you?—you will notice that your client agreed the $500,000 deposit you want returned would serve as liquidated damages if your client failed to complete the purchase of my client's company. Sorry, boys, but you've got a dog here that won't hunt. We're not running a charitable organization. By the way, did we mention we turned down three other offers and went instead with your client because your client said they had never failed to close a deal? I guess there's a first time for everything, huh . . . but it ain't gonna be for free, people." Cliff didn't intentionally try to embarrass anyone, but he could make an adversary feel dumber than Bart Simpson.

In law school Cliff was editor of his law school review and graduated near the top of his class. His professors had predicted great things for Cliff. "He has such potential," they would say. He was heavily recruited by the best law firms in the state, all of which told him, "You've got great potential." In the expectation that law firms would consolidate into larger statewide and regional firms, Cliff went with the local office of a large statewide firm. From his first day on the job different partners repeatedly told him, "You've got a lot of potential, Cliff." He got sick of hearing about it. He was soon ready for all that potential to become some "actual."

Cliff had put in the requisite seventy-hour weeks expected of partner candidates. He made manager right on schedule but couldn't understand why he didn't make partner during his eighth year. Cliff wanted answers. He entered the richly appointed corner office of the managing partner, who suggested they sit in two leather chairs by the window. He was about to hear words that would bring his world tumbling down. The managing partner said, "Cliff, you're one of our best men, but you have a lot of unmet potential."

Unmet potential? thought Cliff. *What's this guy trying to say?* Clearly something wasn't adding up.

Soliciting new business had never been Cliff's strong suit. He was uncomfortable asking people for their business. Instead, he was content to take whatever work the partners assigned him. Actually, many of those assignments had turned into loyal clients who actually preferred Cliff over the partner-in-charge. So in addition to not bringing new clients into the firm, he was viewed as one who took clients away from existing partners. Some of the younger, hungrier partners were not humored. So when partnership status came up at the annual associate review, a small but powerful group of partners always had a knock on Cliff. The unaffected partners didn't want to die on that hill, so they let the blackballers have their way. Cliff was repeatedly passed over for promotion to partner.

For each of the next three years Cliff raised the issue with the managing partner at his annual review. The first year the managing partner parried by saying, "It's something that will happen— but not this year." Cliff thought, *Okay, so I missed it by a year. I'm sure they'll make it right.*

The second year the managing partner said, "Let me be honest and say that a few partners have reservations because you don't bring in new clients." For the next six months he tried to develop some new business, but nothing came of it. Besides, he could barely keep up with the work he already had. So he pulled back from pursuing clients he didn't really want anyway.

The third year Cliff knocked on the managing partner's door. Motioning Cliff in, the managing partner signaled that he was about to wrap up a phone call. He pointed for Cliff to take the chair facing his massive desk instead of the elegant leather chair in which Cliff had sat in previous years. He hung up the phone, cleared his throat, and proceeded with what they both knew was an obvious lie. "Cliff, you're doing a terrific job. We are doing some organizational restructuring right now, however, so we're putting the brakes on a few things." *Blah, blah, blah* . . . He droned on for a few more awkward minutes until they both sensed that enough time had passed to make it comfortable to adjourn the meeting, which they did hastily.

Cliff knew he had been blackballed, but he didn't know by whom—and he really didn't know why either. For the next several months he tried to be philosophical. As time passed, though, he began to resent not only being passed over, but also that the partners had been less than candid with him. What especially galled him was that he knew his work was better than any other associate and nearly every partner in the firm. He hated that he had been manipulated and misled. Even more, though, he hated that he hadn't seen it coming.

Life continued on for Cliff. During his eleventh year in the firm he finally made partner—but his election was a hollow achievement for him. He felt used. Frankly, he was so bitter that he hated all his new partners—the ones who had held him back and the ones who had allowed it to happen. And he had no idea who was who.

When Cliff's meeting with the three hotshot lawyers adjourned, he went straight to the club for his weekly racquetball match with Rick Barrington, his roommate in law school. Rick was everything Cliff would never be, and vice versa. Cliff was thorough, careful, analytical, and serious. Rick was careless, impulsive, and a compulsive party boy. It was only the fate of being assigned roommates that would have ever brought them together, but they clicked. Cliff came from a hardworking middle class family. Rick's father was a nationally prominent heart surgeon. If great things happened for Cliff, it would come as a pleasant surprise; great things were expected of Rick. Rick found it a difficult mantle to wear.

During late-night "share-alls" in law school they had revealed their greatest hopes, fears, and shameful secrets to each other. That had made them soul mates who each felt like the other was the only one he could truly trust. Their other friends saw them as sort of an "odd couple," but their bond of friendship was genuine, forged before any worldly achievements—so neither had to worry about the motives behind the friendship of the other.

Cliff and Rick kept up with each other by playing racquetball once a week. After this week's game they got to talking over beer and pretzels about John Thompson, the client Cliff had just protected from the three sharks. Thompson, one of their classmates, had built a successful software company. In a voice dripping with contempt, Cliff said, "John Thompson and I had lunch last Tuesday. I think John has found religion."

That doesn't sound like such a bad idea, thought Rick.

Rick had recently been reflecting on his own life. He realized it was shallow—futile, really. Most days he felt like the sad clown of a cruel puppeteer who was pulling his strings. He wondered why Cliff would express such a problem with religion. Cliff's life, after all, was no picture of contentment. Rick knew Cliff's marriage was hanging on by a thread. "Cliff," he said, "we've been buddies for a long time, right?"

"That's right."

"Well, don't you ever get frustrated that life seems so pointless? What's so wrong with finding a little relief in religion?" He paused as the waitress brought another round of beer and pretzels.

"Let me just be real honest with you, Cliff. You and I both know that I barely scraped my way through law school. I'm a celebrity sports agent by dumb luck. I careen around town at ninety miles an hour, cell phone constantly ringing. I know everybody, and I'm a favorite on everyone's party list. I've tried a lot of different paths. They've all been dead ends. I've gotten everything I ever wanted, and I'm miserable—just miserable. So here it is: I'm squandering my life. I feel like my soul is wandering around in a wilderness."

Rick had no religious background at all. He had never been to a church service, unless you counted funerals and weddings. Nevertheless, he believed in God.

What Rick could not have known from Cliff's comment about John Thompson was that Cliff secretly envied John. Cliff himself was religious. Always had been, thanks to his mother. Even in college he somehow made it to church about two out of three Sundays—no matter how much of a hangover he had. By disposition Cliff always seemed to be carrying around a burden of guilt about his past. His father drank too much; he thought it was his fault. His parents argued too much; he thought it was his fault. He felt guilty for the money it cost his parents to get him through law school. He felt guilty for doing so well financially while his three brothers all went to work in the same lumber mill where their father worked his entire life. When Cliff climbed on the bus that would take him to college and waved good-bye through the window to his mother, he knew he would never live in that town again. He needed some space.

Cliff had always tried to make his father proud of him, but no matter how much he achieved, his father never praised him. *Once, just once,* Cliff had thought many times, *I wish my dad would say, 'Son, I know we've had our differences, but I want you to know how much I love you, son.'"* It never happened. Then four years ago Cliff's father committed suicide without leaving a note. Cliff was so devastated and embarrassed that he told no one—not even Rick. His father's death happened about the same time he finally made partner, which caused his gaining of the delayed prize to feel even more pointless. Since the funeral—he had played the strong caretaker role then—he repeatedly peppered God, *Haven't I always tried to do the right thing? If you're so good, how could you let all these crummy things happen? And why couldn't you answer the one thing that would have really made me happy—to make partner on schedule?* Over the years Cliff had grown bitter toward God.

"Look, Rick," he said, "I've tried religion. When I was in high school, I attended a weeklong summer camp. When the speaker they brought in asked, 'Does anyone want to give their life to Christ?' I thought, *Sure, why not.* So I prayed the prayer he suggested. But following through on living a religious life once I returned home wasn't as easy as I thought it would be."

Cliff confessed to Rick that he had pretty much put that commitment in the background in order to pursue his dreams. Still, he had never forgotten what he had done. Rick's mournful comments were awakening a hunger for God Cliff had not felt in many years.

Rick was puzzled by Cliff's comment about praying and "giving" his life to Christ. Frankly, Cliff could just as easily have been talking about nuclear physics, because Rick didn't understand a word of what he was talking about.

"Do you know much about the Bible?" Rick asked Cliff.

"Not really. How about you?"

"Actually, I've tried to read it several times recently. But it's hard because I don't have anyone to explain to me what it means. I feel like the secret of life has been encrypted and that maybe the Bible is the decoder. I was wondering. Maybe we could find someone to teach us. What do you think?"

Cliff pondered this for a long moment. He had always hoped religion would be meaningful, but he had never put any genuine effort into understanding what Christian faith would really look like in action. He had set foot on the path but, he had to confess to himself, had "turned back" when the way got tough. Now Rick, his only true friend, was asking him to set out once again. *But Rick is naive,* he thought. Cliff knew there would be many trials ahead.

Cliff was feeling very uncomfortable. Bitterness about his lot in life had created a "wounded pride." He didn't want to "give in" to a God he had doubts about. He reasoned that, because Christianity declares God to be good and powerful, God *could* have prevented all the pain if he is all-powerful and *should* have if he is good. But apart from those worn-out questions, which never seemed to find answers, he also found a desire taking shape inside him that he could only describe as a "thirst" or "hunger" for the One who had let him go through that pain.

"Let me think about it," Cliff said in response to Rick's question.

With that, Cliff and Rick finished their beers and headed out to two very different worlds. Rick was a bachelor again after an amicable divorce three years earlier. He would attend a civic fundraiser at which he would typically drink too much, but not tonight. Cliff would go home to a wife whose heart was breaking as she saw her marriage slipping away. She felt so disconnected. At least Cliff was a good dad. He would play board games with their two children after dinner. He would tousle their hair and read them bedtime stories. It was the one thing that kept a glimmer of hope alive in his wife, Ellie.

A ROSETTA STONE FOR THE SOUL

For over a thousand years ancient Egyptian written culture had been lost because we couldn't understand hieroglyphics. Then in 1799 the Rosetta Stone was discovered near the mouth of a tributary of the Nile.

The Rosetta Stone records three languages—hieroglyphics, demotic, and Greek. Scholars were able to use the Greek language to decipher the hieroglyphs and reconstruct the lost language.

Like Rick, nearly all men reach a point when they feel life is written in some undecipherable code. In my opening chapter I referred to the words of Søren Kierkegaard: "The wisdom of the years is confusing." His complete thought was this: "The wisdom of the years is confusing. Only the wisdom of eternity is edifying."[1] He believed this "wisdom of eternity" is found in the Bible. The Bible makes the astonishing claim to decipher the mysteries of life—a Rosetta Stone for the soul.

The core issue about the Bible, even before the question of Christian belief, is "Am I looking at reliable data?" Since the Bible perfectly explains both the cause and the solution to the problem of futility, it would be of profound interest if it is also true.

HAVEN'T THEOLOGIANS CONCLUDED THAT THE BIBLE ISN'T RELIABLE?

The popular press and broadcast media frequently run articles and specials about Jesus and the Bible. In June 2000, Peter Jennings hosted ABC's landmark television special called "In Search of Jesus." It was exactly the kind of "sound bite" reporting that creates doubts about the truth and reliability of the Bible. Often this type of "reporting with an agenda" makes it sound like only an ignoramus *could* believe, much less *would* believe. I would like to answer just a handful of the questions raised by this particular program—questions that tend to apply to most "popular" reporting on the Bible. You do not need to have seen the program to get the gist:

- **Are the negative things they said about Jesus and the Bible true?** There are both liberal and conservative Bible scholars. Unfortunately, ABC only interviewed liberal scholars. Many, maybe most, liberal scholars do not believe that Jesus is who he claimed to be. Their opinions, therefore, are skewed by their worldview. (I am using *liberal* and *conservative* in a theological and not a political sense. There are, of course, many people who are both politically liberal and theologically conservative.)

- **Isn't it reasonable to assume that all Bible scholars are Christians?** It isn't a requirement. Bible scholars are no more all Christians than all Presbyterians are Christians or than all salesmen are extroverts.

- **Why were the people who were interviewed so skeptical?** Everyone speaks out of their own worldview. It should not be surprising that someone whose private motivations are personal ambition, prestige, and notoriety would attribute those same motives to Jesus. They see him attempting a political revolution. It was exactly *not* that—at least according to Jesus' own words in John 18:36—"My kingdom is not of this world. If it were, my servants would fight to prevent my arrest by the Jews. But now my kingdom is from another place."

- **But these people seemed so persuasive, while the believers in the program were, by and large, not believable?** If you saw the program, I hope you noticed that all of the comments of the skeptics were carefully selected portions of scheduled interviews with educated scholars in their areas of expertise. The comments from the enthusiastic believers—a taxi driver, for example—were all unrehearsed, spontaneous comments from average people on the street (the exception was a well-spoken pastor leading a group to the Holy Land). Personally, I wouldn't go to a taxi driver to learn about archaeology any more than I would go to a Bible scholar for directions if I was lost. The scholar may want to be helpful, but when I'm lost, I'm going to listen to the taxi driver, even if he gives me bad directions. The fact that a Christian taxi driver may be mistaken about an archaeological detail doesn't disprove Christianity. It only proves he doesn't know much about archaeology.

- **What about the differences among the four Gospel stories?** Which would cast greater doubt: that the accounts had differences, or that the accounts were the same? If all four Gospel accounts recorded the same events in the same way, the scholars who now charge that the differences prove they are *fabrications* would no doubt then complain that the similarities prove they are *plagiaries*. Doesn't it seem a bit ludicrous to postulate that since the Last Supper is not included in the Gospel of John, the writers of Matthew, Mark, and Luke fabricated the event? It seems much more satisfying to say simply, "John did not include the Last Supper in his Gospel, and he had a very good reason for not doing so." There are differences because each writer had a different purpose and different audiences. The essential facts are true and rock-solid.

- **When does a scholar cease to be a scholar?** When he or she allows personal belief or unbelief to predetermine his or her conclusions. It is intellectually dishonest to decide what you want to prove and then look for evidence to support the position you have already taken.

- **Was there anything good about "In Search of Jesus"?** I thought it was incredibly interesting that, in spite of these scholars' obvious desire to explain it away, and as theologically liberal as they were, as a matter of intellectual integrity even *they* could not explain away the Resurrection. They didn't go so far as to say they believed, but they at least would admit, "Something happened." Why did they say that? Because it would be the only time in history that a conspiracy of that type had ever held together. If deceivers had intended to devise a false religion, they would not have made up such incredible claims as the Resurrection and the deity of a man or the working of so many miracles. Nor would they have told so much about their own failures, like deserting Jesus in the face of his terrible suffering. Nor would eleven of the twelve disciples have gone to their deaths for a conspiracy. That theory doesn't work, even for a nonbeliever.

THE BIBLE'S INTERNAL CLAIM

Christianity cannot be merely what one wants it to be. It must be what it is, and then one can decide to accept or reject it. Theologian Ron Nash has put it well: "I don't mind if people want to make up a new religion. I just wish they wouldn't call it Christianity." The Bible is the sourcebook for our understanding of Christianity.

Even a casual observer of Christianity knows there is a huge debate about the truth and authority of the Bible. Why is the Bible such a lightning rod? The Bible attracts so much controversy precisely because it does claim to be the word of God. For example, the Bible contains the following verses:

- "Your word is truth" (Jesus—in John 17:17).
- "Every word of God is flawless" (Proverbs 30:5).
- "All Scripture is God-breathed and is useful for teaching, rebuking, correcting and training in righteousness" (2 Timothy 3:16).
- "Everything that was written in the past was written to teach us, so . . . we might have hope" (Romans 15:4).

While an internal claim cannot prove that the Bible is the word of God, it is not insignificant that the Bible makes this claim. In fact, if the Bible did not make this claim, there would be no debate. But since it does make this claim, and since millions of Christians down through the ages have believed the Scriptures to be true, it is a question every thinking person must settle in his or her own mind: Is the Bible true?

The orthodox Christian view is that God inspired human writers with his very thoughts, which they expressed through their own personalities. Christianity teaches that the Bible is true and without error.

Christianity is a "revealed" religion. In an earlier chapter we saw how God reveals himself in nature, and that the idea of God is an intuition we know is true. This is *general revelation.*

The Bible is *special revelation,* which simply means that what cannot be known about God and redemption through nature is "revealed" through the written word. The Bible is so important because it claims to be the map by which we understand the life and work of Jesus, the way to salvation, and the way to godly living. Why should someone who refuses to ask for directions be irritated with the Mapmaker when they arrive at the wrong destination?

TYING IT ALL TOGETHER

Not long ago I went to a favorite garden center to purchase some spring annuals. It was a warm day and, noticing my warm-up suit, the twenty-five-year-old woman (her name was Amy) who waited on me struck up a conversation. "I'll bet you're hot in that outfit," she said.

"Well, it is a little warm," I said. "How about you? You work in this heat all day."

"You don't know the half of it," she began. "I just moved back from Vermont, and I'm having a tough time adjusting to the Florida heat."

"Oh," I said, "what were you doing in Vermont?"

"Well, I had to get away to try and find myself," she offered.

"So how did you do?" I asked.

"Well, to tell you the truth, I'm pretty confused. My father is from India, my mother is a nominal Catholic, and my brother is a Baptist who keeps wagging his finger in my face and yelling that if I don't accept Jesus, I'm going to hell. I've been studying world religions, and I think there are many ways to God. What do you think?"

"Actually, you're probably asking the wrong person," I said. "You see, I'm what you might call a born-again Christian. In other words, I have put my faith in Jesus Christ to forgive my sins and give me eternal life. But it does bother me that your brother would confront you like that. I guess that's not a very sensitive way of making his point, is it?"

"No," she said, "it's not."

"Listen, Amy," I continued. "Your brother is, basically, talking like a nut. Even if he's right, that's no way to talk about matters of faith. Let me suggest a couple of things to consider.

"First, if you go to the tomb of Confucius—occupied. If you go to the tomb of Buddha—occupied. If you go to the tomb of Muhammad—occupied. If you go to the tomb of Jesus—empty. That intrigues me, Amy, and it ought to intrigue you, too.

"Second, in a high school I once saw a poster of the vast cosmos with the caption "'Either we are alone in the universe or we are not. Both ideas are overwhelming.'"

"Wow. That's heavy," said Amy.

"Yes, it is. And I think you owe it to yourself to investigate that issue. Jesus is the only one of those four men who claimed to be God. If that's true, then don't you think you owe it to yourself to find out if he really is who he says he is?"

"Yeah, but there's no way to know for sure," she offered lamely.

"Actually, there is," I suggested. "Do you have a Bible?"

"Oh, yes," she said. "My brother gave me a big, thick Life Application Bible."

I said, "You mean the nut?"

She said, "Yes."

"Okay, then. Let me make a suggestion. Is that all right?" She nodded approval.

"In the Bible there's a short book called the Gospel of John. It contains twenty-one chapters. Why don't you investigate the claims of Jesus for yourself—who he claimed to be, why he came to earth, what belief in him means? You could read a chapter a day for three weeks. John recorded some of Jesus' most remarkable words in those few pages. I would also suggest you begin each time by praying something like *Jesus, if you are God, then I'm asking you to reveal yourself to me in these pages.* Frankly, Amy, I can't do any better than that. If he is who he says he is, then he doesn't need me to argue his case. You can decide for yourself. What do you think?"

"You know, I think I'll do that," she said conclusively.

DECIDING FOR YOURSELF

You can decide for yourself whether or not to believe the Bible is true and whether you can stake your life on it. You could do this by reading it for yourself. Perhaps you'd want to follow the suggestion I made to Amy—reading the Gospel of John, a chapter a day for three weeks. Interact with the text, asking questions like:

- Why did the writer record these particular sayings and events?
- What was his purpose for writing his book?

- What is being said?
- Does what is being said make sense?
- What does Jesus say?
- What does Jesus do?
- Why does Jesus say and do these things?
- How did the people respond?
- How do you respond?
- What does Jesus claim about himself?
- What does Jesus claim about believing in him?
- Does this book hang together?
- Does this book have the ring of authority?
- Does this book seem cogent?
- Does this book have the ring of truth to you personally?

You don't have to trick yourself into Christianity. Let Jesus speak for himself. Once you have come to understand, if Jesus doesn't draw you, nothing I can add will draw you either. There is no sense arguing about it. That would be a waste of time.

PART THREE

COMING BACK TO GOD

11

HOW TO COME BACK TO GOD

On the drive home from racquetball Cliff began thinking again about Rick's question. He was genuinely puzzled and disappointed that he had never been able to integrate his religion and his life. How could he? He had always considered God and faith to be "otherworld" issues and thus kept them in a separate compartment from everyday life.

Cliff had developed a tidy little world that he could control. He had a system. Yet he had no anchor for his soul—nothing that felt solid enough to stand on. At the age of thirty-eight he realized he had overlooked one small potential problem—what if his system didn't work? Truth is, it didn't. His wife was bored with him. He couldn't blame her—he bored himself.

He felt as though there was a hostile "force" that always worked against him, a battle always raging within him. He did not know what that force was. No one had ever explained to him that Christianity isn't magic—not that he had ever given anyone a chance. You have to educate yourself about how it works, just as you would educate yourself about how to be a good lawyer, or plumber, or whatever. Cliff went to church like a lawyer who shows up in court without ever having reviewed his case files—the kind of lawyer Cliff, ironically, would despise.

It dawned on him, *You know, I'm spiritually ignorant. It's never occurred to me that I may have a responsibility to learn how Christianity actually answers the most difficult questions about life.* As this thought entered his consciousness, he felt a heavy wave of emotion sweep over him and envelope him in what he could only describe as a sensation of warm syrup. What Cliff didn't know—how could he?—was that God's Spirit was initiating a process of leading him into the fold.

Cliff had known for several years that his cordial relationship with his wife, Ellie, disguised a much deeper problem. There were whole tracts of territory they had once reveled in together that had now become too touchy and, so, off-limits. He knew he had broken her spirit. Ellie just wasn't the same cheerful, upbeat person he had married fifteen years earlier. Knowing that he was to blame made him ashamed, but he had no idea what to do about it. How do you turn around a battleship, anyway, when you're not even qualified to be on the bridge? So Cliff had been content to let the currents take them where they may. But inside he was sincerely troubled.

Ellie's life revolved around their two wonderful children. Nathan was nine, and Brittany was six. As she felt Cliff slipping away, Ellie made her children the center of her world. She lavished them with the affection she desperately wanted to share with Cliff but couldn't. Ellie herself was genuinely puzzled. She had reached out to Cliff, but that only seemed to make him even more moody. *What does he want?* she would rehearse over and over in her mind. *He has everything in life he ever wanted. He loves law. We have two great children. We live in a wonderful home.* She wanted so much to help him, but she couldn't. No matter what she said or tried, he always seemed just beyond her grasp—just outside the range of her voice. She could never really put into words how she felt, and he could never really appreciate how much she tried.

Cliff came into the kitchen, laid his briefcase on the counter, and gave Ellie a surprisingly sincere kiss on her cheek and said, "I love you"—words she hadn't heard for a long, long time. As she watched him open the refrigerator door, Ellie saw something she hadn't seen in many years. It was a crack in Cliff's armor. The bitterness that usually covered him like a brittle shell wasn't quite so harsh. The effect was like water to a drooping plant. She was startled by the emotion that gripped her heart. She left the room so Cliff wouldn't see the tears running down her cheeks. She had been crying herself to sleep often for the past several months.

Ellie was extremely discouraged. She was right on the verge of becoming clinically depressed. Her marriage was dying, and nothing she said or did seemed to help. In fact, a lot of what she did—like suggesting they go to a marriage counselor—only seemed to make things worse. Cliff only viewed these suggestions as a threat.

Teaching school was a great release for Ellie. She became friendly with another woman who ate lunch at the same time. Over the first couple of years they shared funny and sad stories about their students. Gradually, they got to know about each other's families, too. Something about Vickie made a deep impression on Ellie. She had an inner beauty and calmness that Ellie came to envy. One day Vickie caught Ellie off guard—they had never spoken about personal problems—by asking, "Ellie, you never say much about Cliff. How is your relationship with him?"

Being a very private person, Ellie felt a deluge of conflicting emotions. On one hand, every fiber in her screamed, *Say nothing*. But an equally loud voice shouted, *You've got to tell someone what you're going through*. The two voices were shouting back and forth so loudly she could barely think. The next thing Ellie knew she was sharing the whole bloody mess. Ellie couldn't believe she was doing it, but Vickie just seemed so interested—and so trustworthy and wise, too.

"Ellie," said Vickie, "I know what you're going through. Five years ago I was in your shoes. My marriage had been through its own ups and downs. Something has happened in my life, though, that

has changed all that. I'd love to tell you about it if you'd like to know."
Vickie did not want to cross a boundary without permission.

"Well, of course, Vickie. I want to save my marriage."

"What I'm about to share with you may or may not save your marriage. What it will do is resolve your own personal struggle for a meaningful life. It will allow you to find contentment, regardless of your circumstances. Not to say that things that hurt won't still hurt, but that you will have the strength and faith to carry on, no matter what comes. Do you still want to know?"

"Yes, I do," said Ellie.

Vickie continued, "Five years ago everything started to change when my husband, Jeff, started dabbling with Christianity. He joined a group of guys meeting in a small group once a week at his office before work. Gradually he learned that Christianity isn't at all like what he had seen depicted in popular culture but is instead a belief and trust in the Christ of history. The changes in his life were so profound I couldn't help it—I found myself being attracted to at least explore Christianity. Together we started attending a church that emphasizes worshiping God joyfully; we even joined a Bible study for couples offered by the church, and our faith life slowly changed from dabbling to serious." It showed. This is what Ellie had seen in Vickie but hadn't recognized.

During the next ten minutes Ellie learned a truth so simple and so profound she could hardly believe it. But, in the end, she did.

Now, two weeks later, her husband had kissed her on the cheek, said "I love you," and a glimmer of hope had sprung back to life.

"Cliff, can we talk tonight after the kids go to bed? Some things are happening to me that I want you to know about."

"Sure," said Cliff, a little nervous about what might be coming.

After Ellie shared her experience from a couple of weeks earlier, Cliff almost laughed out loud. *I'm surrounded!* he thought. *They're all going crazy. John Thompson, Rick, and now Ellie. Or maybe I'm the one who's crazy.*

THE BUSINESS OF SOUL MAKING

A man put his "eternal soul" up for auction on eBay.com. He received nine bids—the highest offer was $20.50; eBay then removed the item from their system.

Why would a man want to sell his soul? Only if, because of futility, he thought it was worthless. Christianity solves a number of problems, but the central problem is "What will happen to my soul?"

Christianity claims that every person has a soul, and that God is in the business of "soul making." The soul is that which animates this life and remains in the next. The soul does not dissolve in death. Christianity claims that a single soul is of infinite value and is precious to God. In his own words, Jesus poses the focusing question: "What good will it be for a man if he gains the whole world, yet forfeits his soul? Or what can a man give in exchange for his soul?"[1]

Other systems do capture bits and pieces of truth, but Christianity is the most highly developed of all religious systems—the culmination. The purpose of Christianity is "soul making." God has a "system" by which this is done. Among all religious systems the Christian system is unique; it claims to be perfectly designed to solve the problem of futility. It claims to be a system that leads to an abundant life here on earth (though not without troubles) and, in the world to come, everlasting life.

REVIEW

It is important to believe that which we can reasonably believe is true. So far in this book we have demonstrated that it is reasonable to believe ...

- that God exists.
- that nothing in nature demands a closed system in which God could not supernaturally intervene.
- that we each have a system perfectly designed to produce the result we are getting.

- that even if we get exactly what we want, we will still not be happy apart from God.
- that the Bible is the word of God. It claims to be the word of God, and it is not insignificant that it makes this claim. It continues to change men's lives, while rebuffing attempts to discredit it.
- that Christianity solves the problem of futility, and you don't have to trick yourself into believing it.

Everything we have discussed to this point demonstrates the possibility of a Divine Being intervening in our human affairs to rescue us from our futility and sins. I am not saying anyone has to actually believe these conclusions, but only that it would not be unreasonable if they did. My personal conviction, however, is that we have demonstrated that it is more unreasonable *not* to believe than to believe. In Christianity, the names *Messiah, Christ,* and *Savior* are used to describe the one who makes this intervention into our world to save us.

Interviewer Larry King once said, "As a Jew, I have had nothing but the greatest and most profound respect for Jesus Christ of Nazareth. He was, after all, Jewish—born Jewish, died Jewish. I think Jesus Christ was the greatest single individual of both millenniums, and he had a more profound effect on mankind than any individual ever born. If there's one person in history I would like to interview, it would be Jesus."[2]

There are too many great thinkers who have concluded that Jesus was the Christ for us to dismiss the possibility that Christianity is true. If you have honest doubts about the identity and mission of Jesus, a modest goal might be to spend enough time investigating Jesus so as, if not to believe, at least to doubt the certainty of your doubt.

THE CORRECT INFORMATION

Describing Christianity reminds me of the old story about three blind men describing an elephant. One grabbed its leg and said, "It's like a tree." Another grabbed the trunk and said, "It's like a hose." The third grabbed an ear and said, "It's like a great fan." All true, but only partially.

To understand the Christian system we must first have the correct information. Over the course of the nearly two thousand years since Jesus walked the earth—an established historical fact that scholars no longer debate—thinkers and writers have developed many helpful devices to summarize and explain the system Jesus proclaimed. Tens of thousands of Christian and non-Christian writers have spent millions of hours figuring out how best to explain the Christian system to their readers by means of such things as confessions, creeds, liturgies, catechisms, systematic theologies, and apologetics. All are designed to help ordinary people understand Christianity.

Our task here is much simpler: What is the minimum description of Christianity that still explains the whole? Christianity itself helps us at this point by breaking itself down into two parts: "the gospel" *(kērygma)* and "the teachings" *(didachē)*. You don't need to know how an engine works in order to drive a car. Likewise, you don't need to know all the Christian teachings in order to become a Christian. You only need to understand the gospel, often called "the Good News."

There is no single best way to explain "the gospel" of Jesus. There are, however, some essentials that must be included—universal beliefs that have always been believed everywhere by everyone who professes a Christian faith. These essentials have come to be known as "the rule of faith." The risk in explaining the faith that Jesus proclaimed is to add any "test" or "rule of behavior" that Jesus did not.

THE NECESSARY INFORMATION

Everything I am about to mention can be confirmed by attending an evangelical church service anywhere in America this coming Sunday morning. Read the bulletin, the words to the hymns or choruses, and the creeds. Listen to the Scripture reading, the prayers, and the sermon. Everything can be found there.

The simplest expression of "the gospel" is quoted by the apostle Paul: "For the wages of sin is death, but the gift of God is eternal life in Christ Jesus our Lord."[3] If we step back from this gospel statement, we see three things that need to be fleshed out. The first is *the problem of man,* the second is *the issue of Jesus,* and the third is *the gift of eternal life.* These three elements of the gospel have traditionally had formal names: the doctrine of man, the doctrine of Christ, and the doctrine of salvation. I would summarize this message, and the Christian system, by saying . . .

- Adam failed.
- Jesus nailed.
- Grace prevailed.

Let's briefly look at these three parts.

Adam Failed

The paradox of man is that he is a product of both the Creation and the Fall. The Creation made him like a god, and the Fall made him like a devil.

When we observe the animals, we notice that we are the highest order of creatures by a wide margin. Intuition tells us that human beings have dignity. Christianity teaches that mankind is God's crowning achievement, the full expression of God's creative genius, and that he has good plans for us.

The true tragedy of our existence is not what we have become, but what we could have been. We all sense by intuition that mankind has not reached its potential. We each have an instinct that tells us the human race was destined for better, that our dignity has been tarnished. Logic tells us that something catastrophic has happened to mankind.

Christianity teaches that this catastrophe took place in the Garden of Eden. Evil entered the world, and people began to make sinful choices. A downward spiral of sin continues to the present day.

Christianity teaches that all people are guilty of sin, which halts our progress toward an abundant life. Not only is progress halted, but we also have become alienated from our Creator. It is just this gap—between our sinful state and the abundant life—that creates futility. Futility would not be so horrific if we did not know by instinct what we had lost.

In the first chapter the question was posed, "Why am I still so restless?" Saint Augustine gave the answer in the first paragraph of his book *The Confessions:* "You have made us for Thyself, and our hearts are restless until they rest in Thee." The core solution of Christianity is that no matter how futile your life has become, Jesus Christ wants to restore you to your original dignity and give you rest for your soul both now and forever. This is true Christianity: No matter what you've done, you can be forgiven.

Jesus Nailed

The Christian solution for sin is that God came into the world to be a Savior. Why do we need a Savior? We wouldn't need a Savior if we had done nothing wrong.

Theologian J. Gresham Machen once wrote, "Jesus died—that's history. Jesus died for my sins—that's doctrine."[4] The *history* and *doctrine* of Christ, though intertwined, are different.

The *history* of Jesus is the story of his *Incarnation*. Jesus was a living person who existed in history, performed remarkable miracles, claimed deity, and was resurrected from death. If the birth, life, death, and resurrection of Jesus had never happened in history, there would be no Christian religion. The Jesus of history is the Christ of faith. Christianity *is* Jesus Christ. The *doctrine* of Christ—"he died for our sins"—is understanding that Jesus Christ claimed to make *atonement* for our sins, or to satisfy the "wages of sin is death" problem.

In his own words Jesus said, "I came that you may have life and have it abundantly. I came to seek and to save the lost. For God so loved that world that he sent me into the world so that whoever believes in me will not perish but have everlasting life. I tell you the truth, whoever hears my words and believes him who sent me has eternal life and will not be condemned, he has crossed over from death to life. All that the Father gives me will come to me, and whoever comes to me I will never drive away. I shall lose none of them that he has given me, but raise them up at the last day. My sheep know my voice, and no one can snatch them out of my hand." About his identity Jesus said, "He who has seen me has seen the Father. The Father and I are one. I who speak to you am the Messiah."[5]

These claims, of course, are either true, or they are not true. At this point, however, I am not asking you to believe Christianity, only to understand it.

Why a Human?

Christianity offers two compelling reasons why God sent his Son to become a human being. First, he reduced himself to flesh that we might comprehend him (the *Incarnation*). Second, through Jesus he offered a final, perfect sacrifice for our sins (the *Atonement*).

You might have imagined that if God had, say, one hundred characteristics, that in Jesus you might see ten characteristics on display. It is not like that at all. The Christian system teaches that Jesus is "the exact representation" of God's being, all of God in a human body, and that seeing Jesus is seeing the Father.[6]

A favorite story of unknown origin illustrates the Incarnation of Jesus. Flurries of snow swirled on a chilly Christmas Eve. Standing at the front window a man waved as his wife and children drove away to attend the candlelight service. He couldn't understand all the fuss about Jesus.

Alone, he busied himself decorating the family tree. Suddenly, he heard a *thump* against the window, and then another, and another, *thump . . . thump*. He looked out, and there, shivering on the ground outside the window, lay several tiny sparrows attracted by the light and warmth inside.

Touched, the man went to the garage, turned on the light, and opened the door. The birds didn't move. He got behind them and tried to shoo them in. They scattered. He made a trail into the garage by crumbling some crackers. They wouldn't budge.

He was frustrated as it sunk in that he was a giant, alien creature who terrified the tiny birds. Why couldn't he make them understand that what he wanted more than anything was to help them?

Disheartened, the man went back inside and stared out the window at the frightened little birds. Then, like a bolt of lightning, a thought struck him. *If only I could become a little bird myself— for just a moment. Then they wouldn't be afraid, and I could show them how to find warmth and safety.*

Just then it dawned on him. *Now I understand. That's why Jesus came.*

The Screen People

Physicist Hugh Ross depicted the same point by creating what I'm sure will become a renowned illustration. Imagine a couple of two-dimensional people who live on your computer screen—a couple of "stick" figures.

Suppose you, living in three dimensions, are sitting with your face eight inches away from the screen. To the "screen people," who can only see in height and width, you are invisible. Now suppose you wanted to make yourself known to the screen people. How would you do it? First, you could touch your finger to the screen. How would you be perceived? The screen people would think you were a dot. And when you removed your finger, you would once again be invisible to them.

Now suppose you wanted to try again, so this time you placed your finger lengthwise on the screen. How would you be perceived? The screen people, perceiving only height and width, would think you were a line. Next, imagine that you could actually push your hand through the screen—that it was a liquid surface. If you pushed your finger through, the screen people would perceive that you were a circle. If you kept pushing your arm through, they would perceive you as a bigger circle. But because they are unable to perceive in the third dimension, they will never perceive you as you are. The only way to communicate with them on their level would be to somehow reduce yourself to two dimensions and become a screen person. Then they could perceive you.

Ross makes the point that God, who has many more dimensions than we do, no doubt does interact with us in the same way we might interact with screen people—which would explain why people perceive God so differently, depending on what "part" of his other dimensions he happens to be revealing at the time.

The unique claim of Christianity, however, is that not only does God relate to us from his multidimensionality, but he has also reduced himself in his Son Jesus to *become,* in effect, a screen person so that we might comprehend him.[7]

Grace Prevailed

One day Mark was explaining Christianity to Ed. Ed was interested and said, "But I have nothing to offer!"

"You're beginning to understand," said Mark.

Another man said, "I don't feel like I'm worthy of God." He is close, very close, to understanding Christianity.

The principal requirement for becoming a Christian is to admit that you are not worthy to be one. Christianity is unique among all religions because it is the only religion based on nonperformance. Becoming a Christian is not about "doing" something but about acknowledging one's inability to do *anything* to save oneself. It's not about modifying your behavior to make God happy (more on this in the next chapter).

Rather, the work of salvation is a work of *grace.* The apostle Paul wrote, "But because of his great love for us, God, who is rich in mercy, made us alive with Christ even when we were dead in transgressions—it is by grace you have been saved."[8] Once this simple idea called *grace* is grasped, it begins a chain reaction in the soul. There is no "merit" to be earned. Rather than receiving justice, we have through God's mercy received grace, which leads to godly sorrow and to faith.

The New Testament declares this:

> Therefore, if anyone is in Christ, he is a new creation; the old has gone, the new has come! All this is from God, who reconciled us to himself through Christ. . . . God was reconciling the world to himself in Christ, not counting men's sins against them. . . . God made him who had no sin to be sin for us, so that in him we might become the righteousness of God.[9]

THE MINIMUM BELIEF

The Christian system could be the subject of endless books. On second thought, I should say the Christian system *is* the subject of endless books. What is the minimum, though, that a true Christian believes?

No one can require a more qualified testimony, or can accept less, than "I, _____, a sinner, trust the Savior, Jesus, for the forgiveness of my sins and eternal life." Behind this confession of faith are the following truths:

About Ourselves

- Though created for glory and honor, we have all become sinners.
- No matter what we've done, we can be forgiven.

About Jesus

- Jesus, the Son of God, conceived by the Holy Spirit, became a man, lived a sinless life, was crucified as a sacrifice for the sins of all men, was buried, was resurrected to life, ascended to heaven where he lives today with God the Father, and will come again to redeem those who believe in him and to judge the world.

About Salvation

- Christ Jesus came into the world to save sinners.
- The apostle Paul said he only had one message—the necessity of turning from sin and turning to God, and of faith in our Lord Jesus.[10]
- It is by grace that we are saved, through faith.
- Jesus came to give us an abundant life (contra a life of futility).

COMING BACK, OR COMING, TO GOD

I love a story C. S. Lewis tells in *Prince Caspian* (Book Four of The Chronicles of Narnia). The four heroes, Peter, Edmund, Lucy, and Susan, make an association with a dwarf named Trumpkin—a great warrior.

The five of them take a journey. The four children talk about a lion, Aslan—the Christ-figure in the story. Trumpkin doesn't believe in lions. Peter, Edmund, Lucy, and Susan do, because they have seen Aslan before; yet to this point in their journey they haven't seen him because of their doubts. Then, in the course of their trek, one by one all four children see Aslan; Trumpkin does not.

Susan, the last child to see Aslan, is filled with remorse for having wanted to go in a different direction. She says, "What ever am I to say to him?" Lucy suggests, "Perhaps you won't need to say much."

Then Aslan turns and faces the fivesome, filling them with both gladness and fear. Peter, their leader, approaches Aslan, drops to one knee, and says, "I'm so glad. And I'm so sorry. I've been leading them wrong ever since we started and especially yesterday morning." Aslan says only, "My dear son."

Then Aslan turns to Edmund and says, "Well done."

Then the deep-voiced lion says, "Susan, you have listened to your fears. Come, let me breathe on you. Forget them. Are you brave again?" Susan replies, "A little."

Then, in a much louder voice bordering on a roar, Aslan bellows out to Trumpkin, who now finally can see the lion, "Come here!" Trumpkin gasps, but the children aren't worried because they know Aslan well enough to see that he likes the dwarf very much. Trumpkin, though, has never seen a lion before, especially *this* lion. He does the only sensible thing and slowly obeys Aslan's command.

Aslan pounces. Holding him like a kitten in its mother's mouth, Aslan gives him a shake; Trumpkin's armor rattles, and he flies up in the air. As he comes down, the huge paws catch him as gently as a mother's arms and set him upright on the ground. Then Aslan asks, "Son of Earth, shall we be friends?"

"Ye-he-he-hes" comes the dwarf's response.[11]

And this is how the Lord works with us. When the futility is unbearable, when it looks like we are about to perish, he turns to face us, forgives us, breathes courage on us, and, if we need it, pounces on us. It may feel like he's going to rip us limb from limb. He tosses us, but then he catches us in his soft, velvety paws and sets us upright and asks us if we can be friends. That's the end of living by any other system. Even when we are in utter, complete, total rebellion against God, in his kindness he shakes things up and asks us if we would like to be his friend.

Have you let your fears take you in a wrong direction but now are ready to come back? Perhaps you won't have to say much. Let him breathe on you. Have you been stubbornly going astray? Bow your knee, say I'm sorry, and hear him say "My dear son." Have you not believed in Christ? He likes you very much, and he says, "Come here!" He is the one who by means of futility has shaken you up. And now he is asking you, "Shall we be friends?"

If you are ready to be his friend for the first time, or ready to come back to him, all you have to do is tell him. Tell him you're sorry for your sins, you feel weighed down by them, you want to change, you believe in him now, you want him to save you and be your Lord. If you don't know exactly how to put it, you may want to pray the following prayer (or one similar to it):

> Lord Jesus, I need you. The burden of futility and my sorrow for my sins weigh heavily on me. I believe in you, Jesus. I believe you came and died for my sins. Thank you for giving me the gift of eternal life, as well as the promise of abundant life and rest for my soul. I want to be your friend. I receive you as my Savior and Lord. Change me from the inside out. Amen.

If you have prayed and received Christ, or renewed your relationship with him, welcome to the family, or welcome back. In the next chapter I will suggest a few steps you might take to develop a deepening relationship with him.

How to Have a Deepening Relationship with God

When Rick drove away from the racquetball club, he, too, was pensive. He went on to his dinner party and now sat lost in his thoughts as the speaker rambled on about the virtues of civic pride. *Man, I just don't know if I can take another one of these. I need something with more meat to it.* This wasn't the first time Rick had felt he wanted more out of life.

By nature Rick just wasn't very ambitious. He had never really had to work for grades, girls, or good things. As a result he took the good life for granted. He was much happier hunting and fishing or hitting the nightclubs than engaging in the pedestrian pursuits of law. The one gift that thrust Rick into the spotlight was his throwing arm. He had been the starting quarterback for Clemson University during his junior and senior years. He set several conference records, which earned him a brief mention in the hallowed pages of *Sports Illustrated*.

That's pretty much the way his entire life had gone—a minimum effort producing a charmed result. His football career ended after college, but a network of sports buddies who went pro had begun to blossom. When Rick decided to go to law school—only because his father had made such a big deal out of it—several of these guys wanted Rick to represent them. By a fluke, while still a law student, he had negotiated the largest salary and signing bonus in history for a tight end. And with that, Rick found himself in growing demand as a celebrity sports agent.

In recent months Rick had tried praying to God on several occasions, but it hadn't seemed to work. One of the things he had prayed was *God, if you exist, I want to know you.* Ironically, his racquetball conversation with Cliff was taking him in a direction from which he would never turn back. He had been living far away from God, but he had started a journey that would eventually lead him to the door of Christianity.

Several years earlier his marriage had dissolved as fast as a sugar cube in hot tea. He and his ex-wife, Linda, were on friendly, even charitable, terms. Linda had been the prettiest girl on campus, but she wanted to settle down long before Rick wanted to. He had always been flying "somewhere." She was motivated to start a family partly by her work with special-needs children. She recognized that he was just a big kid she thought would never grow up. It turns out she had been right about the big-kid part but not about the never-grow-up part.

It's time to grow up, Rick thought. *Sunday I'm going to church. I'm going to find out what John Thompson has found out about Christianity. I'm sick and tired of being sick and tired of my life. I need some relief.*

On Sunday morning Rick sat next to a man who was friendly and helpful. *He looks normal enough,* thought Rick. He helped Rick follow the order of worship in the bulletin without smothering him. Rick noticed something in this man he could only describe as a "presence." It was a blend of self-confidence and humility, a genuine interest in others but apparently not for any personal gain and a profound happiness that issued from an inner strength. Rick was captivated. The man's name was Jim.

Jim asked Rick, "Why don't we have breakfast sometime?"

Before he could stop himself, Rick had said, "How about Tuesday at my club. I'll buy."

On Tuesday morning they greeted each other and spent the first cup of coffee on sports. After the waitress brought a second cup of coffee, Jim and Rick exchanged details about their marriages, work, education, and life ambitions. Jim was at peace with himself; Rick was not. It was a simple calculus. Rick wanted to know how to get what Jim had. Rick, however, had no idea how to lead into a conversation about the attractive quality he was observing in Jim's life. Jim helped him out by taking the initiative.

"Rick, I'm glad to hear of your growing curiosity about spiritual things. Perhaps it would be useful for you to hear my story. Interested?"

"Very much so," Rick said.

"Okay then," he began. "I never really chafed against the idea that God exists when I was growing up. Actually, I never thought much about it one way or the other. My parents were agnostics, and I suppose I inherited the same point of view. They believed that God exists and that he created the world but that he isn't involved on a day-to-day basis. They were very moral people.

"I was raised to believe that if you want something badly enough, and if you're willing to work hard to get it, there's nothing you cannot accomplish in life. God gives us talents, and we become what we make of them.

"So I married my college sweetheart, went into business, and started building what I thought was a pretty good life. In fact, I did very well. But the more I achieved the emptier I felt."

At this point Rick, fifteen years Jim's junior, couldn't restrain himself and blurted out, "Yes, that's exactly how I've been feeling."

Jim nodded knowingly and continued, "I tried a lot of different ways to fill the hole. I pursued all the normal avenues—Rotary Club, Chamber of Commerce, sales awards, country club. I accumulated money and bought several expensive toys. We moved into the big house and sent the kids to a private school. Nothing, though, satisfied my deepest longings for significance and purpose."

"That's it," Rick chimed in. "That's exactly what's been happening to me. How did you resolve it? I mean, you seem so at peace with yourself now."

"Well, that's true. I am, Rick. But I took the long road to get here. I really did try every possible avenue to find meaning until, finally, I ran out of options. The one avenue I had not tried was Christianity, because I was afraid I would lose what I thought I was trying to gain. I thought coming to the Christian God would mean I would never be happy—that I would have to live in bondage to rules I didn't think I could keep. I also didn't want to give up my lifestyle.

"Was I ever wrong! I ended up in bondage all right, but it was bondage to monthly payments for a hollow lifestyle that never really got below the surface to anything deep about life and meaning. I thought that money would do what it won't and that God won't do what he will. I thought that money would make me happy and that God wouldn't bring peace and purpose to my life.

"By the ten-year mark in my business life, however, I was weary of it all. Money didn't deliver. I turned to God, and he *did* deliver."

"That's nice," said Rick. "I think that's where I'm at today. I don't know much about God, though. But unlike you, I'd be more than willing to give up my lifestyle if that's what it takes." What Rick didn't say was that he had been drinking too much, trying to anesthetize the intangible pain that gnawed at his gut. In fact, he was drinking alone, keeping a bottle under the front seat of his car and getting blitzed several nights a week. It frightened him. He was close, very close, to becoming an alcoholic.

"It's an interesting thing about lifestyle, Rick," Jim responded. "The guy who helped me get right with God told me, 'You don't have to change your lifestyle at all. God may change what you desire, but it will still be what you want to do. Christianity,' he said, 'isn't about changing your behavior; it's about putting your faith in Christ.' He was right. That's how it happened with me. I still live in the same house, drive the same kinds of cars, have the same job. But some appetites did change. I didn't ask them to change; they just did."

"You know," said Rick, "I've prayed to God several times recently that if he really exists, I'd like to know him. My best friend recently told me he went to a youth camp when he was in high school and prayed a prayer to give his life to Christ, or something like that. Does that make any sense? Is that what you're talking about? Is that the same religion? Because, frankly, I don't have a clue what he was talking about. Are you and he talking about the same religion? If it is, it sure didn't take root for him. He's miserable." After what seemed like a satisfactory answer—though Rick didn't understand a word of it—they finished their breakfast and agreed to meet again in a week.

Meanwhile, Cliff was miserable. After Ellie's late-night talk with him he couldn't get to sleep. He lay there, just staring at the ceiling for over an hour. He may have thought everyone he cared about was going crazy on him, but he was drawn to have what these crazy people had—or were getting.

Ellie just about flipped the next morning when Cliff suggested they attend church that Sunday. A few days later they all got dressed up and went to the 11:00 A.M. service at the church where they had been married. What the pastor said connected with Cliff, as he painted word pictures of God as a loving Father, a forgiver, a healer, and a physician. *Lord knows that's what I need,* Cliff thought, but he struggled to grasp the imagery because of the bad experiences he had had with his own father.

Cliff bowed his head in church and prayed silently, *Lord, I've been a bitter, resentful man. I've blamed you for my problems. But I was wrong. You are not the problem. I am. You are the solution. I've been living by my own best thinking for all of my life. My system hasn't worked. Help me if you can.* It was an honest prayer.

Cliff wrestled with how to tell Rick that he had become religious again. He didn't have to. Three weeks later Rick asked, "Well, have you had a chance to think about our studying the Bible together?"

"Rick, you'll never believe what's happened to me. After our conversation about God, I started thinking about my own life. I realized that everything you were saying about yourself fit me, too. You're quite an evangelist! Even on the drive home that night something came over me. It was like a spiritual experience, a sense of feeling pulled toward God. I felt a love for God and my wife like I had never felt before. It was extraordinary.

"Then I asked Ellie if she'd like to go to church. She about passed out. The pastor really spoke to me. Bottom line is, I'm starting to change. I have become very interested in taking a deeper look at Christianity. I have some doubts, but I think they're honest. I think I can work through them."

Rick couldn't wait another moment. He jumped in and told Cliff the story about his breakfast with Jim. Jim and Rick had already started meeting once a week to explore Christianity. Once Rick explained that Jim had already approved of the idea that Cliff join them, he said, "So what do you say? Want to join us?"

Cliff said, "Yes, I think I'd like that."

JUSTIFICATION AND SANCTIFICATION ...

In the last chapter I mentioned that Christianity breaks itself down into two parts: "the gospel" *(kērygma)* and "the teachings" *(didachē)*. I mentioned that you don't need to know how an engine works in order to drive a car. You do, however, need to know a few things about driving. Embracing "the gospel" is like getting your license; "the teachings" make it safe for you to be on the road.

Salvation includes both *justification* and *sanctification*. The "act" of becoming a Christian is called *justification*—like getting a license to drive. The "process" of becoming a Christian is called *sanctification*.

Christianity teaches that once you have been *justified*—that is, declared righteous before God—you will be a Christian always and forever. That's the "Good News." No man can lose the salvation God grants. Jesus said it this way:

> My sheep listen to my voice; I know them, and they follow me. I give them eternal life, and they shall never perish; no one can snatch them out of my hand. My Father, who has given them to me, is greater than all; no one can snatch them out of my Father's hand.[1]

Christianity also teaches that God will *sanctify* you, or make you holy, and you must also seek holiness, which simply means, "become more like Christ." As someone has said, "God loves you just the way you are, but he loves you too much to leave you that way."

"The teachings" in the Bible tell us how to imitate Christ; it is a system—a worldview. Christian philosopher Francis Schaeffer once observed that after someone becomes a Christian, we have a responsibility to confirm them in a biblical worldview. If we don't, said Schaeffer, we risk losing them to an alien worldview—basically back to a worldly, moral, or religious worldview.

It is not duty that motivates Christians to obey the teachings, but gratitude—a gratitude that grows as the believer increasingly understands the grace given to him.

... NOT BEHAVIOR MODIFICATION

The core value of all religious systems except the Christian system is behavior modification—change and you will make God happy.

After I became a Christian, I assumed the core value of Christianity was behavior modification—to "act Christianly"—a view I mistakenly held for fourteen years. I knew I was saved by grace, but I figured it was up to me to prove that God had not made a mistake.

Exactly *not* that. Christianity is not behavior modification (a thing I do) but heart transformation (a thing grace does). Romans 12:2 does *not* say, "Do not conform any longer to the system of this world *but conform to the system of Christ.*" That would simply be substituting a system that doesn't work with a system we can't keep. It would be using human strength, desire, discipline, and willpower to modify our behavior—a tiring game people can play well for no more than a few hours at a time.

Instead, the essence of what Romans 12:2 teaches is this: "Do not conform any longer to the system of this world *but let God transform you into a new person by changing the way you think.*" Christianity is not what man does for God by intense human effort, but what God does for man by sheer grace. Romans 9:16 puts it this way: "It does not, therefore, depend on man's desire or effort, but on God's mercy."

The core value of the Christian system is not behavior modification but heart transformation. We don't change ourselves; we let God change the way we think. Philippians 2:13 tells us that God is working in us, giving us the desire to obey him and the power to do what pleases him. Behavior does then become "modified," but it is because our *minds* change. We truly, and increasingly, desire to please God from within, not superficially by becoming a martyr or a self-righteous prig.

GOD IS LIKE A PUZZLE

It's fun to be a Christian. But not if you don't know what a Christian is and what he does. Perhaps the only thing more futile than not being a Christian is to be an inept one.

When in despair I first embraced Christ, I started reading the Bible every day and found great comfort. I soon saw that Christianity was made up of a few major themes, which the Bible explains over and over again from different angles. I thought of it as a puzzle, in which, when you get 80 percent of the pieces put together, the whole picture makes sense.

Then it dawned on me that Christianity is more like a cube. In other words, below each puzzle piece there is depth. Each theme is not a single puzzle piece, but rather a sentence or paragraph. Then later I realized, "No, it's more than a paragraph, it's a whole chapter." Later still I saw that each puzzle piece is like the cover of an entire book. Eventually I came to understand that there has been a centuries-long conversation taking place about each of Christianity's great themes—grace, mercy, love, obedience, forgiveness, money, holiness, and so on. An entire library lies beneath the surface of each theme.

THE LORD

John believed that Jesus Christ was his Savior. He assumed it was up to him to live in a way that was worthy of the name Christian. His experience, however, was that he couldn't. He wondered why his life was so powerless—until he attended a college campus-ministry meeting where, he said, "I heard that he was Lord."

Some men know God as Lord and don't live accordingly, but others just don't know. John simply didn't know. The right kind of knowledge changed everything. Usually it's simply a matter of lacking knowledge. The best, and only, way to fully enjoy Christianity is to fully immerse yourself in it. Let's talk about how to do that as a grateful response, rather than merely as a behavior-modification technique.

SPENDING TIME WITH GOD

One thing inexperienced Christians find irritating about experienced Christians is their relentless talk about "spending time with God." A rabid Republican will, of course, irritate even a mild Democrat, and an enthusiastic football fan will unnerve almost anyone pulling for the other team, but why do people on the same team see things differently?

A friend of mine, John Smith, says, "If someone told you that if you would spend thirty minutes a day with a man for one year you would receive $10,000,000, it's pretty certain that at the end of the year you would have $10,000,000." Experienced Christians are so relentless about "spending time with God" because they actually believe they have found something so valuable that they willingly forsake (that is, make secondary) all things to possess it.

In the same way, once a man changes allegiance and embraces Christ, he, too, will find a growing desire—perhaps an ache—to know more about the Liberator of his soul. It has been well said, "The soul that has once been waked, or stung, or uplifted by the desire for God, will inevitably awake to the fear of losing him."[2]

THE PRINCIPLES OF ABUNDANCE

Many books have been written to assist us in the sanctification process, but here are ten basics and a declaration that one could make about each:

- **God:** I will seek to love God with all my heart, and all that this implies.
- **Personal Holiness:** I will seek to lead a holy life, and all that this implies.
- **Marriage:** I will seek to be a faithful, loving husband, and all that this implies.
- **Children:** I will seek to be a godly father and grandfather, and all that this implies.
- **Work:** I will seek to honor God in my work, and all that this implies.
- **Money:** I will seek to be a faithful steward, and all that this implies.
- **Ministry:** I will seek to serve God by building his kingdom, and all that this implies.
- **Health:** I will seek to lead a balanced life, and all that this implies.
- **Church:** I will seek to join and support a church, and all that this implies.

- **Friendship:** I will seek to be a loving, honest friend, and all that this implies.

It would be quite easy to convert these ten areas into a "To Do list" in order to earn favor or merit with God—it happens all the time. That would simply be inserting Christian values into a moral or religious system. I want you to do the right thing but not for the wrong reason. The right reason is because you are grateful to God for salvation.

No man, of course, can do all these things. We are human beings, not machines. For that reason the Holy Spirit offers us ongoing power to obey, and Jesus offers us ongoing forgiveness when we don't. Our calling is to live by the Spirit, not the flesh, but when we sin, which we will continue to do, we must confess it, accept God's ongoing forgiveness, and invite the Spirit of Christ to guide us. The Bible says, "But when he, the Spirit of truth, comes, he will guide you into all truth."[3] And when we fail, Hebrews 5:2 teaches that "[Jesus] is able to deal gently with those who are ignorant and are going astray."

So what *are* the guidelines for Christian behavior? After carefully thinking about this, I offer the following thoughts as a credo for any man seeking to obey God as a grateful response to grace:

1. Some things are specifically commanded in Scripture and must be obeyed.
2. Some things are specifically prohibited in Scripture and must be avoided.
3. Everything not specifically prohibited is permissible.
4. Not everything permissible is beneficial.
5. The Holy Spirit, through the Scriptures privately read or preached, will guide us into proper behavior by his grace.
6. All things must be approached in the attitude of humble submission and obedience to God's will and calling.
7. The goal is to be wise.

THE CIGAR STORY

For twenty-five years I have regularly enjoyed a good cigar—but never more than when traveling abroad, where you can get your hands on some good Cuban stogies.

As almost everyone knows, America has held an embargo against bringing any Cuban products into the United States since 1962. Cigar lovers, though, maintain an underground that keeps these peerless Cuban stogies showing up from time to time.

Two years ago our family undertook a trip to the Holy Land, which I'd been dreaming about for twenty years. Just before returning, I purchased four premium Cuban cigars and put them in my backpack. I did not mention this to my wife or two children.

Thus began a great spiritual battle. No sooner had I buckled my seat belt than the Lord started dealing with me. A great moral test followed.

During the course of the twenty-seven hours it took to get back home I scoured my Bible looking for a loophole. The Holy Spirit kept convicting me of my "little" sin. The more I tried to wiggle free, the tighter the noose around my conscience became.

I would open my Bible to where I had placed my bookmark, read a few pages, put the bookmark back, then rest for a moment with my eyes shut. A few minutes later I would open to the bookmark, read a few more pages, then put it back and rest some more. This went on for several hours.

After hours of reading the Bible and looking for an answer that would make me less culpable, I finally asked the Lord, "What would you have me do?"

Just then I remembered that my two children had given me the wine-colored leather bookmark as a gift a dozen years earlier. It had been in and out of my hand a dozen times already. I glanced down and read its message, "It is a wonderful heritage to have an honest father"—Proverbs 20:7.

That was about as clearly as God had ever spoken to me. I confessed my sin, but, of course, my mind rationalized, *You already have the cigars in your backpack.* It wasn't difficult to go from there to the thought *Okay, I'm going to declare the price of these cigars, but I'll put it in with the leather cigar case I bought as a souvenir of the trip. Then, if they ask me any question whatsoever, not only will I tell the truth, I'll volunteer information. I'll offer them these four contraband cigars for confiscation. In fact, I'm going to put them in the very top of my backpack, where they will be most conspicuous.* These things I did, but I still felt queasy.

We deplaned and started working our way through the customs maze. No one said a word. My guilt was so strong, I almost asked someone to ask me a question. Finally, we had one last stop—the one where they randomly ask some people to open their luggage.

I led our family toward the final exit. About ten steps from the agent my wife looked me straight in the eye and asked, "Are you bringing any Cuban cigars into the country?"

My knees wobbled, and my legs buckled. *I can't believe she did that! Ten steps from the agent!*

We finished running the gauntlet and gave the agent our passports and customs form. She smiled sincerely, gave a quick glance, then waved us through. I couldn't believe it. I wanted to confess! I wanted to turn over those cigars to someone! But, no. She waved us through.

So I kept going, the cigars practically screaming to be noticed.

The next morning, now riddled with guilt like Swiss cheese, I went upstairs and called my two children to my side. "I've done something wrong," I began, then proceeded to confess everything. I even shared the jolt I got when I saw the verse on the bookmark they had given me.

"Will you forgive me?" I asked. They both said of course they would, and it wasn't *that* bad, so don't worry about it.

"Well, what should I do with the cigars?" I asked.

"Dad, you shouldn't have brought them into the country in the first place, but now that they're here, don't worry about it," they told me.

Guilt somewhat assuaged, I thanked them. But I was still troubled.

During the entire trip a portion of Scripture I had memorized twenty-five years ago kept coming to mind, though hazily. The next morning, after a thankful night of good rest in my own bed, I rose early and turned to the passage containing these words of Jesus:

> Whoever can be trusted with very little can also be trusted with much, and whoever is dishonest with very little will also be dishonest with much. So if you have not been trustworthy in handling worldly wealth, who will trust you with true riches?[4]

I was starting to get the message! After my wife and kids stirred to life, I called a family meeting, read them the passage, and told them I had decided that I needed to destroy the cigars.

Let me hasten to point out that I'm not trying to tell anyone else what they should do. I'm only speaking for myself. To be completely honest, I had smuggled a few Cuban cigars into the country on three, maybe four, previous occasions. This particular day, though, God spoke to me in a crystal-clear voice through his Word and Spirit. For me, destroying those delicious but contraband stogies was a test I could not afford to fail.

However, I have enough larceny left in my heart that I wanted to get *some* value in return. So I told the story at the Bible study I teach on Friday mornings, then I cut up the cigars in front of the group. It got a good laugh, so not all was lost.

The lesson for me was simple: *scrupulous obedience.*

As someone has said, "Make sure that your bumper sticker isn't the only thing in your life that tells people you're a Christian."

I don't know about you, but I have so many "big" things I'm dreaming about and working toward, I can't afford to have *any* "little" thing disqualify me. This attitude will ultimately do no good, however, if it's merely behavior modification. It can only come from an increasing desire to please God out of a grateful, transforming heart. It will only come from a growing understanding of the Christian system and a deepening relationship with Jesus Christ.

And when is the best time to do all this? A Chinese proverb says, "The best time to plant a tree was twenty years ago. The second best time is now."

AFTERWORD

As you have been able to see for yourself, it is not unreasonable to believe that Christianity is true. If anything, given the weight of the evidence and the coherence of the arguments, it is more unreasonable not to believe.

What makes the Christian system so encouraging is that it provides meaningful answers to our deepest questions about life—questions for which other systems simply don't have satisfying answers. There are agreeable explanations to resolve the things that create doubt. Christianity is a religion that offers us a hope that quenches—God wants to redeem our lives from futility, despair, sin, and death. We are not alone. Someone cares. God cares. And that's an idea that is overwhelming.

As you now turn your attention to other affairs, let me encourage you to do three things. First, take Jesus Christ with you. Let him transform your heart. Let him increasingly be your first and best thought in every situation. Pray to him about everything. Second, become part of a "community"—a church that honors Jesus Christ and faithfully teaches the Bible. It is doubtful that one can be a successful Christian in isolation. Third, think of someone who needs to read this book, and give it to them.

Keep the faith. God is good. I've been praying for you.

—PATRICK MORLEY

NOTES

Chapter 1—THE SOUL'S SEARCH FOR REST

1. Søren Kierkegaard, *Purity of Heart Is to Will One Thing* (New York: Harper Torchbooks, 1948), 36.

2. Blaise Pascal, *Pensées*, #134 (London: Penguin Books, 1966).

3. I got the idea of co-opting this "business" thought for a spiritual purpose from Dallas Willard in *The Divine Conspiracy* (San Francisco: HarperSanFrancisco, 1998).

Chapter 2—THE FEELING OF FUTILITY

1. Ecclesiastes 2:3.

2. See Ecclesiastes 2:22.

3. Ecclesiastes 2:10–11, 17.

4. *Orlando Sentinel,* September 9, 1999, sec. A, p. 2.

5. Cited in Walter Kaufmann, *Existentialism from Dostoevsky to Sartre* (New York: New American Library, 1975), 345–360.

6. Francis A. Schaeffer, *Escape from Reason* (Downers Grove, Ill.: InterVarsity Press, 1968), 90.

Chapter 3—THE WORLDLY SYSTEM

1. These systems are given various names like phases of the soul, the strands or elements of religion, worldviews, life stages, spheres, or stages along life's way.

Søren Kierkegaard, the Christian writer many also consider the father of existentialism, called his systems the *aesthetic, ethical,* and *religious* spheres, and then further divided his religious sphere into *religiousness A* for what all religions have in common, and *religiousness B* for true Christianity.

C. S. Lewis in *The Problem of Pain* identified three strands or elements in all developed religions, and in Christianity a fourth. He called them the experience of the *numinous* (which I will explain in a bit more detail in chapter 5), the consciousness of a *moral law* at once approved and disobeyed, and making the numinous power of which we feel awe the *guardian* of the morality to which we feel obligation. The fourth strand—*Christianity*—is based on a historical event. Elsewhere he identifies the unbeliever as a *pagan*.

The apostle Paul, using categories he writes about in the Bible, calls his stages the *flesh,* the *law,* and the *Spirit.*

This table compares these four systems:

	One	*Two*	*Three*	*Four*
Kierkegaard	Aesthetic	Ethical	Religiousness A	Religiousness B
Lewis	Pagan	Moral Law	Numinous Guardian	Christianity
Apostle Paul	Flesh	Law I	Law II	Spirit
My Categories	Worldly	Moral	Religious	Christian

For our purposes I will call these four systems *worldly, moral, religious,* and *Christian.*

2. C. S. Lewis, *God in the Dock* (Grand Rapids: Eerdmans, 1970), 202.

3. Blaise Pascal, *Pensées,* #136 (London: Penguin Books, 1966), 68.

4. See Romans 12:2.

5. See Galatians 5:16; Ephesians 2:3

Chapter 4—The Moral System

1. C. S. Lewis, *The Problem of Pain* (New York: Macmillan, 1962), 21.

2. Lewis, *The Problem of Pain,* 21.

Chapter 5—The Religious System

1. Rudolph Otto, *The Idea of the Holy* (London: Oxford Univ. Press, 1923), 12–13.

2. Discussed in C. S. Lewis, *The Problem of Pain* (New York: Macmillan, 1962), 22.

Chapter 6—Giving the Christian System Another Look

1. C. S. Lewis, *God in the Dock* (Grand Rapids: Eerdmans, 1970), 127.

2. Blaise Pascal, *Pensées,* #427 (London: Penguin Books, 1966), 155.

3. Pascal, *Pensées,* #136, 67.

Chapter 7—Is the Idea of God Logical?

1. I will attempt to show the reasonable grounds for concluding that Christianity is true. My goal will be to increase the reader's confidence in what can be known about Christianity by presenting a progression of proofs and probabilities, the most persuasive and compelling first, the end result being a movement in the reader's mind from possible to plausible to probable to certain belief. In our look at the Christian system it is not one piece of evidence but the cumulative weight of all the evidence that brings us to a point of saying, "Yes, the weight of the evidence has moved me beyond reasonable doubt." Each proof gives a degree of confidence, not completely, but the accumulation of the partials is complete. First, I will begin with the most certain facts and proofs and proceed to the least certain. In this way we will never lay a stronger brick on top of a weaker one, thereby giving the strongest structural integrity to our case at any particular point. Second, I will blend systems together, freely picking out ideas that are most helpful to whatever stage we are in at a given point. For example, we will begin in the rationalist mode of Descartes and end in the third order of Pascal's system.

2. Here I am consciously selecting Descartes' term *intuition* because I am at this point using his method of rational doubt to arrive at an idea with such absolute clarity and distinctness that it can be taken as a certain truth immediately apprehended by any honest person. This gives us a surefooted starting point of absolute certainty. Though our ultimate goal is to prove Christianity beyond reasonable doubt (probability), at this early point we have found an idea about which we can have certainty. Descartes would say that the value of a conclusion depends on whether the premise is true or not. I agree. I disagree that for a premise to be true it must be demonstrated as true. However, at this point we do have a premise that can be shown as a clearly true idea. From this foundation we can reason and build in a progressive and orderly manner.

3. If there were "nothing," then there would be no necessity of a Necessary Being (but then, of course, you wouldn't exist to talk about it).

4. The idea of a Necessary Being, what I call God, includes at least two subintuitions: a "creative" power and a "sustaining" power. The

Bible, for example, refers to God and Jesus as Creator and Sustainer. We do not find in intuition, however, the necessity of a "redeeming" power. Notwithstanding, the Bible also refers to God and Jesus as a Redeemer. This I will explore throughout the remainder of the book.

Chapter 8—SHOULDN'T SCIENCE RULE OVER THEOLOGY?

1. These numeric values were determined in 1999 by astronomers making measurements using the Very Long Baseline Array, a system of ten large radio-telescope antennae placed 5,000 miles across the United States from the U.S. Virgin Islands to Hawaii. Working together as a single unit, the antennae can measure motions in the distant universe with unprecedented accuracy.

2. Cited in Kitty Ferguson, *Stephen Hawking: Quest for a Theory of Everything, The Story of His Life and Work* (New York: Bantam Books, 1991), 94.

3. Stephen Hawking, *A Brief History of Time: From the Big Bang to Black Holes* (New York: Bantam Books, 1988), 174.

4. Stephen Hawking, *The Illustrated A Brief History of Time* (New York: Bantam Books, 1996), 163.

5. This assertion grows out of the doctrine of creation and the doctrine of natural law.

6. Science grew out of a culture that required answers from beyond, from something transcendent.

7. For this section I have depended on my lecture notes from Dr. Charles MacKenzie, professor of philosophy at Reformed Theological Seminary/Orlando.

Chapter 9—SINCE LIFE IS SO FUTILE, WHY SHOULD I BELIEVE GOD CARES ABOUT ME PERSONALLY?

1. See Romans 8:19–21.

2. Ecclesiastes 3:14.

3. See C. S. Lewis, *The Problem of Pain* (New York: Macmillan, 1962), 44.

4. Cited in Philip Hughes, *A Commentary on the Epistle to the Hebrews* (Grand Rapids: Eerdmans, 1977), 149.

Chapter 10—HOW CAN A MAN STAKE HIS ENTIRE LIFE ON BELIEVING THE BIBLE IS TRUE?

1. Søren Kierkegaard, *Purity of Heart Is to Will One Thing* (New York: Harper Torchbooks, 1948), 36.

Chapter 11—HOW TO COME BACK TO GOD

1. Matthew 16:26.
2. Cited in a press release on the Jesus Film Project, March 23, 2000.
3. Romans 6:23.
4. J. Gresham Machen, *Christianity and Liberalism* (Grand Rapids: Eerdmans, 1923), 27.
5. See John 10:10; Luke 19:10; John 3:16; 5:24; 6:37, 39; 10:27–28; 14:9; 10:30; 4:26.
6. See Hebrews 1:3; Colossians 2:9; John 14:9.
7. Hugh Ross, *Beyond the Cosmos* (Colorado Springs: NavPress, 1996), 74–76, 89–100.
8. Ephesians 2:4–5.
9. 2 Corinthians 5:17–19, 21.
10. See Acts 20:21.
11. C. S. Lewis, *Prince Caspian,* in The Chronicles of Narnia (New York: HarperTrophy, 1951), 152–55.

Chapter 12—HOW TO HAVE A DEEPENING RELATIONSHIP WITH GOD

1. John 10:27–29.
2. C. S. Lewis, *Prayer: Letters to Malcolm* (London: Fountain, 1963), 73.
3. John 16:13.
4. Luke 16:10–11.

ACKNOWLEDGMENTS

Special thanks to Ben Clark and David Popper for reviewing key parts of the manuscript; Charles MacKenzie for teaching me about the symbiosis between theology and science; Chuck Mitchell for handling a complex business transaction that came up in the middle of writing this manuscript; my colleagues at Zondervan for their commitment to excellence: John Sloan, Dirk Buursma, John Topliff, Greg Stielstra, and Scott Bolinder; and the staff of Man in the Mirror for permitting me the time to pursue this joy of writing: Pam Adkins, BJ Belton, Corey Brewer, Marie Bussell, Chris DeBaggis, Brett Clemmer, David Delk, Dick Dishneau, Betty Feiler, Cheri Hulke, Karen Mroczkowski, Peggy Morrison, Kelly O'Byrne, Phil Steele, Andrew Templeton, Brian Tinker, Mary Triller, and Jess Wolfe. Thank you so much.

PATRICK MORLEY

Since the late 1980s, Patrick Morley has been one of America's most-respected authorities on the unique challenges and opportunities that men face. After spending the first part of his career in the highly competitive world of commercial real estate, Patrick has been used throughout the world to help men think more deeply about their lives.

In 1973 Patrick founded Morley Properties, which for several years was hailed as one of Florida's one hundred largest privately held companies. During this time he was the president or managing partner of fifty-nine companies and partnerships. In 1989 he wrote *The Man in the Mirror,* a landmark book that burst forth from his own search for meaning, purpose, and a deeper relationship with God. This best-selling book captured the imaginations of hundreds of thousands of men worldwide. As a result, in 1991 Patrick Morley sold his business and founded Man in the Mirror, a ministry to men. Through his speaking and writing, he has become a tireless advocate for men, encouraging and inspiring them to change their lives in Christ. He has now written nine books.

"Our ministry exists," says Patrick Morley, "in answer to the prayers of all those wives, mothers, and grandmothers who have been praying for the men in their lives for decades."

Man in the Mirror's faculty members conduct church-sponsored men's events nationwide. Patrick's dream is to network with other ministries and churches of all denominations to reach every man in America with a credible offer of salvation and the resources to grow in Christ.

Patrick Morley graduated with honors from the University of Central Florida, which selected him to receive its Distinguished

Alumnus Award in 1984. He has completed studies at the Harvard Business School and Reformed Theological Seminary. Every Friday morning Patrick teaches a Bible study to 150 businessmen in Orlando, Florida, where he lives with his wife, Patsy, and his dog, Katie. Patrick and Patsy have two grown children.

Patrick's Web site can be found at: *www.maninthemirror.com*

Want a Deeper
Walk with God?

Practical Theology

Devotional

Want a Stronger
Marriage?

For Her

For Both
of You

The Man in the Mirror

Patrick Morley

"Uncommon wisdom ... stirring, disturbing, and abundantly encouraging."
—Dr. R. C. Sproul

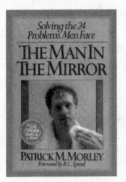

This book has established itself as a cornerstone in men's literature since its 1989 release. Winner of the prestigious Gold Medallion Award and appearing on the best-seller list eighteen times, it has helped thousands of men understand the person who stares back at them from the glass each morning and know what to do about their twenty-four most difficult problems.

The Man in the Mirror invites men to take a probing look at their identities, relationships, finances, time, temperament, and, most important, the means to bring about lasting change.

If life's demands are constantly pressuring you to run faster and jump higher, this book is for you. Rich in anecdotes, thought-provoking questions, and biblical insights, and featuring focus questions in each chapter suitable for personal or group use, this book offers a penetrating, pragmatic, and life-changing look at how to trade the rat race for the rewards of godly manhood.

Softcover 0-310-21768-7
Mass Market 0-310-23493-X
Audio Pages 0-310-24207-X

Pick up a copy today at your favorite bookstore!

ZondervanPublishingHouse
Grand Rapids, Michigan 49530
http://www.zondervan.com

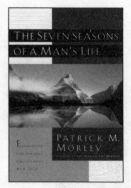

Walking with Christ in the Details of Life

Patrick Morley

Putting Christ first in every dimension of life is one of the toughest challenges Christians face. For a Christian, each day is an opportunity for a vital, daily walk with the Lord. Yet there are so many things that are hard to understand and that pull a follower away from the daily path with Jesus. Total fulfillment for the Christian comes by walking with Christ in all these details of life.

Author Patrick Morley shows you how to gain maximum personal fulfillment by totally surrendering the details of your life to Christ. Morley reveals how to transform your life from partial to total obedience by confronting the temptations, the problems, and the doubts that keep Christians from this kind of surrender.

Walking with Christ in the Details of Life provides the insights and tools you need to enrich your life and experience a satisfying transformation to total surrender.

Softcover 0-310-21766-0

Pick up a copy today at your favorite bookstore!

ZondervanPublishingHouse
Grand Rapids, Michigan 49530
http://www.zondervan.com

The Rest of Your Life

Patrick Morley

Are you completely satisfied with the way your life is turning out? If not, maybe it's time to do something extreme.

Do you hunger for personal, spiritual revival? A reawakening in your life? Do you desire to recover a craving for the things of God? This longing in your heart for "more" can be completely satisfied. The life-changing passion you hunger for is actually available to you. You really can walk with Christ.

The Rest of Your Life will guide you from where you are now on your Christian journey to greater meaning and purpose, based on sound biblical truth. It will move you to authentic Christianity in lifestyle and thinking.

Softcover 0-310-21767-9

Pick up a copy today at your favorite bookstore!

ZondervanPublishingHouse

Grand Rapids, Michigan 49530

http://www.zondervan.com

We want to hear from you. Please send your comments about this book to us in care of the address below. Thank you.

ZondervanPublishingHouse
Grand Rapids, Michigan 49530
http://www.zondervan.com

Found Art
Mosaics

Found Art Mosaics

Suzan Germond

Sterling Publishing Co., Inc.
New York

Prolific Impressions Production Staff:

Editor in Chief: Mickey Baskett
Copy Editor: Phyllis Mueller
Graphics: Dianne Miller, Karen Turpin
Photography: Thomas McConnell Photography
Administration: Jim Baskett

Library of Congress Cataloging-in-Publication Data Available

2 4 6 8 10 9 7 5 3 1

Published by Sterling Publishing Co., Inc.
387 Park Avenue South, New York, NY 10016
©2007 by Prolific Impressions, Inc.
Distributed in Canada by Sterling Publishing
c/o Canadian Manda Group, 165 Dufferin Street,
Toronto, Ontario, Canada M6K 3H6
Distributed in the United Kingdom by GMC Distribution Services,
Castle Place, 166 High Street, Lewes, East Sussex, England BN7 1XU
Distributed in Australia by Capricorn Link (Australia) Pty. Ltd.
P.O. Box 704, Windsor, NSW 2756, Australia

Printed in China
All rights reserved

ISBN-13: 978-1-4027-3505-9
ISBN-10: 1-4027-3505-7

For information about custom editions, special sales, premium and corporate purchases, please contact Sterling Special Sales Department at 800-805-5489 or specialsales@sterlingpub.com.

Acknowledgments

I wish to recognize the following companies for their excellent products which I used in this book:

Crystal tiles:
    www.marylandmosaics.com
Colored mirror and Van Gogh tiles:
    www.mosaicsbymaria.com
Vitreous glass tile: www.sqtile.com
Epoxy, universal tints:
    www.artstuf.com
Smalti and cement colorant:
    www.mosaicsmalti.com
Mosaic mounting paper:
    www.venturetape.com
Faux china tile: www.kptiles.com
Buttons:
    www.susanclarkeoriginals.com
Cement foam board (Wediboard®):
    www.mosaictilesupplies.com
Aluminum board (Hexlite):
    www.dimosaico.com
Collage material:
    www.artchixstudio.com
Specialty mosaic glue for glass:
    www.macglue.net
Mosaic supplies:
    www.mosaicsupply.com
You can find further resources on
    Suzan Germond's website
    (www.majormosaics.com).

About the Author

Suzan Germond

Suzan Germond is a Canadian living in Austin, Texas. Her substantial art background includes a Ph.D. from Stanford University in Art History with a specialization in 17th century Italian art, but until she discovered mosaics her focus was academic.

After graduating in 1995, Suzan moved with her family to Austin. Discovering few jobs were available in her field, she changed course, became a certified art appraiser, and founded her own business, Germond Art Services. In 1998, during a lull in appraising, Suzan took a mosaics class at a community college on a whim. She was drawn to the possibilities of color, pattern, and shape while working with tangible dimensional materials like china and glass. Almost immediately she knew mosaics would consume and redirect her life. Since then, she has studied at numerous mosaic workshops and classes, including a Master Program at the Orsoni Glass Studio at Venice, Italy.

Suzan's mosaic work focuses on the colorful and whimsical and has been recognized for its vibrancy, intricacy, and craftsmanship. Her work is represented by galleries, she regularly participates in juried art festivals, and has been filmed creating a mosaic chair for HGTV's *That's Clever*. She teaches locally and, because she believes strongly in mosaics as a public art form, she has donated her time and expertise to create large outdoor mosaics at local public schools in Austin, TX. Suzan is a member of the American Craft Council and the Society of American Mosaic Artists.

Special Thanks...

I thank my dentist, Dr. Robinson, for his continuous supply of dental tools, and I thank Ellen Blakeley for sharing her tempered glass mosaic technique.

And to the online mosaic groups – mosaicartistsorg@yahoogroups.com and mosaic_addicts@yahoogroups.com, communities of thousands of devoted mosaic artists always eager to share their ideas and experiences.

A heartfelt thank-you to my editor Mickey Baskett for choosing me and having faith.

Finally, special thanks to Ginger, Pixie, KC, and Prince for the company.

Dedication

This book is dedicated to my family and special friends. To my husband, Ken Germond, who good-naturedly tolerates ever-increasing piles of mosaic material; to my children, Alex and Mimi, who are my biggest cheerleaders; to the unwavering support of my parents and three brothers, which means the world to me; to my best friend and assistant, Donna Attwell, who constantly provides laughter and joy in my life. To my husband's family, Kay, Ken, and Nancy, who make a point of coming to all my art shows.

Contents

PAGE 68

PAGE 70

PAGE 105

PAGE 30

Mosaics Are Magical

Mosaics play with your perception. As you view a mosaic, you become aware of a collection of individual small pieces that have been carefully positioned and adhered to a surface. Once arranged in a pattern, the pieces become a greater decorative whole design, yet each piece remains separate and unique, creating a constant tension between the distinct elements and the whole design. Your eye and brain can switch back and forth between the two with great delight.

Mixed media mosaics take this exercise in observation one step further. Like two-dimensional collage and three-dimensional assemblage, they arrange diverse materials to create new imagery and provoke new associations. The viewer is not only aware of the individual pieces but of the choices made by the artist in the mosaic building process.

Experimentation with different types of mosaic ornamentation began in the 19th century, expanded in the 20th century and continues to this day. China, crockery, mirrors, and natural and found objects have been used by artists to create unique architectural environments. A few of the fantastic mosaic monuments around the world include Ferdinand Cheval's Palais Ideal, Antoni Gaudi's architectural masterpiece Parc Gueli in Barcelona, Spain, Niki de Saint Phalle's Tarot Garden in Tuscany, Italy, and Simon Rodia's Watts Tower in Los Angeles.

Contemporary mosaic artists continue to explore and push the limits of construction and materials. Mosaics are used for interior and exterior decoration and are gaining recognition as a fine art category separate from, but equal to, other mediums. As architects, artists, and craftspeople widen their creative boundaries, new materials come into play. Access to new materials via the Internet has encouraged the growth of mosaic making industries.

Mosaics are made even richer, in my opinion, when the items they are made of have a previous history. A toothbrush holder, a bag of beads, grandma's costume jewelry, or a discarded knickknack can be recycled and reinterpreted to create found art mosaics. Past references and personal memories add another layer of meaning to the creative process. Using found objects is a way of renewing the past and combining our history with our present material world.

Re-using and rehabilitating old or discarded things appeals to many artists – it's a challenge to create something new and meaningful from something useless and rejected. It can be seen as a reflection on our consumer culture and how quickly things are disposed of and no longer regarded as valuable. Some artists use artifacts as they find them, making rusted, tarnished, or damaged elements part of their artistic statement. Other artists (like me) enjoy upgrading and enhancing found objects with shiny and colorful precious materials like gold tiles, colored mirror pieces, and glittering tiles. My mosaics are purposefully whimsical, optimistic, and decorative. I want my pieces to look vibrant to emphasize how far they have traveled in the recycling journey.

Acquiring & Collecting Materials

Finding material to work with is almost too easy. The process of discovery begins when you look at your physical world and its discards and ask, "How can this be reclaimed and reinvigorated?"

Secondhand surfaces for mosaics can be found in any number of places: on the street, in thrift shops and attics, and at online auctions, salvage yards, garage sales, or recycling centers. (I always travel with gloves, safety glasses, and a plastic box in case I find a treasure in a trash pile. And I always ask permission from the establishment to be sure it's okay to remove items from the property.)

Objects used to cover the found pieces can be tile, glass scraps, broken china, jewelry, old buttons, hardware, shells, stones, trinkets, marbles, old tools, mirror, magnets, game pieces, toys, and – well, the list goes on and on. Collectively, they are called "tesserae."

Be warned! You may excitedly (perhaps obsessively) begin to accumulate and recycle everyday items with the thought, "Someday I might use this." (I think that is the epitaph I want on my tombstone.) Mosaic goodies can fill boxes and rooms and take over the garage, and a perpetual scavenger can drive family and friends crazy. (I speak from experience.)

But collecting has an upside, too. Sometimes it is the random odd thing that you uncovered six months ago at a garage sale that triggers a project or inspires you to finish a piece. The creative spark can happen spontaneously – that is the beauty of working with found objects.

Using This Book

In this book are 27 mosaic projects – each includes something that was used, abandoned, or intended for a different purpose. The "something" may be the surface, the tesserae, or both. You'll also find information about mosaic materials and tools, and detailed instructions on different techniques.

You can find images of contemporary mosaics and further details of techniques in the many excellent mosaic books and encyclopedias available. I encourage you to take classes and workshops to learn new techniques. For clarification or direction, contact me via my website, www.majormosaics.com. There are mosaic organizations and online resources where you can interact with others who have discovered this meaningful art form.

An important thing to keep in mind is that you want your mosaics to last. Work with things that are clean, safe, and sturdy. Use the proper preparation procedures, adhesives, tools, and safety precautions outlined in this book. Approach the projects with an open mind, allowing for spontaneous changes or reinterpretations to make the work your own. Relax and feel comfortable with where your intuition takes you.

Suzan Germond

Materials for Mosaics

The bits of material that are glued to a surface to form a mosaic are called **tesserae** (the word has its origins in Latin and means "cube"). Historically, tesserae were small squares of stone and glass used by Greek, Roman, and Byzantine artists to decorate architecture.

Glass

Glass is typically made from silicate and oxides that are melted, then cooled until hard and brittle. As a mosaic medium glass is impermeable (hence, it is referred to as vitreous). Because it is easy to cut and will not fade, it is a good choice for outdoor projects. There are several types of glass available.

Vitreous Glass Tiles

This type of solid-colored tile is machine made from molds. It is 1/8" thick and comes in 3/8", 3/4", or 1" squares. Typically the underside is grooved for better adhesion. Vitreous tiles can be purchased mounted on paper sheets or loose by the pound. The sheets are an industry standard – they measure approximately one square foot and contain 225 tiles that can be removed from the paper by soaking in water. The quality and variety of color is enormous; the tiles are manufactured all over the world, in Italy, France, China, Mexico, and other countries. Lesser quality tiles contain more silica; they are grainier in appearance and more brittle. Higher end tiles have a smooth surface and come in a variety of finishes, such as two-tone, metallic, or iridized.

As demand for glass tiles has increased, several innovations have appeared on the market. There is recycled glass tile. There are thick cubes of colored transparent glass. There is clear glass tile that has been melded with decorative backings. The result can be tile that glitters or looks painted or has an antique appearance. Given the decorative possibilities of glass tile, new colors and sizes are introduced every season. Visit a local tile shop to see samples of current production.

Pictured above: vitreous glass tiles.

13

Glass, continued from page 13.

Smalti

Smalti are handmade enamel glass pieces made by firing molten glass with metallic oxides. Out of the furnace comes a thick sheet of pure color that is cooled and then cut into 1/2" rectangular pieces. Tiny air pockets in the glass (a result of the firing) make it highly reflective so smalti are rarely grouted. They are usually laid in an adhesive bed with the pieces touching. Smalti are produced in Italy and Mexico. They are sold loose in 1/4 or 1/2 pound increments.

Gold smalti are made by placing 24 karat gold leaf between two sheets of transparent glass (one sheet is very thin and the other is much thicker). When fired in a furnace, the glass fuses, permanently encasing the gold. A few gold smalti add a touch of luxury to your mosaic. Because their manufacture is labor-intensive, smalti are expensive.

Stained Glass

Stained glass may be machine rolled or hand made into large sheets. If you visit a stained glass store you will see the hundreds of choices available: colored translucent, opaque, opalescent, iridescent, dichroic, textured clear, and more. Stained glass can be purchased by the pound as scrap pieces, or in sheets. Some online retailers sell pre-cut squares of glass in various sizes (typically 1/2" to 1"). Pre-cut stained glass shapes of flowers and animals are also readily available.

Millefiori

Millefiori are thin rods of patterned glass that are cut into small discs and used in fusing and glass blowing. The material can be traced back to ancient Egypt, although it is associated most commonly with Venetian glassmaking. (The name is Italian; the English translation is "a thousand flowers.") Millefiori come in various sizes and transparencies. They make colorful additions to mosaic projects and can be purchased online in small increments.

Mirror

Reflective glass that has been coated on its back with silver or aluminum can add a sparkle to any mosaic project. Colored mirror, in particular, is very popular. Like stained glass, colored mirror can be found pre-cut online. **Always** use an appropriate adhesive such as silicone or mirror mastic with mirror glass. Other glues will chemically alter the coating and cause the mirror to de-silver.

Other Types of Glass

I learned about the possibilities of **tempered glass** at a workshop with California artist Ellen Blakeley, one of the first to work with this unusual material. Tempered glass, a type of transparent sheet glass tempered by sudden cooling, is manufactured to meet safety standards and cannot be broken unless it is hit hard on one corner with a hammer. The glass breaks into interesting small pieces with a transparent crackled design. You can paint or draw on a surface and cover it with the glass or use tempered glass in collages to create layered effects. **Be careful!** Use appropriate tools and safety measures – the glass can literally explode and shatter. (Don't confuse tempered glass with windshield glass, which is a composite of two sheets of glass with an intermediate layer of transparent plastic.)

Continued on next page

Continued from page 15

Flat-backed glass marbles are made from molten glass blobs that are cooled on a flat surface so their tops are rounded and their bottoms are flat. They come in a variety of colors and finishes and are typically sold in mesh bags in the floral sections of crafts stores. You can also find **molded glass shapes** like hearts, animals, and squiggles that can enhance a mosaic design.

In addition to real **beach glass** that has been tumbled in the surf over time and washes up on the beach, there is commercially produced beach glass, which has a frosted appearance and rounded edges to imitate the look of the surf-tumbled original. Beach glass provides a muted effect in a mosaic and is often paired with shells.

Fused glass is made from small pieces of compatible glass that are layered and heated in a kiln so that they melt together. Often used for jewelry,

fused the glass has become popular with mosaic artists because of the rich patterns and shape possibilities. Making your own fused glass tiles allows you to personalize in color and design – check for a class near you.

Imitation Glass

Acrylic and plastic can be used to create mosaic shapes without the dangers of working with sharp glass. Plastic colored tiles and flat-back beads that look like glass are sold in small packets in craft stores. Mosaic mirror tile made from polished metallic plastic is an alternative to mirror glass. These materials are easy to cut with scissors and a great resource for children's mosaics.

16

Ceramics

Ceramics are made from firing clay with minerals. The result can be earthenware (including terra cotta), stoneware, or porcelain. Each type has a different level of porousness. The location of your finished mosaic piece dictates the type of material you choose.

Ceramic tiles can be glazed (either matte or shiny) or unglazed. Typical tiles sold in home improvement stores that measure 4" square are low-fired with a surface glaze and intended for indoor use. Crafts stores offer low-fired ceramic tiles in multiple small shapes (leaves, hearts, and circles) and colors; many come with stamped designs that make interesting additions to mosaics.

Tile shops offer many interesting tile shapes with luscious glazes and patterns. A higher firing temperature produces a more impervious product that is waterproof and frostproof. Porcelain tile, which is fired at the highest temperature, typically is unglazed and a pure color throughout. It is an ideal material for outdoor mosaics because it is resistant to weather.

Online auction sites are excellent sources for handmade painted and stamped ceramics – just make sure the surface has been treated to withstand grouting.

China & Tableware

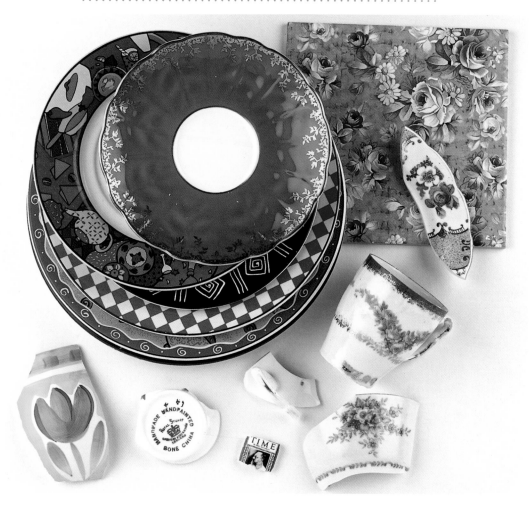

China, tableware, and pottery are among the most readily available mosaic materials. Like tile, china and tableware are fired at different temperatures with varying results and for a variety uses. Abundant and inexpensive, they appeal to those with a sentimental streak – broken or cracked wedding gifts or family heirlooms can be reinvigorated in an artwork.

China varies from translucently thin bone china to thick, heavy stoneware with different levels of quality and permeability. This very range allows for many appealing patterns and colors that can be mixed and matched. One disadvantage in using a variety of cut china pieces is that they may not be uniformly thick; glue may be needed to build up thinner pieces, and this can get messy. One solution is to substitute china-pattern ceramic tiles – they are 8" square and 1/4" thick.

Because most china has a surface glaze, it may not be the ideal material for long term outdoor use. A woman once phoned me, hoping that I could repair an outdoor cement mosaic table her grandmother had made in the 1950s. It had been covered with china shards and all that remained were blank white pieces.

Mosaics composed primarily of pieces of dishes and vessels are called *pique-assiette*, a French term that means "plate taker." The term was originally applied to Raymond Isodore, a Frenchman, who dug up shards around the fields of his home near Chartres over thirty years (1930s-1960s). Isodore completely covered the outside (and inside!) of his house with the shards. Called *La Maison Picasiette*, it is a mosaic shrine. The eccentricity of covering a home with found china bits appeals to mosaic artists because it confirms that there are no boundaries in either the material used or where it is placed.

Natural Materials

The outdoor world offers a variety of materials, including shells, stones, fossils, marble, granite, and slate. Mosaics made with natural materials may be muted in color and quite elegant in design. The attraction of natural materials is their texture, variety of shapes, durability, and accessibility.

Some natural materials are difficult to cut without specialized cutting tools such as a wet saw or hammer and hardie. Luckily, pre-cut cubes of marble and stone are available at tile shops, at home improvement centers, and online. If you do not live close to a beach or park, shells and polished stones can be purchased at craft stores. Bead shops offer beautiful pieces of mother-of-pearl and abalone shell. A rock tumbler is a good investment if you choose to work with stones.

Found Objects

Found objects are my favorite materials. The category includes pretty much everything dimensional – things like buttons, watches, jewelry, figurines, beads, crystals, toys, game pieces, wire, cutlery, keys, bones, cork, wood, seeds, and refrigerator magnets. You can also make your own objects and shapes to add to mosaics with plaster, polymer clay, and molds.

When you incorporate these odds and ends it is important to make sure they are stable. It is also necessary to have the proper tools to prepare the pieces. If you grout your mosaic, the process will require more planning and clean-up when you incorporate mixed materials.

Metal & Wood

Many new styles of tesserae are introduced each year at "covering" conventions. Handcrafted tiles of various metals and finishes – stainless steel, bronze, pewter, and aluminum – and wood tiles are available. They can make stunning contrasts and accent pieces. They can be costly.

Less expensive and unusual materials found closer to home that can be cut into random mosaic shapes include linoleum, metal sheeting, and rubber. Again, it is important to use the proper tools, adhesives, and safety equipment.

Breaking & Cutting Tools

A variety of hand tools are used for cutting and breaking glass, tile, and china.
These are the tools I used for the projects in this book.

Pictured above, clockwise from top left: Wheel cutters, two types of wire cutting nippers for hard tiles, tile nippers, glass scorer, running pliers, grozing pliers.

Nippers

Tile nippers are a two-handled tool with a spring and carbide steel blades that do not close completely. They can be used to cut tiles or dishes into shapes. To use them, simply insert one-fourth of the tile or china piece and, keeping your arm relaxed, squeeze the handles together. The material will break where the blades are positioned.

A type of **nippers designed for wire cutting** can be used for cutting hard unglazed tile. They have carbide steel blades like tile nippers, but the blades are adjustable and can be replaced. They are more expensive and less readily available, but if you choose to work with unglazed porcelain, they may be worth the investment.

Cutters

Another key tool for breaking glass, smalti, and thinner china is **wheel cutters**, which have two wheels at the end of a two-handle spring. The wheels are replaceable and adjustable. For cutting, the material is placed completely under the wheels. A quick squeeze gives a clean break. Delicate china should be cut with wheel cutters; tile nippers will cause it to shatter.

Larger tiles can be shaped into smaller squares, rectangles, or triangles with a **tile cutter**. This tabletop device scores and breaks – you line up the tile, run the scorer across it, and press on the breaking handle. The tile is cut along the scored line.

Hammers

A blow from a **hammer** can break china, terra cotta, and tempered glass. Wrap the piece in a towel to protect yourself from shards.

The **hammer and hardie** originated in antiquity. These tools are designed to cut hard materials like marble and smalti. A chisel tip (the hardie) is set into a log for stability. When the tessera is positioned on the tip and hit with the specialized hammer, the force cleanly breaks the piece. This tool is expensive and requires patience and practice. I have seen a mosaic master cut a 2" cube of smalti into a perfect, tiny 1/4" circle.

Just for Glass Cutting

Cutting glass into specific shapes requires a **glass scorer**, **ruler**, and **running pliers**. There are many types of glass scorers – it's a good idea to visit a stained glass shop to experiment with the various styles.

I use the scorer to cut glass into squares this way: after I have drawn vertical and horizontal lines on the glass with a wax marker, I align the ruler and push the scorer along the length of the glass against the ruler, then across the glass so that I have a checkerboard of etched lines. I then use running pliers to break each line, starting in the middle of the glass piece and working outward. Once I have broken the glass into vertical strips, I break it along the horizontal lines.

If you plan on making lots of squares, you can invest in a **cutting system** that makes this process more efficient. It comes with breaking tools and a grid cutting surface.

Smoothing Tools

Cutting glass and tile can create sharp edges. **Grozing pliers** can remove the rough edges left by imperfect breaks. A **whetstone**, like the kind used to sharpen knives, can smooth sharp edges. You can also use a diamond file.

Some artists put their pieces of cut glass in a closed container with water, soap, and salt or sand and shake the container. The mild abrasion dulls the edges. A **glass grinding machine**, used primarily by stained glass artists, can be used to smooth rough edges.

Specialized Tools

Working with found objects often requires taking apart jewelry or dissembling something. **Jewelry making tools**, **long nose pliers**, **wire cutters**, and **button shank removers** all come in handy.

Saws

The **ring saw**, **wet saw**, and **diamond band saw** are electric tools that all work with water to keep the blades from overheating while cutting the material. Ring saws are typically used for stained glass shapes. The wet saw cuts thicker material like ceramic tile and marble. The diamond band saw cuts everything and allows intricate designs.

Additional Tools & Supplies

This list includes items I use on a regular basis in mosaic making.

- **Metal fine point tool**, for cleaning adhesive from grout lines. (You can also use **dental tools**.)
- **Tweezers**, for moving and placing pieces of tesserae. Double-hinged tweezers are best because they lock in place.
- **Craft sticks**, for applying adhesives and stirring grout and thinset mortar.
- **Cotton swabs**, for cleaning up wet adhesives.
- **Craft knife or single-edge razor blades**, for removing dried adhesive.
- **Transfer paper**, for transferring designs that have been photocopied.
- **Lazy susan**, for holding three-dimensional pieces while you work.
- **Sponges**, for wiping.
- **Notched trowel**, for spreading thinset mortar on flat surfaces.
- **Ruler**, for measuring.
- **Wax crayon**, for marking glass.

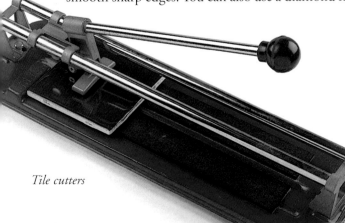

Tile cutters

Surfaces

When I teach a mosaics class, the complaint I hear most often is that the pieces pop off or the grout cracks. More often than not, the problem is with the substrate – the surface on which the mosaic was created was inappropriate to begin with or was not properly prepared.

All bases must be clean, dry, and free of dust. There are many options available for cleaning: all-purpose cleaners, diluted vinegar, rubbing alcohol, trisodium phosphate (TSP), and non-soapy detergents. After cleaning it is imperative to seal any porous object to be covered in mosaic so that it cannot absorb moisture from the adhesive or the grout. There are several methods; the most common are white paint primer, clear grout sealer, or white PVA glue diluted with water (1 part glue to 4 parts water).

■ Wood

Almost any wood that is at least 5/8" thick can be used as a base for a mosaic as long as the item is kept indoors. Even with the best preparation, wood will eventually warp or rot if left outside. Certain products that are advertised for outdoor use, such as backer board and marine plywood, contain cellulose, which will expand and contract over time, particularly with extreme changes in temperature.

Many fun pre-cut wooden shapes are available at craft stores and online. For indoor use, plywood, medium density fiberboard (MDF), and woods like oak need to be covered front, back, and sides with an appropriate sealer. Paint primers designed for wood are readily available at home improvement centers. I prefer

a spray can of white primer because I can quickly cover a surface and transfer my design afterward, if necessary.

Wood furniture is an ideal candidate for mosaic makeovers, but make sure all the joints are solid before you start and that the piece can hold the weight of a mosaic. Unfinished furniture needs to be sanded and sealed. Old furniture needs to be cleaned with a degreaser. If the old finish is flaking or cracked, it will need to be removed.

■ Other Types of Boards for Bases

Cement board can be used outside and does not need to be sealed. It comes in 1/4" and 1/2" thicknesses and can be cut into shapes using a jigsaw with a masonry blade. The drawback to this material is that it is heavy and requires some type of framing, **Caution!** When you saw the board there will be a lot of cement dust so it is imperative that you wear a respirator-style face mask.

Backer board, a combination of cement and other substances including cellulose, is commonly used in home construction. It is lighter and smoother than cement board, comes in the same thicknesses (1/4" and 1/2"), and can be cut using the same methods. It has a grid pattern on one side for easy measuring.

Cement foam board such as Wediboard® is waterproof, extremely lightweight, and easy to cut. It is made of dense polystyrene foam that is covered with a thin layer of fiber mesh and coated with cement. It comes in five thicknesses (1/4" to 1"). It should not be used for outdoor horizontal applications like tabletops and requires some forethought for hanging and framing.

Aluminum board is lightweight, rigid board with an aluminum honeycomb core and a skin of glass fiber and epoxy resin. It's expensive, and it's less widely available than some other boards.

Glass & Mirror Glass

Glass tabletops, panes of glass, and mirrors can be used as bases for mosaics as long as they are thick enough to support the weight. Likewise, plastic glass (Plexiglas®) is an option as long as it is thick enough so that it does not flex. Glass vases with a smooth surface are also good candidates. For a transparent glass-on-glass effect, it is important to use the proper adhesive for clarity.

Metal

Metal can react to temperature changes so it is important to use a flexible adhesive like silicone. Old metal should be cleaned, and all metal should be treated with a rust proofing coating before applying the primer. Metal shapes with lots of openings can be covered with wire mesh and coated with a layer of cement to create a solid surface to cover with tesserae.

Fiber Glass Mesh

Fiber glass mesh is an ideal surface for making a mosaic in one location and then transporting it to another location for installation. Vertical projects like kitchen backsplashes are perfect candidates for the mesh method – you glue the tesserae on the mesh and then, at a later time, mount the mesh on a bed of permanent adhesive, let dry, then grout in place. Do not use wire or cloth that will rust or disintegrate.

Concrete

Concrete is a mixture of cement, sand, and water. When fully cured, it is a strong and stable surface. Many three-dimensional concrete forms like birdbaths, stepping stones, and garden statuary are available at home centers and garden shops. You can also cast your own simple shapes. For mosaics, avoid concrete items with intricate detailing or cover them with an additional thin coat of cement to smooth out the surface.

Because concrete has a rough, grainy surface, I seal it with clear grout sealer (not primer) before I attach the tesserae.

Terra Cotta

Terra cotta items like flowerpots and ceramic garden ornaments will absorb moisture from adhesives and grout and must be covered completely on all sides with a sealer. I use grout sealer since it is fully absorbed into the surface.

Ceramics

Glazed ceramics like vases are appropriate surfaces for mosaics. They don't need to be sealed and can be lightly sanded to create a fine "tooth" so the adhesive will bond securely. Be sure ceramics are clean and free of cracks. Certain flaws or chips can be covered by a mosaic, but a major imperfection will not hold up over time.

Plastic Foam

Plastic foam, such as Styrofoam®, is lightweight and inexpensive and can be carved into shapes. Use safety precautions to avoid toxic fumes if you use a heated instrument for cutting. Since solvent adhesives will melt plastic foam, it is important to choose the right glue. It is very helpful to cover the foam with silver tape or wrap it with plaster cloth to protect the surface and create a more rigid base.

Many mosaic artists use plastic foam heads to make interesting portraits with mixed materials.

Papier Mâché

Papier mâché can be used as a mosaic base for three-dimensional forms if it is completely sealed and protected with silver tape or a thin layer of cement. Of course, the form itself must be durable and well built or grout cracks will appear over time.

Plastics

Rigid plastic plumbing pipes, available at home improvement centers, are stable enough to use as a mosaic base, but most plastic surfaces are too thin. (When they flex, they cause the grout to crack.) An alternative to plastics is cast resin and fiber glass shapes. They are often sold as lightweight garden ornaments. Prepare the base by sanding and priming, and use a silicone adhesive.

Grout

Grout is a cement-based substance that is used to fill the joints between the tesserae after the tesserae pieces are glued to the surface. Grout adds cohesion and strength to the mosaic form. Depending on the spacing of the tesserae, the grout lines can play an obvious visual role – they might be as wide as the tile or disappear as hairline cracks.

Most grouts have added polymers to enhance their strength and flexibility. Grout, like thinset mortar, is sold premixed in containers and as a powder you mix yourself. I prefer the powdered form that is mixed with water. Grout has a shelf life – use it quickly and store it in plastic containers with tight-fitting lids. If you leave grout in its original paper bag on the garage floor, it will harden into a brick within months.

Types of Grout

There are two basic types of grout, non-sanded and sanded. **Non-sanded grout** has a smoother, stickier feel and is typically used for very fine grout lines or to avoid scratching precious materials such as the gold edging on fine china. **Sanded grout** has a coarser texture and, because of the addition of sand, provides more structural support for larger grout lines. Sanded grout typically contains added polymers for flexibility.

Sanded epoxy grout, first used in commercial kitchens, never needs to be sealed. It requires mixing two powders together and is more difficult to clean up. However, you can choose to add specialized ingredients (sold with the grout) to make it glitter gold or glow neon. (Envision the possibilities for nighttime mosaics!)

Colorants

Grout color is an important aesthetic choice in creating a mosaic. Gray grout is considered neutral, black grout creates a dramatic effect, and white grout, which is more delicate, draws attention to the individual tesserae. In addition to these basic choices, there are many other colors of grout available.

If you want a color that is not available commercially, you can mix a light-colored grout with powdered cement colorants, pure color tints, or acrylic paints. I mix the grout with water first and then add the colorant. It is important to keep a record of the amounts you used in case you need to make more at a later date to replicate the original batch. You may wish to make a small board with grout samples – when grout dries, the color is lighter than when it is wet.

How to Mix & Apply Grout

YOU'LL NEED:

Powdered grout
Water
A disposable container
A dust mask and gloves, to protect your lungs and hands while mixing
A measuring cup
A stirring tool
A spreading tool, such as a flexible foam spatula or a grout float (I prefer to use my fingers – I put adhesive bandages on the tips and wear a tight-fitting rubber glove. Other options for spreading include pieces of bubble wrap, foam sheets from packaging, or small flat-head instruments.)
Vinegar, for rinsing your hands after grouting
Cellulose sponge and paper towels or cheesecloth, for wiping
Soft cloth rags, for polishing, *optional*
Newspaper, to cover your work surface or work area

HERE'S HOW:

1. **Prepare.** Assemble your supplies and tools. Cover your work surface or work area – the place where you'll be grouting your mosaic – with newspaper.
2. **Measure.** Following the grout manufacturer's guidelines, measure the grout powder and place it in the mixing container. With experience, you will learn how much grout to make; initially, it's a good idea to make more than you think you'll need.
3. **Mix.** Measure the water and begin adding it *a little at a time*. Stir, adding small increments of water, until the mixture is like mud and will not fall off your stirring tool.
4. **Let it slake.** Leave the grout alone for five minutes so the necessary chemical interactions can take place. (This is called "slaking.")
5. **Apply.** Stir the grout again. To spread the grout, grab a handful with your gloved hand and place it on the surface of the mosaic. Use a spreading tool or your protected, gloved hand to slide the grout over the mosaic and press it into the crevices between the tesserae. Work one area at time, completely filling each crevice.
6. **Wipe.** When the mosaic is all grouted, remove the excess grout immediately. Wipe the surface first with a damp (just barely damp, almost dry) sponge, wiping in circles to smooth out the joints and pick up the grout from the face of the tiles. (Too much water in the sponge can dilute the grout and cause sinking and cracking.) When most of the excess grout has been removed, rinse the sponge in a bucket of water and put it aside.

Continued on next page

Continued from page 23

7. Use paper towels or cheesecloth to rub off the rest of the grout and polish the face of the tesserae.

8. **Let dry and clean up.** Let dry. Fold up the newspaper – with the grout remnants – and put it in the trash. **Never** put grout down a sink. Leftover grout can be mixed with white glue to form a shape you can add to a mosaic at a later date. (Think small heart, flower, cross.) Once the grouting is complete, rinse your hands with vinegar to restore the pH of your skin.

9. **Polish.** When the grout is dry, rub away any haze with soft cloth rags. (You can use vinegar to wipe haze from the tesserae as long as you rinse it off afterward.) For more problematic grout remnants use an acidic cleaner that can be found in the tile section of home improvement stores. Follow safety precautions.

Tips & Techniques

▦ Using Two or More Grout Colors

Sometimes you may want to use two or more different grout colors to highlight or blend a portion of your mosaic. Here's how:

1. Mix and apply the darker grout first, clean it up, and let it dry for 24 hours.

2. Cover the top edge of the dark grout that will be next to the lighter grout with painter's tape. Burnish well.

3. Apply the lighter grout up to and onto the tape. Once it is dry, remove the tape. You should have a clean line between the two grout colors.

▦ Protecting Tesserae & Dimensional Objects

There are several ways to protect tesserae and dimensional objects in your mosaic that might be damaged during grouting. Here are some suggestions – it's worth experimenting to see what works best for you.

Sealing with Glue.

1. Seal porous tesserae or object with a coat of grout sealer.

2. Brush the covered surface with a coat of PVA white glue. Let the glue dry completely to a clear state.

3. Grout the piece and let dry fully.

4. With a wet cotton swab, begin rubbing slowly over the covered object. The glue will become white and sticky again and can be wiped off with repeated applications of the wet cotton swab.

Covering with Pliable Putty.

1. Work a small piece of putty or plasticine until it is soft and pliable.

2. Cover the tesserae or other object.

3. Grout the piece and let dry completely.

4. Remove the protective putty covering.

Covering with Tape.

1. Cover the tesserae or other object with painter's tape so that the grout cannot touch the edges.

2. Grout the piece and let dry completely.

3. Remove the tape after the grout has dried.

Removing and Replacing.

1. Place the object temporarily on the surface to "reserve" its space. Remove it when you're ready to grout.

2. When you grout the project, cover the empty area with a layer of grout and press the object into the wet grout to leave an impression. Remove the object and clean off any grout on it. Let the grouted project dry completely.

3. Glue the object in the reserved space.

▦ Changing the Grout Color

If you are not satisfied with the final grout color, there are several remedies:

• Use a sharp tool to scratch away a thin layer of the grout, then cover it with a new batch.

• Brush acrylic paint (diluted or full strength) on top of the grout. (This changes the appearance of the grout and gives a more plastic appearance. It will also fade with time.)

• Use a metallic rub-on wax. (These require some maintenance, i.e., repeat applications.)

Adhesives

The tesserae pieces are glued to your surface before grouting. Because there are many adhesive products on the market, it is important to choose the appropriate one for the type of mosaic you are making, the materials you are using, and where the mosaic will be displayed. Adhesives may be water-based or solvent-based. If you have questions or safety concerns about an adhesive, contact the manufacturer (via the telephone number on the package) and request the Material Safety Data Sheet.

▣ Thinset Mortar

Thinset mortar is a powdered mixture of portland cement and sand. Gray or white in color, it is called "thinset" in the United States and "cement adhesive" in Europe. Its chemical reaction is activated by the addition of a liquid – it can either be water or a latex (to enhance flexibility). Although premixed thinset is available, it is always better to mix your own in small batches. The mortar and fluid are stirred together to a peanut butter consistency. The mixture has a limited working time before it dries out. Many artists extend its working time by placing the thinset in a transparent plastic bag, nipping off a corner like a pastry bag, and piping it onto the surface or tiles.

The name thinset refers to the way the mortar is applied for best adhesion (i.e., thinly, with a trowel). For outdoor mosaics, this is one of the best adhesives because it is waterproof and very strong. Thinset is also ideal for the self-grouting or "push method" of setting objects into an adhesive; the pieces are embedded and do not need to be grouted. When thinset will be visible, it can be colored with powdered cement colorants.

▣ Silicone

This polymer adhesive is a popular choice because it is suitable for almost every surface except rubber and some plastics. It is durable yet remains flexible when dry, allowing for expansion and contraction. It is sold as a sealant and comes in a variety of colors. For mosaic purposes, clear or transparent silicone is a good choice. Silicone has several advantages: it is waterproof, it has immediate vertical hold, it dries clear (depending on the brand), it protects the backing of mirrors, and it can be used outdoors.

Continued on next page

Adhesives, continued from page 27

Silicone can irritate eyes and skin, and it has a distinct odor so good ventilation is necessary. It is tiresome to clean up once it has dried because it has a strong rubbery adhesion. The most effective clean-up tools are acetone and a single-edge sharp blade (mini window scraper).

PVA

Polyvinyl acetate (PVA) is an ideal adhesive for horizontal indoor mosaics that will not be exposed to moisture. Designed to work with porous materials, it is a non-toxic, water-based white glue (but don't confuse it with popular white school glue). Polyvinyl acetate gains strength as it dries, but it is not entirely waterproof and is not intended to support heavy objects.

When diluted with water (1 part glue to 4 parts water), it functions as a sealer on porous surfaces. Given its skim milk consistency, it is absorbed into the surface as opposed to sitting on the top.

Epoxy

This is a two-part glue that requires mixing a resin and a hardener in very specific amounts. The keys to success are accurate measuring and thorough mixing. It comes in three forms: individual liquids that are mixed together in a ratio determined by the manufacturer, side-by-side barrels, and squeeze pouches or tubes that are kneaded vigorously to activate. Epoxy provides a stronger bond than almost any other glue, and the liquid form can be used as a protective finish. However, epoxy resin can cause allergic reactions, and safety precautions are necessary.

Ceramic Tile Adhesive

Commonly referred to as "mastic," tile adhesive may be solvent- or water-based. It comes premixed in plastic containers and is popular in the tile industry. Easy to use, it has good vertical hold but it does not have the longevity of other glues. It should not be used outdoors, near heat, or on an item that would be immersed in water. When it dries it shrinks and can become brittle. It is easy to remove.

Specialty Adhesives

Adhesives intended for jewelry making, boat building, and small construction jobs can also be used for mosaics. They are advertised as rubber-based or solvent-based **contact cement glues**, meaning they are most effective when the adhesive is applied to both pieces and allowed to dry slightly before the pieces are joined together. They clean up with mineral spirits. Contact cement glues tend to be very strong smelling and their labels carry warnings about fumes and toxicity.

New clear-drying **acrylic adhesives** are appealing to mosaic artists who like to work with glass on glass.

Adhesives to Avoid

There are certain types of adhesives to avoid: **hot glue, glue that dries instantaneously** (e.g., "super" glues) and **glue that expands as it dries**. Either their chemical components or lack of longevity make them inappropriate for mosaic use.

Tile Cleaners

To remove stubborn grout remnants or to clean a mosaic, use a tile cleaner – you'll find it in the tile sections of home improvement centers. Use caution – they are strong, acidic chemicals – and follow the manufacturer's instructions.

Sealants

One type sealant is used at the beginning and another type at the end of a mosaic project. One is to prepare the surface before the mosaic is applied and the other is to protect the grout from potential stains and exterior elements after the mosaic is complete. Tabletops, trays, and outdoor pieces should always be sealed.

Two coats of **liquid penetrating sealer** should be applied after the grout has dried at least 24 hours. It can be brushed over the whole project and then wiped off the tesserae. The sealer will be fully absorbed by the porous grout and will not change the grout's appearance. If you prefer a glossy finish and your mosaic will be displayed indoors, there are sealers that can be applied to the grout to add protective shine. **Epoxy resins** can be poured over flat projects for a shiny, protective surface. Always follow the manufacturer's instructions precisely for good results.

Tile Cleaner & Sealant

Using Patterns

Many designs in this book include patterns. If you like, you can draw the design on the surface, using the pattern as a guide. Use a pencil, not a black marker, when you draw – the marker ink could seep through the grout over time.

If you do not feel comfortable drawing you can photocopy and enlarge the pattern provided. Place a sheet of black transfer paper on the surface and cover it with the photocopy. Outline the shape using firm pressure with a pencil.

Safety Gear

You need to protect your eyes, lungs, and hands when cutting hard materials, working with sharp edges and smelly adhesives, and mixing powder products – your safety gear should include safety glasses, a quality mask, and protective gloves. Always carefully read and follow the instructions for using any product or tool, and be aware that there can be long term health consequences from making mosaic art. Many adhesives contain carcinogens, and their intense odors make good ventilation imperative. Every time you cut glass and tile, microscopic dust is produced, and powdered cement and grout can create a fine mist in the air as they are mixed.

For protection, **always** wear a rated respirator mask, and use a shop vacuum and/or damp wipes to clean dust from your workspace on a regular basis.

Mosaic Technique
Direct Method

The direct method, where the tesserae are applied
directly to the surface, is the most straightforward and
most common mosaic technique. After materials are cut
to fit, they are glued and grouted. This section shows
you how, step by step.

This **Mixed Media Butterfly Tray** is used as an example to show the steps for the direct method mosaic technique. A variety of tesserae were used to make this tray: vitreous glass, stained glass, china, and buttons. Except for the china and the grout, all the materials can be purchased at a crafts store.

In this example, wheel cutters are used for all the cutting. You'll see how to break a square tile in half, create a circle from a tile, and lay tiles to fit a curve. The process can be used to make any direct method mosaic project.

Supplies for Tray

Surface:
1 wooden tray, 9-1/4" x 12-1/2"

Tesserae:
25 metallic black vitreous tiles, 3/4"
24 metallic purple vitreous tiles, 3/4"
Opaque orange stained glass, 8" square
12 orange plastic buttons, 1/2"
4 china plates, dinner size

Other Supplies:
White PVA adhesive
Black sanded grout
Distilled water
Tile sealer
Optional: White primer
Purple acrylic paint
Varnish
Carpenter's level
Tack cloth
Tile cleaner
Safety gear

Tools:
Wheel cutters
Button shank remover *optional*
Brushes
Glass scorer, ruler, and running pliers
Optional: Tile nippers
Pencil

Prepare the Surface

1. Sand any rough spots on the tray and wipe clean with a tack cloth.
2. Seal the entire tray with diluted white glue (1 part glue to 4 parts water) or white primer. Let dry completely.
3. Draw the butterfly on the bottom of the tray *or* trace the pattern for the butterfly and transfer to the bottom of the tray with a pencil, centering the design. Outline the shape with a pencil, using firm pressure. (Photo 1) NOTE: Do not use a marker – the ink could seep through the grout over time.

Photo 1 – Outlining the butterfly design on the bottom of the tray.

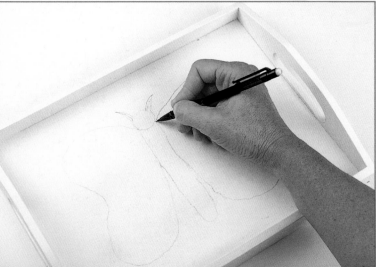

Prepare the Tesserae

Photo 2 – Using wheel cutters to cut a tile.

Photo 3 – Scoring the glass for the wings.

1. The black tiles form the border at the edge of the tray. Use wheel cutters to snap each black tile into two rectangular pieces. (Photo 2) To do this, turn the tile upside down so you can line up the cutters with the adhesive lines on the underside, make sure the tile is centered between the wheels, and press firmly.

2. The purple tiles are used to make the butterfly's head and antennae and to outline the butterfly's wings. Set aside two tiles – one for the head, the other for the antennae. Then use the wheel cutters to snap the rest of the purple tiles into two rectangular pieces. (You'll do more trimming on these pieces later when you fit them to the pattern.)

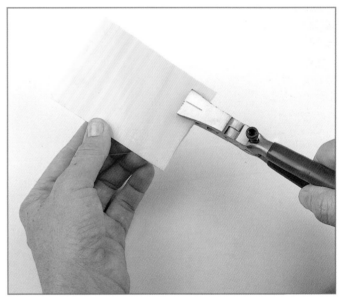

Photo 4 – Positioning the running pliers on the scored line.

3. To cut the circular head, take one of the purple square tiles you set aside and make angle cuts on all four corners. Then use the wheel cutters to take tiny "nibbles" along the straight edges to make a circle. TIP: Don't despair if your first circles look misshapen. Circle cutting has a definite learning curve. The joy of mosaics is that the pieces do not have to be perfect.

Continued on next page

Preparing the Tesserae, continued from page 33

4. To create the antennae, cut the remaining purple tile in half. Cut each half in half again so that you have four thin strips of tile. You'll use two of these for the antennae. TIP: The pieces are usually not completely straight; they typically have an angled or curved appearance. Take advantage of that in choosing the pieces for your design.

5. Snap off the shanks of the buttons with a button shank remover tool.

6. Cut the orange glass into random shapes for the wings. Use the glass scorer and ruler (Photo 3), to score a 1" wide strip of glass. Position the running pliers on the score (Photo 4) and squeeze the handles of the pliers to break the glass. (Photo 5) Repeat the process to cut the glass into 1" square pieces. Using the wheel cutters, break the glass into random shapes of about the same size. (They will be used to fill in the wings.)

7. Pieces of china plates are used for the background. If the china is thin, use wheel cutters to cut each piece into three to four large pieces. (Photo 6) (You'll cut them into smaller pieces later.) If the china is thick, you can use tile nippers.

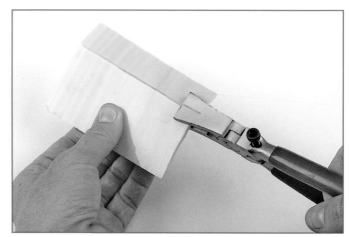

Photo 5 – Using running pliers to break the glass.

Photo 6 – Using wheel cutters to cut a china dish.

Attach the Tesserae

There are different schools of thought about laying down tesserae – how you choose to do it is a matter of personal preference. Some people spread a layer of adhesive over a portion of the surface and place the tesserae one after the other. (Photo 7, Photo 8) Others (myself included) usually butter the back of each tile and place it. (Photo 9, Photo 10) I prefer this method in most circumstances because I don't want excess glue oozing up between my tiles, and I don't want to obscure my pattern with adhesive.

Photo 7 – Spreading glue along the edge of the tray with a craft stick.

Attach the tesserae in this order:

1. Lay the black border tiles.
2. Place the purple tiles to outline of the butterfly's wings. As you lay the purple tiles, you'll need to cut some of the rectangles and angle their edges so that they follow the curve of the wings. This is an important detail for the flow of the piece. Cutting tesserae into wedges that are wider at one end than the other to fit around a curve adds a level of sophistication to your work.
3. Attach the tiles for the butterfly's head and antennae.
4. Glue six buttons on each wing.

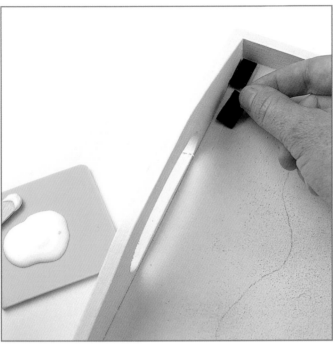

Photo 8- Placing the black border tiles.

Photo 10 – Placing the glass piece.

5. Fill in the wings around the buttons with pieces of orange glass. Use wheel cutters to nip pieces to size. As you place the pieces, try not to create long straight lines. Once grouted, these lines become "rivers." Don't cut the pieces too small. Both distract the eye once the mosaic is grouted.
6. Cut the china plates into smaller pieces to fit the background spaces. Be aware that plates break differently – some fracture straight across, and others break along the rim. The pieces need to be cut small enough to remove the curve in the china so the pieces will lay flat. You can cut a lot of pieces at one time and search for the shape you need *or* cut the pieces to fit one-by-one. *TIP: For tabletops and trays, use a level as you adhere the tesserae to make sure the surface stays even.* When you are using china with different thicknesses, build up the adhesive under the thinner pieces so surface will be level.

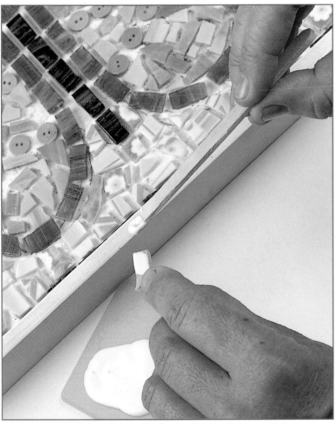

Photo 9 – Applying glue to the back of a single piece of glass.

Grout & Clean

How much grout a project needs depends on the thickness and the spacing of the tesserae. For a tray of this size, with thin glass and china pieces and narrow grout lines, a plastic quart container about three-quarters full will suffice. For more information, see "Grout" and "How to Mix & Apply Grout" in the Mosaic Materials section.

1. Mix the grout. When mixing a dark grout, I use distilled water instead of tap water to avoid the mineral deposits that eventually effloresce on the surface.
2. Use your gloved hand or a spatula to place about a handful of grout on the surface. (Photo 11) Press the grout into the spaces between the tesserae. (Photo 12) Repeat until all areas of the mosaic have been grouted.
3. With a slightly damp sponge, wipe away excess grout. Make circular strokes. (Photo 13) If a tile pops off while you're grouting, set it aside. Once the excess grout has been wiped off, clean out the spot and re-attach the tile, then add grout around it.
4. Use paper towels to wipe off the rest of the excess grout.
5. Polish off the haze, rubbing the mosaic until it shines. Let grout dry 24 hours.(Photo 14)

Photo 11 – Placing a handful of grout on the surface of the mosaic.

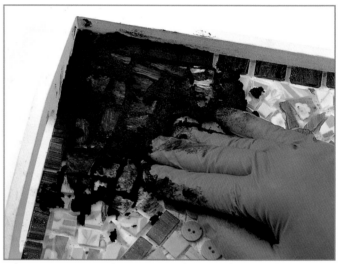

Photo 12 – Pressing the grout into the spaces between the tesserae.

Photo 13 – Using a sponge to wipe away excess grout.

Photo 14 – Polishing the mosaic.

Finishing

1. Paint the remaining exposed wood of the tray with purple acrylic paint. Let dry.
2. Varnish the painted wood. Let dry.
3. Seal the grout with grout sealer. (Photo 15) Let dry. ❑

Photo 15 – Apply grout sealer.

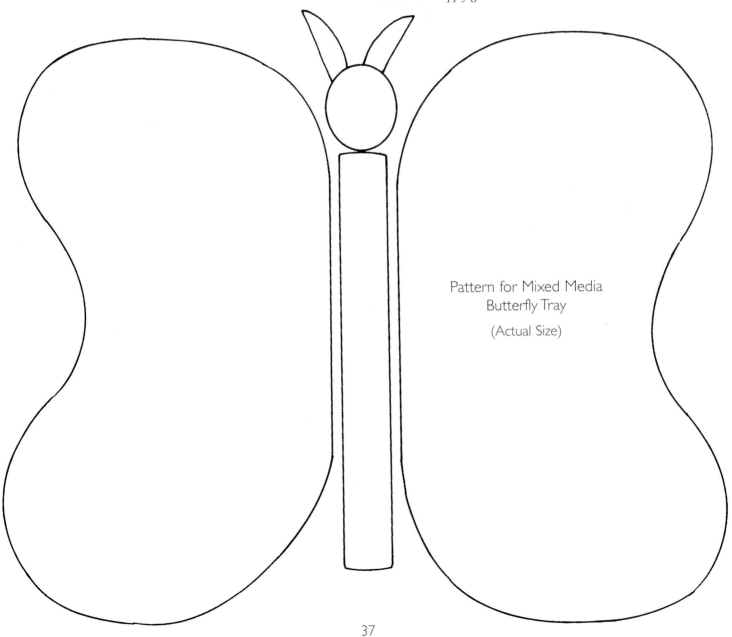

Pattern for Mixed Media
Butterfly Tray

(Actual Size)

Mosaic Technique

Indirect Method

Indirect mosaic methods should be used when you want to create a mosaic with a flat surface, such as a tabletop or chair seat, using materials of varying thicknesses or when you want to create your mosaic in one location and install it elsewhere. There are several different techniques.

In the **reverse method**, you temporarily glue tesserae upside down and backwards on brown kraft paper. After the glue dries, you pre-grout the mosaic, prepare the surface with adhesive mortar, and turn the mosaic onto the mortar adhesive. When it dries, you wet the brown paper, remove it, then grout.

The **double reverse method** is simpler and less intimidating because you always see the front of your project. You create the mosaic on a low density polyethylene mounting paper. This transparent, waxy paper has a smooth side and a sticky side, much like clear self-adhesive shelf paper,

but with different adhesion and release properties. (Tesserae won't remain attached to regular self-adhesive paper throughout this process.) You place your tesserae on the sticky side of the mounting paper and cover it with another piece of mounting paper with the sticky side down so the mosaic is sandwiched between the two pieces of mounting paper. To install the mosaic, you flip it over, remove the bottom piece of mounting paper, and turn it over into a bed of cement adhesive and level the surface. When it dries, peel off the top piece of mounting paper and then grout.

Supplies for Stool

The **Black & White Mosaic Stool** is used as an example to show the indirect mosaic technique.

Surface:
Wooden stool with round seat

Tesserae:
5 black-and-white patterned plates, 12" diameter
6 plates with black-and-white patterned rims, 6" diameter
1 plate with black-and-white patterned rim, 8" diameter
9 round mirror pieces, various sizes (1/4" to 2")
4 white plastic buttons, 1-1/4" diameter
3 polymer clay beads with yin-yang pattern
7 round black ceramic tiles, 1/2"
8 black-and-white buttons, 3/8" diameter
13 small black-and-white patterned millefiori

Other Supplies:
2 sheets mosaic mounting paper (sold online)
White thinset mortar
Sanded grout – White
Cement colorant – Yellow
Grout sealer
Acrylic paints – Black, cream
Paint brushes
Painter's masking tape
Sandpaper
White primer
Tile cleaner
Safety gear

Tools:
Wheel cutters *and/or* tile nippers
Button shank remover *optional*
Notched trowel
Level

Prepare the Stool

1. Clean, sand, and prime the stool.
2. Design a pattern for your stool. Draw the design on white paper, using the photo as a guide.
3. Cut out two circles of mounting paper, each 12-1/2" diameter. Set one aside. Remove the protective film on the other piece of mounting paper (Photo 1) and place it, sticky side up, on top of the pattern.

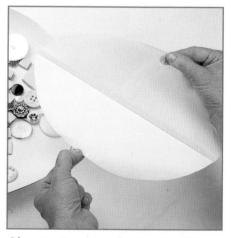

Photo 1 – Removing the protective film from a piece of mounting paper.

Prepare the Tesserae

1. Use either wheel cutters (for thinner plates) or tile nippers (for thicker plates) to break the rims from the plates. (Photos 2 & 3)
2. To make the pieces for the outer border of the stool, cut pieces from the larger plates, alternating pieces of china with two different patterns. In the example, the tesserae with the swirls are 1-1/4"; the diamond-pattern pieces are 1" long and 1/2" wide.
3. Cut 1/2" square pieces of china to make two rings inside the border. Choose four motifs for these pieces; you will alternate the two motifs on each ring.

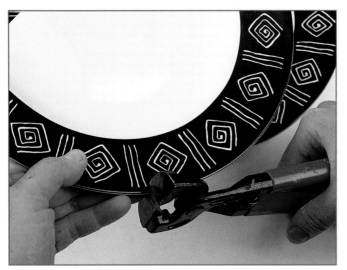

Photo 2 – Cutting a section of the plate

Photo 3 – Cutting the section into smaller squares

Position the Tesserae

1. Beginning with the outer ring, select pieces of cut china one at a time and press firmly on the sticky paper that is on top of the pattern. (Photo 4)
2. When the outer border pieces are in place, position the next two rings of cut pieces. (Photo 5)
3. Fill the center area of the mosaic with buttons, beads, mirror circles, millefiori, and round black tiles.
4. When all the pieces are attached, take the second circle of mounting paper and remove the protective film.
5. Lay the mounting paper, sticky side down, on top of the mosaic. (Photos 6 & 7) Press to adhere so the mosaic is sandwiched between two pieces of mounting paper. Because the pieces are not uniform in height, be sure to individually burnish each piece to the mounting paper. (Photo 8)

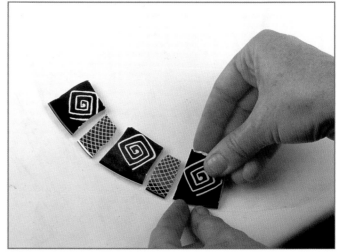

Photo 4 – Adhering the outer ring.

6. Turn over the mosaic, which is sandwiched between the two pieces of mounting paper. The tesserae will now be upside down. (Photo 9) TIP: This is easier, particularly if your mosaic is a large one, if you place the mosaic between two pieces of board when you flip it.

7. Peel off the mounting paper from the bottom of the mosaic. (Photo 10) Your tesserae are now upside down, still adhered to the second sheet of mounting paper.

Photo 5 – Positioning the next two rings of tesserae.

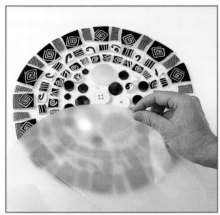

Photo 6 – The backing has been removed from the second piece of mounting paper.

Photo 7 – Positioning the second piece of mounting paper over the mosaic.

Photo 8 – Burnishing each piece to the mounting paper.

Photo 9 – Turning the mosaic. (It is upside down.)

Photo 10 – Peeling off the mounting paper from the bottom of the mosaic.

Apply the Mortar Base

1. Mix two to three cups of white thinset mortar. Tint it with cement colorant to achieve a pale yellow color.
2. Use your hands or a large spoon to place the thinset mortar on the seat of the stool. (Photo 11)
3. Spread the mortar with hands to evenly distribute it. (Photo 12)
4. Use a notched trowel with widely spaced teeth to level the thinset, dragging the trowel across the seat so it creates ridges and evenly distributes the adhesive mortar on the surface. (Photo 13) NOTE: This mortar bed must be slightly thicker than your thickest tesserae so the surface of the finished mosaic will be flat. Remove extra mortar from sides of stool.
5. Flip the tesserae, still attached to mounting paper, onto the seat of the stool. (Photos 14 & 15)

Photo 11 – Placing thinset mortar on the surface.

Photo 12 – Spreading the mortar with hands to evenly distribute

Photo 13 – Leveling and evening up the mortar with trowel.

Photo 14 – Flipping mosaic piece over.

Photo 15 – Positioning the mosaic on the stool.

Photo 16 – Pressing the mosaic piece in place.

Photo 17 – Using a level to make sure the mosaic is flat.

Photo 18 – Using a sponge to wipe away excess thinset mortar from around the edge of the mosaic.

Photo 19 – Peeling off the mounting paper on top of the mosaic.

6. Press the mosaic in place. Do not press too hard because you don't want the thinset to ooze up too far between the tiles. (Photo 16)

7. Use a level to make sure the top of the mosaic is flat. (Photo 17)

8. Use a sponge to wipe away excess thinset from around the edge of the mosaic. (Photo 18) Let dry completely (24 hours).

9. Peel off the mounting paper. (Photo 19)

Grout the Mosaic

For more information, see "Grout" and "How to Mix & Apply Grout" in the Mosaic Materials section.

1. Mix the grout, using the same proportion of colorant to white grout powder that you used to tint the white thinset. (You only need a small amount of grout. Because the colored thinset will be exposed along the edge of the stool it is important to use a grout that matches the thinset color.)

2. Use your gloved hand or a spatula to place about a handful of grout on the surface. Press the grout into the spaces between the tesserae. Repeat until all areas of the mosaic have been grouted.

3. With a damp sponge, wipe away excess grout. Use circular strokes.

4. Use paper towels to wipe off the rest of the excess grout. Let dry.

Finish

1. Use painter's tape to mask off wide bands on the legs of the stool, using the photo as a guide. Paint the stretchers, the edge of the seat, and the bands with black paint. Remove tape and let dry completely.

2. Mask off and paint the remaining areas of the stool with cream paint. Let dry.

3. Varnish the painted portions. Let dry.

4. Seal the mosaic grout with grout sealer. Let dry. ❏

Mosaic Projects

In this section are 27 mosaic projects using found materials. They vary in level of difficulty and time needed – some require no cutting or grouting; others demand more time, patience, and acquired skills.

Each project includes step-by-step instructions and a list of the necessary supplies. Not listed are the basic supplies you need for every project: safety gear such as gloves and a mask, clean-up items (sponges, paper towels), craft sticks, plastic containers, measuring cups, and newspaper.

If you cannot find the same materials or surfaces I used, feel free to experiment with other surfaces and tesserae. The wonder of mosaics is its versatility!

Pictured at right: Garden Fantasy Gazing Ball –
Instructions begin on page 48.

Garden Fantasy
Gazing Ball
....

Bowling balls can be recycled to make gorgeous mosaic garden ornaments. They can be found in thrift shops and at bowling alleys. There are many techniques for covering the three finger holes, including wood filler, thinset mortar, and aluminum foil. I thought it would be fun to use one hole in the design to hold the beaded wire bouquet. The other two holes were completely covered with yellow glass circles. To keep the ball from rolling around while working, lay it between two rolled towels, lay it on a piece of bubble-wrap, or place it in a sturdy, flat-sided bowl with a towel, then place on a lazy susan for ease.

SUPPLIES

Surface:
Bowling ball

Tesserae:
Crystal glass tiles, 3/8" – Red, magenta, yellow, light blue
Crystal glass tiles, 1" – 2 yellow, 4 purple, 1 blue
Crystal glass tile, 3/4" – 1 red
Opaque colored glass, 8" square pieces in a variety of colors
Mustard yellow glass, 10" square
Dark green mirror, 1/4" squares
Purple mirror, 8" square
Gold mirror, 12" square

Other Supplies:
16 head pins
16 wire clothes hangers
35 (approx.) beads and colored crystals for the dangles
Silicone adhesive
White marker
Sanded grout – Black
Black enamel spray paint
All-purpose cleaner and degreaser
Optional: Small marbles, to help hold the wire bouquet in place
Leather gloves

Tools:
Wheel cutters
Glass scorer, running pliers
Wire cutters
Long nose pliers

INSTRUCTIONS

Prepare the Ball & Wires:
1. Clean the bowling ball with an all-purpose cleaner and degreaser.
2. Following the pattern, draw the outlines of the design in white marker on the ball.
3. Using long nose pliers, untwist the hangers and straighten them. From the hangers, cut 16 lengths of wire between 10" and 20", using wire cutters.
4. Using the pliers, curl one end of each wire piece to form a loop for a beaded dangle.
5. Wearing gloves, join the hangers together at their other ends (like a bouquet) and wrap the bottom 2" with a piece of wire. (This wrapped portion will be placed inside one of the finger holes of the bowling ball.)
6. Spray paint the wire bouquet with black enamel. Let dry.
7. Using the photo as a guide, make 16 beaded dangles on head pins. Make a loop for hanging at the top of each dangle.

Prepare the Tesserae:
1. Cut the mustard yellow glass into 13 circles ranging in size from 1/4" in diameter to 1-1/4" in diameter.
2. Cut purple and light yellow glass into long triangular shapes for stars.
3. Cut the blue mirror glass into seven triangles. *The remainder of the glass will be cut or broken to fit areas.*

Attach the Tesserae:
1. Using silicone adhesive, glue the red and maroon 3/8" tiles along the swirl motifs in the design.
2. Glue two mustard glass circles over two of the finger openings.
3. Fill in the orange band with small random cuts of glass.
4. Following the pattern, glue the remaining glass, cutting the pieces with wheel cutters to fit as you work. Let dry.

Grout:
1. Mix black sanded grout and spread it over ball. Keep the remaining finger hole open.
2. Wipe away the excess grout.
3. Clean up with paper towels. Let dry.

Finish:
1. Fill the remaining finger hole 3/4" full with silicone adhesive. Place the wire bouquet in the hole. *Option:* If the wire wiggles, add a few small marbles to keep the wires upright in the center of the hole.
2. Mix a small batch of black sanded grout to fill in the remainder of the hole. Fill the hole and smooth the top so there are no seams. Let dry.
3. Seal the bowling ball with grout sealer. Let dry.
4. Slip the loops of the beaded dangles over the loops on the ends of the wires and close with pliers. ❑

Pattern #1
(Actual Size)

Pattern #2

(Actual Size)

Instructions begin on page 54

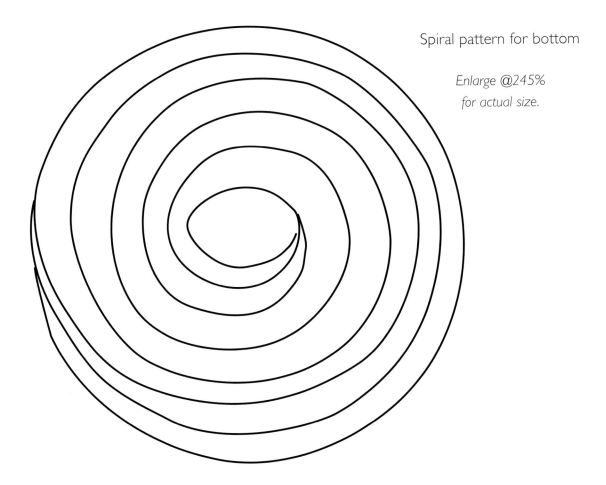

Spiral pattern for bottom

Enlarge @245%
for actual size.

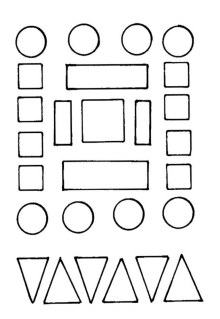

Pattern for Rim

(Actual Size)

Fantastic Fish
Tabletop Birdbath

This birdbath was inspired by the chipped ceramic fish toothbrush holder that I placed in the center. I thought the fish would look appropriate in a water environment – instead of holding brushes, they are burbling glass "bubbles." The colors of the toothbrush holder dictated the color scheme of orange, pink, green, and blue. The mirror details add a touch of sparkle and reflect the sunlight.

Pattern appears on the previous page.

SUPPLIES

Surface:
Resin or concrete tabletop birdbath, 16" diameter

Tesserae:
Ceramic toothbrush holder with 4 openings
Opaque colored glass, 12" square – Royal blue, pink, dark orange, light orange (1 each)
125 (approx.) lime green flat-back glass marbles
Orange mirror, 6" square
Blue mirror, 8" square
36 peppermint pink mirror squares, 1/2"
75 (approx.) lime green vitreous glass tiles, 3/4"

Other Supplies:
Thinset mortar
Silicone adhesive
10 ft. of 18 gauge copper wire
12 flat back clear blue marbles
12 small blue glass beads
1 tube royal blue seed beads
Wax crayon
Sanded grout – Antique white
Universal tint – Yellow, blue
Grout sealer
Outdoor acrylic paints – Bright orange, coral, hot pink, lime green, royal blue
Exterior varnish
Optional: Concrete sealer (if you're using a concrete birdbath)

Tools:
Wheel cutters
Glass scorer, running pliers
Pencil or tracing tool
Paint brushes
Wire cutters

INSTRUCTIONS

Prepare the Birdbath:
1. Clean the birdbath, if necessary. If your birdbath is concrete, seal it and let dry. (If your birdbath is resin, it doesn't need to be sealed.)
2. Position the toothbrush holder in the center of the basin. Use a wax crayon to trace around its base.
3. Transfer the spiral pattern to the basin.

Make the "Bubbles":
1. Cut 12 strips of copper wire, each approximately 10" long.
2. Wrap one end of each piece of wire around a flat-back blue marble to create an X-design with the wire.
3. Add one small glass bead on the end of the wire. Twist the wire around a pencil to create curls. Set aside.

Attach the Tesserae:
Use wheel cutters or glass scorer to cut the tesserae.

1. Cut the blue and pink glass into rectangles 1/2" wide, varying in size between 3/4" and 2". Nip the ends so that the pieces are angled to follow the curve of the spiral. Glue the pieces on the two spiral outlines with silicone adhesive.
2. Cut the two shades of orange glass into 1-1/2" triangles. Glue them on the inner edge of the basin, alternating the colors.
3. Adhere the ring of green flat-back marbles along the top edge. (I used 57 here.)
4. Cut strips of blue mirror 1" x 1/4".
5. Cut the orange mirror into 1/4" squares.
6. Glue strips of blue mirror outside the ring of green marbles, alternating the blue mirror strips with 1/4" squares of orange mirror.
7. Under each blue mirror strip, glue a 1/2" square of peppermint pink mirror.
8. Under each small orange mirror square, glue a 1/4" piece of light orange glass, followed by another 1/4" piece of orange mirror.
9. Create another row of 1" blue mirror strips, alternating them with 1/4" squares of light orange glass.
10. Glue another ring of green flat-back marbles. (I used 65 here.)

Continued on page 56

Continued from page 54

11. Cut the pink glass into 1/2" triangles and glue them in a ring, alternating point up and point down. Let dry 24 hours.
12. Mix enough white cement adhesive to fill the toothbrush holder. Tint with blue colorant.
13. Fill the toothbrush holder with the cement.
14. Push the strips of curled wire with the marbles and beads into the cement. Distribute them equally and make sure the wires are secure. Let dry.
15. Cover the dry blue cement with a thin layer of silicone. Pour on blue seed beads to cover the cement.
16. With silicone adhesive, glue the toothbrush holder at the center of the basin. Let dry 24 hours.

Grout:

For more information, see "Grout" and "How to Mix & Apply Grout" in the Mosaic Materials section.

1. Mix the antique white grout. Add a few drops of yellow tint to create a lemon yellow color.
2. Apply grout to the basin and the rim of the birdbath. Wipe away excess with a sponge.
3. Clean up with paper towels. Let dry 24 hours.

Finish:

1. Seal with grout sealer.
2. Paint the base of the birdbath with outdoor acrylic paints, using the photo as a guide. Let dry.
3. Varnish for protection. Let dry. TIP: When the birdbath gets dirty it can be soaked and scrubbed with a diluted bleach-and-water mix. Rinse thoroughly. ❏

Buttons & Pebbles

Vase

Here's a way to use and enjoy a button collection. Because this project is not grouted, use buttons that are the same color as the object you are covering. Be sure to place the buttons as close together as possible. Here, I covered an old white pitcher with a variety of white buttons and white pebbles.

SUPPLIES

Surface:
Vase or pitcher, 10" high (20" circumference, 5" opening)

Tesserae:
300-400 white buttons, various sizes
16 oz. white floral or aquarium pebbles

Other Supplies:
Silicone adhesive
Fine grit sandpaper
All-purpose cleaner and degreaser

Tools:
Button shank remover
Toothpicks *or* dental tools
2 cloth towels

INSTRUCTIONS

Prepare:
1. Use the button shank tool to remove the backs of the shank buttons so they will lay flat.
2. Clean the vase or pitcher with an all-purpose cleaner and degreaser.
3. Lightly sand the exterior to give the smooth surface some texture ("tooth") to hold the adhesive.
4. Lay the vase or pitcher on its side between two rolled towels.

Attach the Tesserae:
1. Working from the bottom upward, glue the buttons, one at a time, to the surface with small dabs of silicone.
   • You do not want glue oozing up between the buttons. Should this occur, use a toothpick or other thin tool to scrape away excess glue.
   • Try to arrange the buttons randomly, rather than in rows. Fill in any small spaces with the smallest buttons.
   • Let one side of vase dry completely before turning it over to work on the other side.
2. When the body of the vase or pitcher is covered with buttons and the adhesive is fully set, apply a thin layer of silicone with a craft stick around the base and cover the glue with white pebbles. Because the pebbles are small, it is not necessary to glue each one individually.
3. Use the same technique to apply pebbles around the neck of the vase or pitcher. Leave the very top of the rim uncovered. Let dry. ❏

Bright Geometrics
Hat Rack

This project recycles a door from an old wooden nightstand. Turned horizontally, with a variety of glass tiles covering the wooden inset panel and with added knobs, it becomes a charming hat rack.

The secret is to use different sizes of tiles in rich colors and textures to break up the horizontal lines. The number of rows of tesserae depends on the height and width of the panel in the door. For this 4" panel, there are six rows of tile of different sizes. There is minimal cutting.

Instructions begin on page 60

Bright Geometrics
Hat Rack

Pictured on pages 58-59

SUPPLIES

Surface:

Wooden cupboard door, 19" x 9"
  with 4" panel

20" piece of decorative molding

4 decorative knobs or hooks

Tesserae:

21 yellow glass tiles, 3/4"

27 blue iridium glass tiles, 1/2"

43 silver glass tiles, 1/4"

21 red glass tile, 3/4"

16 purple glitter crystal glass tile, 1"

40 gold smalti with alternating
  shades of green and teal on the
  underside, 1/4"

Other Supplies:

PVA white glue

White spray primer

Wood filler (if necessary)

Acrylic paint – Yellow

Matte varnish

Sanded grout – Black

Distilled water

Sandpaper

Tack cloth

Finishing nails and hammer

2 D-rings and picture wire (for
  hanging)

Painter's masking tape

Tools:

Wheel cutters

Paint brushes

INSTRUCTIONS

Prepare:

1. Remove any hardware from the door. Clean the surface and fill holes with wood filler. Let dry. Sand and wipe clean with tack cloth.

2. Seal the door and the piece of molding with white primer. (I like to use a spray can for quick coverage.) Let dry.

3. Paint both pieces with two coats of yellow acrylic paint. Let dry.

4. Attach the molding with four finishing nails. Counter-sink the nails. Fill the holes and smooth the filler. Let dry.

5. Attach the 2 D-rings and wire on the back for hanging.

Attach the Tesserae:

1. With white glue, glue the smalti, undersides up, on the bottom, with the tiles almost touching. If a complete tile does not fit at the end of a row, nip it in half and place that piece somewhere within the row. Avoid cutting the tiles on the ends of the rows.

2. Glue a row of purple glitter crystal tiles above the smalti.

3. Glue a row of red glass tiles above the purple tiles.

4. Glue the silver glass tiles above the red glass tiles.

5. Glue the blue tiles above the silver tiles.

6. Glue the yellow glass tiles above the blue tiles. Let dry.

Grout:

For more information, see "Grout" and "How to Mix & Apply Grout" in the Mosaic Materials section.

1. Tape off the inner edges of the panel to avoid grout stains.

2. Mix the black grout.

3. Spread the grout over the tesserae. Sponge away the excess and wipe up with paper towels. Let dry.

Finish:

1. Touch up paint as needed. Let dry.

2. Apply two coats of matte varnish to the painted surfaces. Let dry.

3. Screw the four decorative knobs in the wood below the mosaic panel, spacing them evenly. ❏

"Home Is Where the Heart Is"
Souvenir Plate Panel
....

Here's another way to use an old door from a cabinet or discarded piece of furniture. Because of its size and weight, this door panel can accommodate several souvenir plates. You can use your own collection or find the plates at thrift stores and flea markets.

If you have access to a ring saw or wet saw you can cut out the plate centers in one piece. If not, you can break the plates with nippers or a hammer and glue the pieces close together. Since this is a wall piece, it doesn't have to be completely flat.

Pictured on pages 62-63.

SUPPLIES

Wooden door, 23" x 15", 1-1/2" thick

Tesserae:
33 (approx.) souvenir china plates, mugs, and bowls
Round metal picture frame, 5" diameter, glass and backing removed
Plastic or wooden letter tiles, 1/2", to spell out "Home Is Where the Heart Is" or other message (available at craft stores)

Other Supplies:
3 large metal hooks
PVA white adhesive
Silicone adhesive
Sanded grout – Tobacco brown
Grout sealer
Acrylic paints – Dark chocolate, bright red
Matte varnish
Wood filler
Sandpaper
White spray primer
Painter's masking tape
White crayon
2 D-rings and picture wire (for hanging)

Tools:
Tile nippers
Wheel glass cutters
Paint brushes

INSTRUCTIONS

Prepare:
1. Remove any old hardware from the door. Clean the surface. Fill any holes with wood filler. Let dry.
2. Sand the door and wipe with a tack cloth.
3. Spray with white primer. Let dry.
4. Brush two coats of brown acrylic paint over the entire surface. Let dry.
5. Attach hanging hardware to the back of the door.
6. Measure and mark the area for the mosaic. (Mine is 22" x 12". I left a 3-1/2" space at the bottom for the hooks and used the routed line on the door in the design.) Mask off the perimeter of the mosaic with painter's tape.
7. Position the 5" frame in the center of the taped-off area. Draw around it with white pencil. Remove the frame. (The frame and lettering will be installed after the mosaic is grouted.)
8. Cut or break the china into pieces.

Continued on next page

continued from page 61

Attach the Tesserae:

Use the photo as a guide for placement.

1. Starting in one corner, glue the china. Keep the pieces close together so that the names of the states and any text are readable. If the china piece is flat, use PVA glue; if the china piece is curved, use silicone. Don't glue any china in the marked area where the frame will be.
2. Fill gaps or small areas with small pieces of china, using images, words, or colors, as appropriate. Let dry.

Grout:

For more information, see "Grout" and "How to Mix & Apply Grout" in the Mosaic Materials section.

1. Mix the brown sanded grout. After it slakes, cover the china. Grout right up to edge of the center circle.
2. Wipe away the excess grout with a sponge and clean up with paper towels. Make sure the outside edge of the grout is tidy with no ragged edges. Let dry.

Finish:

1. Position and glue the word tiles inside the frame area with white glue.
2. Place the frame around the text and secure with silicone glue. Let dry.
3. Touch up the grout, as necessary, around the outside of the frame. Let dry.
4. Seal the grout. Let dry.
5. Remove the painter's tape. Touch up the door with brown paint, as needed.
6. Highlight the routed groove with bright red paint. Let dry.
7. Apply a few coats of matte varnish to the painted area. Let dry.
8. Screw the three hooks, spacing them evenly, along the bottom of the panel. ❏

Time Is Precious
Picture Frames

Old wooden frames and discarded watches are combined for these projects. One frame has round watch faces; the other has square and rectangular faces. Look for wooden frames 1-1/2" to 2" wide with a rim. They do not need to be painted; the wood tones complement the watches. It may take several trips to thrift shops to collect enough watch faces, but the result is worth the effort.

I used rubber stamps and sayings about time to temporarily fill the frames. (You could also print words and images on a computer.) These frames make great retirement and bon voyage gifts.

"Time Flies When You Are Having Fun" Frame

SUPPLIES

Surface:
Wooden frame, 5" x 7" opening, 1-1/2" border with lip
Card stock, 5" x 7"

Tesserae:
20 (approx.) watches with round faces
10 to 12 gold and silver acrylic tile pieces
Watch parts (available online)
5 charms related to time (clocks, quotes, timers)

Other Supplies:
Epoxy adhesive
Foam brush
Painter's tape

Continued on page 66

Continued on page 66

Time is precious. What are we waiting for?

continued from page 64

Small container
Cotton swabs
Denatured alcohol
Rubber stamps and ink

Tools:
Tweezers
Long nose pliers
Scissors
Single edge blade

INSTRUCTIONS

Prepare:

1. Make sure the frame is clean and in good repair. Tape the inside edge of the frame with painter's tape to pre-vent the adhesive from running over the edge.
2. Using pliers, remove the watch faces from the watch bands. Save the metal bands for another project.

Attach the Tesserae:

1. Mix about 1/4 cup epoxy in a small container. Using a foam brush, paint a thin layer of epoxy over the inside border of the frame.
2. Starting in the lower corner and working clockwise, position and glue the watch faces close together along the border of the frame.
3. Leave space at the top center for the charms. If anything slides in the epoxy, temporarily tape it in place.
4. When the watches are attached, use tweezers to place gold and silver tile pieces to fill the empty spaces. These tiles can be cut to fit with scissors, if necessary. Be careful not to get epoxy on the tops of the tiles.
5. Use tweezers to pick up small watch pieces and place them around the frame. Let dry 24 hours.

Finish:

1. Scrape away any epoxy that has dried on the surface of the tesserae with the single edge blade.
2. Stamp images and a quotation on the card stock. Place it in the frame under the glass.
3. Replace the backing and frame hardware. ❏

"Time is Precious. What Are We Waiting For?" Frame

SUPPLIES

Surface:
Wooden frame, 3-1/2" x 5" opening with 1" inner border
Card stock, 3-1/2" x 5"

Tesserae:
18 watches with square or rectangular faces
9 gold glass tiles, 1"

Other Supplies:
Epoxy adhesive
Foam brush
Painter's masking tape
Rubber stamps and ink

Tools:
Wheel cutters
Tweezers
Long nose pliers
Scissors
Craft knife *or* single edge blade

INSTRUCTIONS

Prepare:

1. Clean the frame as needed. Affix painter's tape to the edge of the inside border to prevent epoxy spills.
2. Remove the watch bands from the faces. Set aside the metal bands for another future project.
3. Cut the glass tiles in half.

Attach the Tesserae:

1. Mix 1/4 cup of epoxy. With a foam brush, brush a thin layer evenly along inside border of frame.
2. Using the photo as a guide, place the watch faces and gold tiles in the epoxy, alternating the watch faces and strips of gold tile. Tape any pieces into place if they slip. Let the frame dry for 24 hours.

Finish:

1. Use a craft knife or blade to scrape away any excess dried epoxy.
2. Stamp an image and a quote on the card stock and place it in the frame under the glass.
3. Replace the backing and reattach any hardware. ❏

Glittering Jewels
Belt Buckle

Mosaics can decorate any size surface, from the side of a building to a small piece of jewelry. This mosaic belt buckle uses old costume jewelry – brooches, earrings, and some beads – glued on a crystal glass tile mosaic. Blank belt buckles are popular with artists who fuse glass and are available through stained glass suppliers. Look for one with a lip or rim to protect the edges. Belts with removable buckles are also readily available online. One of my customers displays her buckles on small easels when she is not wearing them.

SUPPLIES

Surface:
1 blank belt buckle, 3" diameter

Tesserae:
Crystal glitter tiles, 1" – 1 royal blue, 1 turquoise, 1 sage green
2 gold brooches, 1" diameter, with blue and green stones or beads
1 gold brooch of figure (Mine is a dancer.)
Fire opal cabochon, 1/2"
2 blue opal cabochons, 1/4"
3 earrings – Butterfly, star, flower

Other Supplies:
Sanded white grout
Acrylic paint – Lime green
PVA white adhesive
Epoxy adhesive (Two-barrel epoxy may be the best choice – you only need a small amount.)
Jewelry cleaner

Tools:
Long nose pliers
Wheel glass cutters
Craft knife *or* single-edge blade

INSTRUCTIONS

Prepare:
1. Using pliers, remove the backs of the brooches and earrings so they lay flat.
2. Clean jewelry, if necessary, so it sparkles.

Attach the Tesserae:
1. Nip the three crystal glass tiles into random shapes.
2. Glue on the belt face with white glue, arranging them randomly with even grout lines throughout. Let dry.

Grout:
For more information, see "Grout" and "How to Mix & Apply Grout" in the Mosaic Materials section.
1. Mix 1/2 cup white grout with green acrylic paint to make a pale lime color.
2. Spread over the tesserae. Wipe away the excess. Clean with paper towels. Let dry.

Finish:
1. Following the product instructions, mix about one teaspoon of two-part epoxy.
2. Use a craft stick to apply a small dab of epoxy to the back of each brooch and arrange on top of the crystal tile mosaic.
3. Add the earrings and beads until you have covered most, but not all, of the tiles underneath. If anything starts to slip, tape it in place. Let dry 24 hours.
4. Carefully remove any excess dried epoxy with a craft knife or blade. ❏

Kitty Dreams
Framed Mirror

I discovered this small arch-shaped framed mirror at one garage sale and a bag of fish refrigerator magnets at another sale down the street. The two called out to me to be combined since I had found them on the same day. This project involves grouting around the dimensional fish. To avoid staining them with the black grout, the fish need to be protected. See "Protecting Tesserae & Other Dimensional Objects" for more information.

SUPPLIES

Surface:
Arch-shaped frame, 9-1/2" x 6" with a 6" x 3" mirror

Tesserae:
Royal blue stained glass, 8" x 10"
Mustard yellow stained glass, 6" square
4 fish-motif magnets (Ideally, they all face the same direction.)

Other Supplies:
Black sanded grout
Distilled water
PVA white adhesive
Silicone glue
Acrylic paint – Black
White pencil
Painter's masking tape

Tools:
Wheel cutters
Paint brush
Optional: Ring saw

INSTRUCTIONS

Prepare:
1. Clean the frame, if necessary.
2. Mask off the mirror with the painter's tape. Don't cover the inside edges of the frame.
3. Paint the entire frame with black acrylic paint. Let dry.
4. Using the pattern as a guide, draw the kitty outline on the frame with a white pencil.
5. Remove the magnets from the backs of the fish.

Attach the Tesserae:
1. Cut the yellow glass into small random shapes. Glue them inside the outline of the kitty's head and paws with white glue. *Options:* Use a ring saw to cut the head and paws pieces. Or have the pieces cut at a glass shop. (You'll pay a small fee.)
2. Using silicone, glue the fish in place.
3. Cut the blue glass into random small shapes and glue them around the cat and the fish. Let dry.

Grout:
For more information, see "Grout" and "How to Mix & Apply Grout" in the Mosaic Materials section.
1. Cover the fish to protect them. See "Protecting Tesserae & Other Objects."
2. Mix the black sanded grout.
3. Apply the grout to the frame, working right up to the fish.
4. Wipe away the excess with a sponge and clean up with paper towels. Let dry.

Finish:
1. Seal with grout sealer. Let dry.
2. Remove the protective covering from the fish. Clean up as necessary.
3. Remove the tape from the mirror and polish.
4. Touch up the sides and the edges of the frame with black paint, if needed. Let dry. ❑

Pattern for Kitty Dreams
Framed Mirror

(Actual Size)

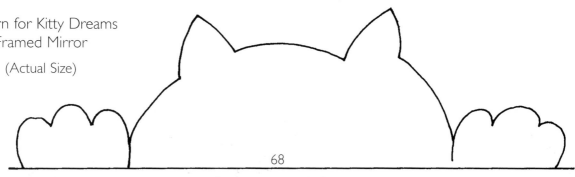

Violet Textures
Picture Frame

Odds and ends of mosaic materials that don't necessarily seem to belong together can be combined to make decorative picture frames. For this frame, I decided on a purple and white color scheme and found all kinds of goodies in those two colors: tiles, earrings, buttons, charms, beads, cabochons, parts of Christmas ornaments, and millefiori. The combination of materials gives the frame a rich texture. There is no set method for arranging so many different pieces – my rule of thumb is to work in one direction and place the pieces until the frame is full. Because the piece is not grouted it is important to use a strong adhesive and place the pieces as close together as possible. You can always go back and fill blank spots.

SUPPLIES

Surface:
Frame, 8" square with a 3" opening and 2" border

Tesserae:
Approximately 4 cups of small purple and white objects, such as:
4-5 purple glass tiles (various sizes)
14 buttons (random sizes)
16 glass beads
1 small pearl necklace, taken apart
Opaque violet glass, 2" square
Opaque white glass, 2" square
Purple mirror, 2" square
4 earrings
3 glass flowers
2 glass butterflies
10 plastic beads
2 plastic icicles
4 sequin flowers
Lavender seed beads
1 baby rattle charm
1 charm with Chinese character
8 cabochons
1 large painted flat-back marble
3 millefiori

Other Supplies:
Acrylic paints – White, lavender
Silicone glue
White PVA glue *or* epoxy adhesive

Tools:
Pliers
Button shank remover *optional*
Tweezers
Wheel cutters
Craft knife *or* window scraper
Paint brushes

INSTRUCTIONS

Prepare:
1. Clean the frame, if necessary. Paint with white paint. Let dry.
2. Using tools, take apart all brooches, earrings, and necklaces so individual beads and pieces can be used. Remove shanks from any buttons you might be using.

Attach the Tesserae:
1. Choose a starting point on the frame. Apply a 2" square of adhesive with a craft stick and begin laying the various pieces side by side, alternating colors and shapes. Repeat until the frame is covered. TIPS: For balance, place larger items on each side of frame. Awkwardly shaped pieces may require epoxy for good adhesion.
2. Using tweezers, place the smallest beads into the little spaces. Let dry for 24 hours.

Finish:
1. Clean off any excess dried glue with a craft knife or window scraper.
2. Touch up the paint.
3. Paint lavender stripes along the edges of the frame. Let dry. ❑

Tea in the Garden
Flower Pot

This project recycles all those handles left over from breaking up china cups and mugs. I also included plaster teacups made from molds and leftover tile from a neighbor's swimming pool project. Tile stores often sell remnants from jobs and sample boards they no longer need – they are an inexpensive way to get interesting material. My favorite tile store has a discard area where you can fill a substantial cardboard box for very little money. The colorful little teacup shapes were made of plaster. You can mold these yourself using plastic molds and plaster found at craft shops.

SUPPLIES

Surface:
Terra-cotta flower pot, 10" tall, 11" diameter
Terra-cotta saucer (to fit the pot)
4 self-adhesive plastic "feet" (for the pot)

Tesserae:
25 teacup and coffee cup handles, mostly white and cream color
200 round royal blue swimming pool tiles, 1" diameter
12 flat-back clear marbles – Pink and blue
For the teacups:
Plaster
Teacup mold, 1" x 1-1/2"

Other Supplies:
Thinset mortar
Latex admixture
Tile sealer
Grout sealer
Outdoor acrylic paints – Pink, red, black, royal blue
Exterior varnish
Painter's masking tape

Tools:
Variety of brushes (foam, fine tip)
Wheel cutters
Tile nippers
Lazy susan
Paint brushes

INSTRUCTIONS

Prepare:
1. Using a brush, fully cover the entire pot (inside, outside and bottom) with penetrating tile sealer. Seal the saucer too. (This will prevent moisture from seeping through the porous terra cotta and causing tiles to loosen.)
2. Following the plaster manufacturer's instructions and using the molds, make eight plaster teacups. Let dry. *Option:* Make polymer clay teacups.
3. Paint the teacups with the outdoor acrylic paints, using the project photo as a guide.
4. Varnish the teacups and let dry.
5. Cut up enough cups to get 25 intact handles. See "How to Cut Cup Handles." Put aside the remnants of china for another project.

6. Place the terra-cotta pot on a lazy susan for easy access.

Attach the Tesserae:
1. Mix together about one cup of thinset and latex admixture. (Note the time – the chemicals in thinset remain active for 20 to 30 minutes; make new batches as necessary.)
2. Apply the mixture to the back of each teacup handle and position the handles on the rim of the flower pot, using the photo as a guide. Tape the handles in place to avoid slippage. Let dry at least 24 hours.
3. Make a fresh batch of thinset and affix the eight teacups around the body of the flower pot.
4. Fill in the spaces around the teacups with round tiles and the occasional flat back marble. Space the tiles evenly. Let dry for 24 hours. *TIP: Since you are working vertically, it's best to apply the adhesive individually to the back of each piece.*

Continued on page 74

Continued from page 72

Grout:

For more information, see "Grout" and "How to Mix & Apply Grout" in the Mosaic Materials section.

1. Mask off the teacups. See "Protecting Tesserae & Other Objects."

2. Mix several cups of white sanded grout in a large disposable container.

3. Apply the grout first to the body of pot. Wipe away excess and clean up with paper towels.

4. Mix a second batch of white sanded grout and apply to the rim, pushing the grout in and around each handle. Be sure to wipe the grout from the lip of the pot.

5. Wipe away the excess grout with a sponge and clean with paper towels. Let dry.

Finish:

1. Apply two coats of grout sealer. Let dry.

2. Paint the interior of the pot and a saucer with royal blue exterior paint. Let dry.

3. Varnish the painted areas and let dry.

4. Attach plastic "feet" on the bottom of the pot so that it does not sit flat in the saucer. ❏

How to Cut Cup Handles

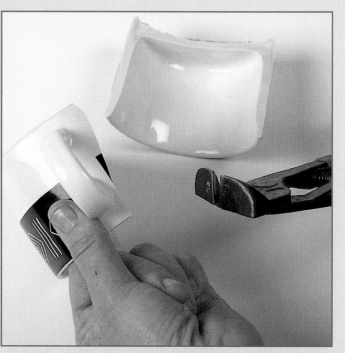

1. Position the tile nippers at the top of the cup next to the handle. Press your thumb along the other side of the handle. Squeeze the nippers to cut the china. A section of the cup will break away.

2. Use the nippers to cut along side the handle, then across the bottom, and up the other side to get an intact handle.

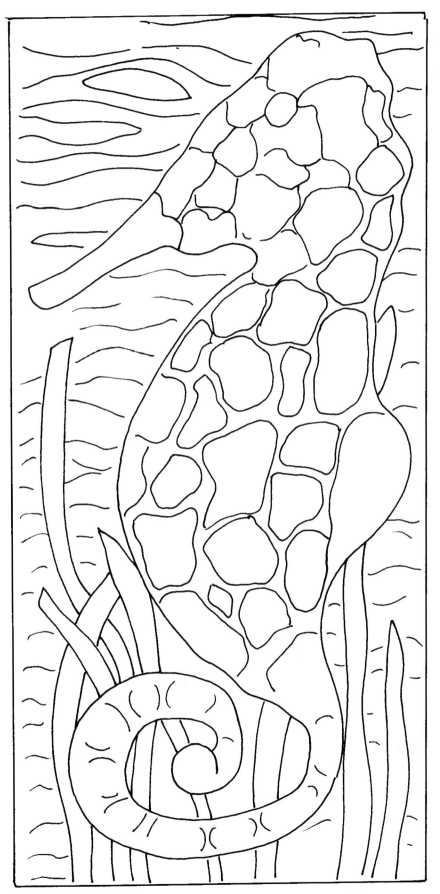

Pattern for Seashell Seahorse
Wall Piece

Enlarge @240% for actual size.

Instructions begin on page 76.

Seashell Seahorse
Wall Piece

I found many interesting shapes of coral, small shells, and debris while beachcombing on the Florida coast. Because the pieces were too large to use on the side of a frame or vase, I laid them out to form the shape of a seahorse – the long coral pieces worked perfectly. The size of the piece was determined by an old frame that I found at an estate sale. I didn't want to grout around the coral and shells and I didn't want to mask off each piece so I used a self-grouting technique to attach them. So that the piece could be used in a bathroom or other moist location, I used waterproof cement foam board as the base. I cut the foam board to fit the frame before I began.

Pattern can be found on page 75.

SUPPLIES

Surface:
Frame, 26" x 13-1/2" with 1" border
Cement foam board, 11" x 24", 1/2" thick (Cement board may be used if cement foam board is not available.)

Tesserae:
60 (approx.) pieces of coral, shells, and beach debris, ranging in size from 1/4" to 5"
Opaque green iridescent glass, 12" square
3 opaque turquoise glass, 12" square (each a different shade, one iridized)
8 large blue millefiori *or* blue flat-back marbles
160 (approx.) small millefiori *or* blue glass beads
2 tubes turquoise seed beads
1 tube purple sparkle seed beads

Other Supplies:
Enamel acrylic paint – Topaz blue
Acrylic paint – Cream
Cement adhesive
Thinset mortar
Adhesive for glass
Cement colorant – Plum
Sanded grout – White
White primer

Black transfer paper
Pencil

Tools:
Spatula
Wheel cutters
Glass cutters
Syringe *or* toothpicks

INSTRUCTIONS

Prepare:
1. Make two photocopies of the pattern. Enlarge as directed or to fit your frame.
2. Prime the cement foam board. Let dry.
3. Place black transfer paper on the board and, on top of that, place one photocopy of the pattern. Use a pencil to outline the seahorse, the seaweed, and the waves. Remove the transfer paper and the photocopy.
4. Position the shells on the second photocopy temporarily.

Attach the Tesserae:
1. Mix approximately 3 cups of thinset and add colorant powder to create purple adhesive.
2. Apply colored thinset to the seahorse outline with a small spatula. Stay within the design lines and make the adhesive bed about 1/4" thick.
3. Pick up the shells from the pattern copy and place them in the same position on the adhesive on the board. Lightly push each piece into the adhesive. The coral and shells should be almost touching, but the adhesive should be visible between the pieces. Let dry.
4. Use a syringe or toothpicks to cover the exposed purple adhesive around the tesserae with white glue. Sprinkle purple sparkle seed beads generously over the glue. Let dry.
5. Cut the green glass into 2" x 1" strips. Nip the glass to create tips and curves to suggest seaweed. Glue in place with glass glue.
6. Cut the blue glass to follow the water pattern, alternating the shades of blue. Leave 1/4" of space along the outside edge of the board to accommodate the edge of the frame. Also leave 10 to 15 curved spaces empty to place millefiori after grouting. Use the photo and patterns as guides for placement.

continued on page 78

continued from page 76

Grout:

For more information, see "Grout" and "How to Mix & Apply Grout" in the Mosaic Materials section.

1. Mix white grout. Tint with topaz blue paint.
2. Apply the grout to the glass and seaweed, pushing right up to the edge of the seahorse.
3. Wipe away the excess with a sponge and clean with paper towels. Let dry.

Finish:

1. Cover the grout and the porous shells of the seahorse with grout sealer.

2. With glass glue, attach the millefiori in the empty spaces.
3. Fill any spaces around the millefiori with turquoise seed beads.
4. Apply silicone adhesive to the 1/4" of space at the edge of the board. Set the frame in place over the board. Let dry.
5. To create a clean edge, run a thin bead of glass glue where the frame and board meet. Apply a single row of turquoise seed beads.
6. *Option:* Apply a line of silicone glue along the back of the board where the board meets the edge of the frame. Let dry.
7. Using the photo as a guide for color placement, paint the frame with cream paint. Add topaz blue borders. Let dry. ❑

Sparkle & Glow
Lamp Base

I discovered this striped paper lamp shade at a vintage store and picked up a simple ceramic lamp base at a thrift shop. The shade inspired the color choice of the crystal tiles. (You could decorate a plain shade if you cannot find a funky one.)

SUPPLIES

Surface:
Lamp base, 8" high, 13" circumference
Lamp shade, 8" high, 20" circumference

Tesserae:
40 metallic green crystal tiles, 3/4"
100 crystal tiles in the same colors as the lamp shade, 3/8"

Other Supplies:
Silicone adhesive
Sanded grout – Terra-cotta
Acrylic paint – Terra-cotta
Sandpaper

Tools:
Tile cutters *or* tile nippers

INSTRUCTIONS

Prepare:
Since the lamp is a glazed ceramic surface, sand it lightly for better adhesion. Wipe away dust.

Attach the Tesserae:
1. Adhere the 3/8" tiles in rows along the base. (I tried to place them in a sequence that corresponded with the stripes on the shade.)
2. Cut the 3/4" metallic green tiles into random shapes and cover the rest of the lamp base. Occasionally intersperse one of the 3/8" tiles for color contrast. Let dry.

Grout:
For more information, see "Grout" and "How to Mix & Apply Grout" in the Mosaic Materials section.
1. Mix the sanded terra cotta grout.
2. Cover the lamp base, taking care not to damage the cord.
3. Wipe away the excess with a sponge and clean up with paper towels. Let dry.

Finish:
1. Paint the exposed portions of the lamp base with terra-cotta acrylic paint.
2. Top with the shade. ❑

Snazzy Salad Set
Decorative Kitchen Utensils

Here's a great way to reinvent those big old decorative wooden utensils with mirror and china. I found a large broken piece of amber-tinted 1/4" thick mirror in the reject pile behind a glass store. This thick mirror works well with pieces of thick china.

Since these types of utensils often have intricately carved handles it is best to cover them with a layer of wood filler to make a smooth surface for the mosaic pieces. Most of these utensils have holes drilled through the top of the handles. On these, I covered the holes on the front but left them exposed on the backs for hanging. If you want the utensils to hang upside down (with the mirrored ends up), use two-armed bicycle hooks to hold them where the head meets the handle.

SUPPLIES

Surface:
Wooden utensils, 24" long with 2" wide handles and 9" heads

Tesserae:
1 sq. ft. mirror, 1/4" thick
Red and white checked china (4 dinner plate rims)
Vegetable-patterned china (10 to 12 large shards for each utensil)
Small refrigerator magnets, small wooden fruit, and/or polymer clay veggies

Other Supplies:
Wood filler
White spray primer
Silicone
Black acrylic paint
Black sanded grout
Distilled water
Grout sealer
Sandpaper
Tack cloth
Painter's masking tape

Tools:
Tile nippers
Wheel cutters
Small spatula *or* putty knife
Whetstone (for smoothing glass edges) *or* diamond file

Tips for Working with Sharp Pieces

When you are working with materials that have sharp edges, it's a good idea to take precautions. Here are some tips:

- **Tumble the pieces.** After you cut pieces of glass and china, put them in a jar with a lid. Add some dish soap and water and a little salt or sand and shake. This tumbling action will remove some sharp edges. (Think of beach glass.)

- **Use a whetstone or file before gluing.** File the edge of a sharp piece by stroking a whetstone along the edge of the piece. Move the stone in one direction.

- **Smooth after grouting.** Once a piece is grouted, if you still have sharp edges, use a file to smooth.

- **Be safe!** When grouting sharp edges, I put adhesive bandages on the tips of my fingers before I put on my gloves. That way, if the glove tears, my fingers are still protected.

INSTRUCTIONS

Prepare:
1. Make sure the wooden utensils are clean. Spray them with white primer. Let dry.
2. Using a small spatula, apply a layer of wood filler over the surface of the handles to fill in crevices. Let dry 24 hours. Sand smooth. Wipe with a tack cloth.
3. Prepare the vegetable shapes – e.g., remove magnet pieces or pin backs – so that the backs are flat.

Cut & Apply the Mirror Tesserae:
The cuts do not have to be perfect, but be very careful of sharp edges. See "Tips for Working with Sharp Pieces" before you begin gluing.

1. Being careful of sharp edges, cut the mirror with tile nippers into about thirty 1/2" pieces for the spoon face.
2. Glue each piece in place individually with silicone, laying them to make a border on the edge of the bowl of the spoon. Nip the edges to make angled shapes as necessary.

Continued on page 82

continued from page 80

3. Fill in the rest of spoon with mirror pieces cut into random shapes. Make sure they are small enough to lay flat and accommodate the slight curve of the spoon.

4. Cut nine 1/2" mirror squares for the inner tines of the fork. Glue them on with silicone.

5. To cover the outer tines of the fork, cut small pieces of mirror for the top. Gradually increase the size of the mirror pieces as you work downward. (The biggest pieces are about 1".)

6. Cut a piece of mirror for the center of the fork. (Mine is 2" x 1-3/4".) Cut a piece (1" x 1-1/2") to place beside it. Let the mirror tesserae dry for 24 hours.

Cut & Apply the Remaining Tesserae:

1. Cut the checked china into 1/4" to 1/2" pieces.

2. Glue the pieces with silicone to the sides of the spoon and fork handles. Let dry.

3. Cut 1" x 1/2" pieces of vegetable-patterned china. If the china is thick use, use tile nippers. If the china is thin, use wheel cutters.

4. Glue approximately nine pieces down the front of each handle, adding a dimensional piece here and there.

5. Fill in any small spots with leftover china pieces. Let dry.

Grout:

For more information, see "Grout" and "How to Mix & Apply Grout" in the Mosaic Materials section.

1. Mask the surfaces of any piece you do not want to be grouted. Use painter's masking tape or see "Protecting Tesserae & Other Objects."

2. Mix the black sanded grout with distilled water.

3. Working one utensil at a time, cover the mirror and china pieces with grout. Be careful and remember the sharp edges.

4. Wipe smooth with a sponge and clean up with paper towels. Let dry.

Finish:

1. Seal with grout sealer.

2. Paint the backs and any exposed edges with black paint. Let dry. ❏

Black & White & Yellow
Domino Box

I made this as a gift for a fanatic domino player to store his game pieces. It started out with three objects: a simple wooden box with a hinged lid, a square candle holder base, and a metal flower. I wanted the box's purpose to be obvious so I covered it with game pieces that, conveniently, are the same thickness as the yummy yellow smalti. They make a nice contrast to all the black and white. This quick and easy project does not require cutting or grouting. I painted the inside of the box with fire engine red for another jolt of color.

SUPPLIES

Surface:
Wooden box with hinged lid, 8" square, 6" tall

Tesserae:
36 dominoes
54 pieces bright yellow smalti
38 white flat-back marbles, 1/4"
28 black flat-back marbles, 1/2"

1 flat metal candle holder with ball feet, 4" square
1 metal flower
Decorative center for flower (flat-back marble, bead or jewel)

Other Supplies:
Acrylic paints – Black, red, white, yellow

Metal paints – White, yellow
White primer
Metal primer
Thinset mortar

Tools:
Paint brushes
Artist's paint brush *or* pencil

INSTRUCTIONS

Prepare:

1. Prime the wooden box. Let dry.
2. Paint the interior with red paint.
3. Paint the exterior with black paint. Let dry.
4. Prime the candle holder and the flower with metal primer.
5. Turn the candle holder upside down. Paint it white with black feet.
6. Paint the flower yellow. Let dry.

Attach the Tesserae:

1. Lay the box on its side. Glue the dominoes and smalti in rows, starting on the bottom left. Use this sequence: 1 vertical piece of smalti, 1 horizontal domino, 1 vertical piece of smalti, 2 horizontal dominoes. Alternate the pattern by one space on each subsequent row.

2. Adhere one row of yellow smalti horizontally along the top.
3. Glue the small white marbles along the edge of the lid. Let the glue dry.
4. Turn the box and glue another side, repeating until all sides are covered. Let the glue dry before turning to the next side.
5. Glue the candle holder upside down on the center of the lid. Let dry. Glue the flower at the center of the candle holder.
6. Glue black flat-back marbles along the edge of the lid to fill in the space between the edge and the candle holder. Let dry.

Finish:

1. Add white polka dots to the flower with the handle end of a paintbrush.
2. Touch up the paint, as necessary. Let dry. ❏

Garden Delights
Stepping Stones

These four stepping stones were a project for a friend's garden. We found the cement stones and tiles at a hardware store and then went to a thrift store to select some china. We found just enough china to cover all four with the same range of colors and patterns. My challenge was to create a different design on each stone – I started with a group of flowers, then a single flower, then a swirl, and finally (with what was left) a random pattern.

Outdoor mosaics made with china are not permanent; most china loses its surface glaze over time. Porcelain china lasts longer than stoneware with transfer patterns.

SUPPLIES

Surfaces:
4 cement stepping stones 12" diameter

Tesserae:
8 to 10 dinner plates – Black, blue, yellow, and red designs
1 brown porcelain tile

Other Supplies:
Thinset mortar
Latex admixture
Sanded grout – Natural gray
Grout sealer
Exterior paint in colors that complement the china

Tools:
Tile nippers
Wheel cutters
Level

INSTRUCTIONS

Prepare:

1. Seal the concrete with grout sealer. Let dry.
2. Break the china rims into 1" to 2" pieces with tile nippers or wheel cutters, depending on the thickness of the china.
3. Copy, enlarge, and transfer the provided patterns *or* draw them freehand on the stepping stones *or* use the patterns as guides for placing the tesserae.

Attach the Tesserae:

Glue the tesserae to the stones, following the instructions and the photos on the following pages. Let the adhesive dry completely before proceeding.

- Following the package instructions, mix a small container of thinset with the latex admixture.
- If your china is of varying thicknesses, build up the thinner pieces to the level of the thicker pieces with additional adhesive.
- Use a level to make sure the surface remains flat.

Grout:

For more information, see "Grout" and "How to Mix & Apply Grout" in the Mosaic Materials section.

1. Mix the gray grout.
2. Working one stone at a time, spread the grout over the tesserae. Take care to fully grout the edges.
3. Wipe away the excess with a sponge and clean up with paper towels. Let dry for 24 hours.

Finish:

1. Seal each stone with grout sealer.
2. *Option:* If the stepping stones will be sitting above the ground, paint the sides of the stones with exterior paint in a colors that complements the china. ❏

Pattern for Single Flower Stepping Stone

(Actual Size)

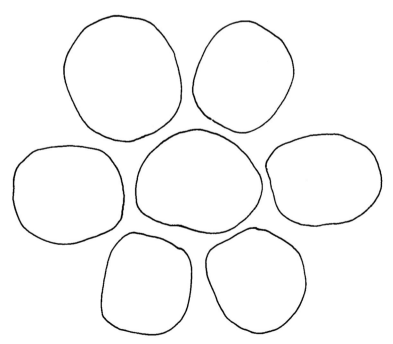

Floral Bouquet Stepping Stone

1. Use the rim of a blue checkerboard plate to create a border around the outside edge, cutting the china into wedges to fit the angles. Leave 2" to 3" along the bottom for brown tile.

2. Break the brown porcelain tile into random shapes to create the "dirt."

3. Nip a circular center for each flower and petals of different colors.

4. Cut green pieces of china to create stems.

5. Use the centers and undersides of plates for the white pieces. ❑

Single Flower Stepping Stone

1. Use the rims of two different black and white plates and alternate pieces to create a border. Nip angles so the curve flows smoothly.
2. Make a second border inside the first with smaller pieces of china, alternating the colors.

3. Cut a circle from black china for the flower center and six petals from bright colors. Glue at the center.
4. Use a contrasting color (here, two shades of blue) to fill the area between the flower and the inner border. ❑

Swirl Stepping Stone

1. Place a 1" piece of black patterned china in the center of the swirl.
2. Use small pieces of china to make the swirl. Angle china pieces with nippers so the swirl maintains a smooth curve.
3. Use white pieces from the plates to fill in around the swirl. ❑

Random Pattern Stepping Stone

1. Glue china pieces along the edge of the stepping stone.
2. Fill in the entire surface with random leftover pieces in various colors and shapes. Watch for "rivers" – long lines of grout that can detract from the tesserae. ❑

Pattern for Swirl Stepping Stone

Enlarge @125% for actual size.

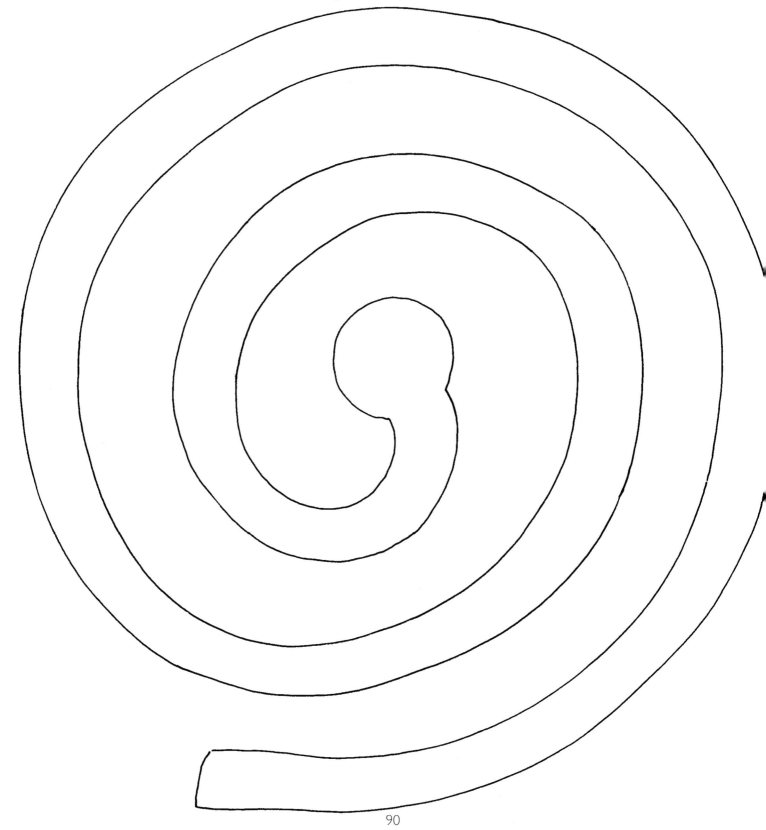

Garden Delights Stepping Stones

Pattern for Floral Bouquet
Stepping Stone
(Actual Size)

Mosaic Bouquet
Wall Art

This mosaic project showcases many techniques for laying tile and using grouts of different colors side by side. The grouting is a two-part process – the vase is grouted first with darker grout; later, the tiles laid around the vase are grouted in a different color. I permanently glued the frame to the plywood base before I began. I invite you to "think outside the box" when gathering pieces to compose the bouquet. The key is layering and more layering.

SUPPLIES

Surface:
Wooden frame with 12" x 16" opening
1/4" plywood, 12" x 16" to fit frame

Tesserae:
30 (approx.) dark moss green vitreous glass tiles, 3/4"
40 (approx.) medium moss green vitreous tiles, 3/4"
40 (approx.) light moss green vitreous glass tiles, 3/4"
Black and white rim from a 12" dinner plate
8 pink millefiori beads, 1/4"
50 (approx.) pieces for the bouquet, 1/4" to 4" (e.g., buttons, brooches, a place-card holder, beads, cabochons, coral, bone, charms, plastic leaves, polymer clay pieces, vinyl, a zipper-pull, ceramic flowers)
Strips of opaque green glass with tapered ends, 6-1/2" x 8" (for stems)

Other Supplies:
White spray primer
1-1/3 yds. pink cording
White PVA adhesive
Silicone adhesive
Epoxy adhesive

White sanded grout
Green universal tint *or* moss acrylic paint
Black sanded grout
Painter's masking tape
Hangers and picture wire
Copper wire

Tools:
Wheel cutters
Tile nippers
Pencil

INSTRUCTIONS

Prepare:
1. Seal the front and the back of the board with primer. Let dry.
2. Glue the board inside the frame with silicone or epoxy adhesive.
3. Attach hangers and wire to the frame before you start the mosaic.
4. Copy, enlarge, and transfer the pattern *or* draw with a pencil. (It is 7" tall and 3-1/2" wide at its widest point.)
5. Cut the plate rim into random pieces, 1/4" to 1/2".

Glue & Grout the Vase:
1. To make the vase, glue down the pieces of china and the millefiori with white glue. Let dry.

2. Mix black sanded grout and cover the vase. Wipe away the excess and clean with paper towels. (For more information, see "Grout" and "How to Mix & Apply Grout" in the Mosaic Materials section.) Let dry.
3. Seal the vase with grout sealer.

Glue & Grout the Background:
1. Starting at the bottom, glue the three shades of green vitreous tiles in a pattern called "opus tessellatum" around the vase. (The alternating rows resemble the bricklaying pattern called "header bond.") Cut the tiles where necessary to fit around the vase. Some tiles will need to be cut in half to complete a row.
2. When you reach the top of the vase, glue strips of green glass to suggest stems and leaves coming out of the vase. Let dry.
3. Continue gluing the green vitreous tiles to complete the background. Cut tile pieces to fit around the green glass pieces. You don't need to cover the area where the bouquet will be.
4. Cut strips of painter's tape and lay them flush along the flat outer edge of the vase to cover the black grout.

continued on page 94

continued from page 92

5. Mix white sanded grout and color with green tint or moss green acrylic paint. (Your goal is a lighter green hue than the tiles.)

6. Spread the grout over the green tiles and the green glass pieces, pushing it right up to the edge of the painter's tape on the vase.

7. Wipe away excess with a sponge and clean up with paper towels. Let dry completely.

8. Remove the painter's tape from the vase.

Create The Bouquet:

This is the fun part! Use the photo as a guide.

1. Use silicone glue (epoxy for heavier pieces) to adhere the materials to create a bouquet. Glue the pieces on top of the green glass pieces, allowing the "leaves" to show in some places. Start with larger flat pieces and add smaller pieces on top. Keep everything as close together as possible.

2. Make a curlicue from beads and copper wire. Glue in place, using the photo as a guide. Let dry.

Finish:

1. Paint the frame with the moss green paint you used to tint the grout. Let dry.

2. Glue the pink cord along the inner edge. ❏

Pattern for Mosaic Bouquet
Wall Art

(Actual Size)

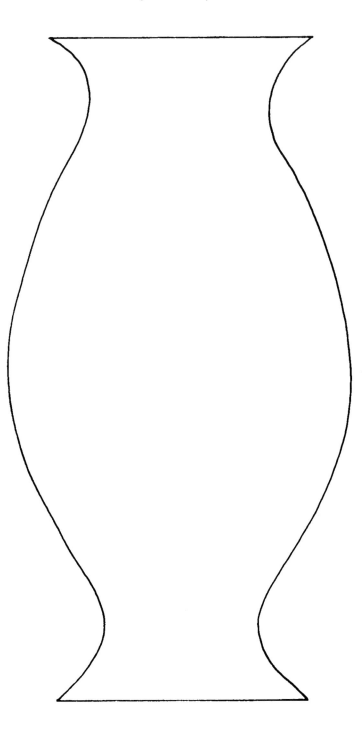

Pattern for Pearls & Periwinkle
Mosaic Cross

Instructions begin on page 96.

Enlarge @125% for actual size

Pattern for cutting your own
cross. Use wood that is 1/2"
thick and cut with a jigsaw.

Pearls & Periwinkle
Mosaic Cross

I made this cross for an elderly lady who loves pearls and periwinkle blue. She donated an old pearl necklace that added sentimental value to the project. The design incorporates jewelry, buttons, pearls, beads, an itty-bitty angel from an ornament, and a polymer clay flower. The wooden shape can be cut with a jigsaw using the pattern provided, or you can buy a pre-cut cross at a crafts shop – just be sure it is wide enough to hold all the tesserae.

Pattern can be found on page 95.

SUPPLIES

Surface:
Wooden cross, 11" x 8", 1/2" thick

Tesserae:
Use a mix of costume jewelry, cabochons, buttons, beads. I used these items.
1 costume pearl necklace, 18" strand with knots
1 pearl bracelet with 20 oval white beads, 1/4"
2 white plastic buttons, 1"
3 white/clear/silver buttons, 3/4"
5 teardrop pearl button covers
20 oblong pearl beads, 1/4"
4 round small pearl beads, 1/2"
1 3-piece dangle pearl earring
2 oval mother-of-pearl earrings
1 pearl and iridized glass earring, 1/4"
1 silver and pearl brooch with blue glass, 1-1/2"
2 squares of mother-of-pearl, 1/2" (from a necklace)
8 white iridized tube beads, 1/2" long
8 blue teardrop cabochons, 1/4"
4 blue cabochons, 1/2"
2 white plastic leaves, 1-1/2"
60 blue beads, various sizes and colors

1 kneeling angel (from Christmas ornament), 1" tall

For the clay flower:
1 small block of polymer clay
1 flower cookie cutter, 2-1/2" diameter

Other Supplies:
1 tube contact cement adhesive
Acrylic paints – Periwinkle blue, white
Varnish
Primer

Tools:
Button shank remover
Long nose pliers
Brushes
Polymer clay tools

INSTRUCTIONS

Prepare:
1. Seal the cross completely with primer. Let dry.
2. Paint the front of the cross with white paint.
3. Paint the sides and the back with periwinkle blue acrylic paint. Let dry.
4. Following the clay manufacturer's instructions, roll out clay to 1/4"

thick. Using a cookie cutter, make a 2-1/2" flower. Bake and let cool *or* let dry according to the clay manufacturer's instructions.
5. Paint the flower with periwinkle blue paint. Set aside.
6. Remove the backs from the buttons and the button covers. Cut the pearl necklace into two pieces, one 12" long and one 6" long. Take apart the jewelry pieces.

Attach the Tesserae:
1. Glue the polymer clay flower on the center of the cross.
2. Run a bead of glue along the edges of the vertical arm of the cross. Position the two pieces of the pearl necklace over the glue, with the longer piece on the longer part.
3. Add the brooch, tube beads, and teardrop blue cabochons to the flower.
4. Arrange and glue the rest of the jewelry pieces and other tesserae to the cross, using the photo as a guide. Fill gaps with small glass jewels and beads.
5. Fill any small spaces with blue seed beads. ❑

Chandelier Mosaics
Lamp Shades

Mosaic lamp shades on a chandelier are a jazzy alternative to fabric shades or plain glass shades.
To make these, cover glass shades (found inexpensively at home recycling centers or thrift shops) or hard plastic shades (available at craft stores) with glittering colored mirror, glass, and flat-back beads and finish with beaded fringe.
Be sure to use silicone adhesive – it works best with mirror tesserae and will withstand the heat of light bulbs. So more light will shine through the shade, I used silver seed beads to fill the "grout" spaces for a more transparent effect. Beads can replace grout on many indoor projects (tabletops are an exception), but the process requires a little more time and patience than the usual grouting. Depending on the look you want to achieve, you can use micro glass beads (the tiny kind that don't have holes), seed beads, or tiny pearls.

SUPPLIES

For one shade
Surface:
Glass or plastic chandelier lamp shade, 5" tall

Tesserae:
20 squares colored mirror in variety of colors, 1/2"
26 squares blue-purple Van Gogh glass, 1/2"
80 random-shaped pieces champagne gold mirror
70 (approx.) flat-back beads of various colors

Other Supplies:
2 tubes silver glitter seed beads (for the "grout")
105 (approx.) assorted beads (for the fringe)
16 gauge wire

Continued on page 100

continued from page 98

2 oz. plastic bottle with a fine metal tip, or syringe
Silicone adhesive
Adhesive for glass
Painter's masking tape
Acetone
2 towels

Tools:

Long nose pliers
Lazy susan
Empty jar or glass (to hold the shade while you work)
Toothpicks *or* dental tool
Craft knife *or* single-edge blade

INSTRUCTIONS

Prepare:

1. Place the shade on the jar or glass. Place the jar or glass on the lazy susan.
2. Divide the area of the shade to make five bands with a 1/2" mirror band along the center. TIP: Use painter's tape to temporarily mark the divisions.

Make the Beaded Dangles:

The fringe is made up of beaded dangles.

1. Cut a 3" piece of wire.
2. Thread a small bead on the wire, 1/4" from the end. Fold the 1/4" end of the wire back over the bead and twist the wire so the small bead is secured in place.

Photo shows "before" and "after" adding seed beads between tessarae.

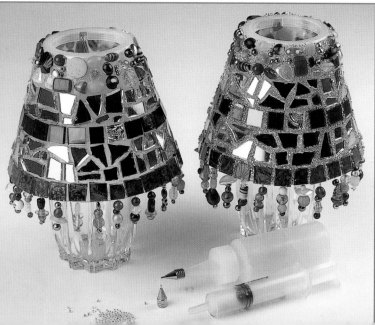

3. Add a larger bead that covers the twisted wire. Add three more beads and set aside.
4. Repeat to make 26 beaded dangles, each 3/4" long.

Attach the Tesserae:

1. Glue a row of colored mirror squares along the center of the shade with dabs of silicone. If excess silicone oozes up between the tesserae, remove with a toothpick or dental tool. (It is important to keep the "grout" spaces clean for the beads.)
2. On the bottom edge of the shade, apply a small dab of silicone and position one beaded dangle with the end of the wire in the silicone and the top bead right at the bottom of the shade. Put a square of blue-purple glass over the wire. Repeat all the way around the shade. Let dry 24 hours. Cut off any excess wire that extends above the glass squares.
3. Glue pieces of gold mirror to form a band between the two rows of square tesserae.
4. Glue a second band of gold mirror pieces the same width as the previous band above the row of colored mirror squares.
5. Finish the top of the shade by gluing flat-back beads along the top 2". Let dry.

Fill the Spaces:

1. Carefully place the shade on its side between two rolled towels. Fill the 2-oz. bottle with glass glue and attach the fine metal tip.
2. Working one small area at a time, apply glue in the grout lines between the tesserae and sprinkle with silver seed beads, allowing the beads to cover the glue and fill the spaces between the tesserae. Let that part of the shade dry before turning it to apply more beads.(This may seem time-consuming but in the long run is more efficient and less messy than covering the whole grout area with glue and pushing on lots of beads at once.) *Options:* Instead of the metal tip, use a toothpick or a veterinary syringe to apply the glue.
3. Repeat until all areas between the tesserae are filled with glue and seed beads. Let dry.

Finish:

1. Touch up any blank spots with more beads.
2. Remove excess silicone with acetone and a craft knife or blade. ❑

Philosophical Baggage

Instructions begin on page 102.

Philosophical Baggage
Suitcase
....

This project is a work of art and a conversation piece, and it can be used
to store memorabilia if you cover it so that it can be opened. Choose a
suitcase with a sturdy frame and a hard surface that will not flex.
For the mosaic, I used tiles from old ceramic sample boards I found at a tile
discount warehouse and a box of unusually shaped wooden knobs I was lucky
to find (at a greatly reduced price!) at a hardware store. Unpainted wooden
knobs can be purchased at craft stores and personalized for mosaic projects.
Put a monogram on one side or a clever saying. Use your computer to print out a
monogram or verse. Enlarge it to the size needed for the size suitcase you are making.

Also pictured on page 101.

SUPPLIES

Surface:
A sturdy suitcase

Tesserae:
For Side One, pictured opposite
Tin picture frame with mirror and
    doors, 7" x 8" (found at Mexican
    import stores)
30 iridized brown flat-back marbles
8 clear flat back marbles, 1"
Paper map pieces
40 (approx.) earth-tone ceramic tiles,
    2" (various colors)
50 burgundy wooden pointed knobs
60 pale yellow unglazed ceramic
    tiles, 3/4"
40 mottled brown unglazed ceramic
    tiles, 1"

*For Side Two, pictured on the previous
    page*
1 small travel pin, back removed
3 sheets bronze colored mirror, 12"
32 iridized golden brown flat-back
    marbles

30 bronze unglazed ceramic tiles, 3/4"
32 dark yellow unglazed ceramic
    tiles, 1"
10 burgundy glazed china plates
4 burgundy wooden pointed knobs

Other Supplies:
Silicone adhesive
Epoxy adhesive
Adhesive for glass
Primer for plastic and vinyl
Sanded grout – Tobacco brown
Painter's masking tape

Tools:
Wheel cutters
Tile nippers
Hammer
Pencil
Scissors
Measuring tape
Large old books

INSTRUCTIONS FOR SIDE ONE

Prepare:
1. Clean the luggage inside and out.
2. Prime the outside with plastic and
   vinyl sealer. Let dry.
3. Design a pattern and transfer it to
   the suitcase side if needed.
4. Place the eight 1" clear flat-back
   marbles on the map pieces and trace
   around them. Cut out the pieces.
   Glue them with glass glue to the
   backs of the clear flat-back marbles.
   (These are the "map marbles.")
5. Break the earth-tone tiles into
   random shapes, using a hammer.
   (You'll nip them into shapes with
   the tile nippers as you place them.)

Attach the Tesserae:
1. Lay the suitcase on its side. Using
   silicone, glue the frame mirror at the
   center.

Continued on page 104

continued from page 102

2. Glue the small iridized marbles around the top and bottom of the frame.

3. Glue the eight map marbles in a loose circle around the frame.

4. Measure and mark a 4" border around the sides and top edges of the suitcase. Cover the rest of the face of the suitcase with earth-tone ceramic tile pieces, mixing the colors.

5. Along the 4" border, glue a row of pointed knobs, alternating each one with a 3/4" yellow unglazed tile.

6. Make a second row, alternating each knob with two 3/4" yellow unglazed tiles, placing the knobs so they are offset to the first row.

7. Add a third row of knobs alternated with two 1" unglazed mottled brown tiles. (These knobs should line up with the first row, taking into account the larger circumference.)

8. Fill in the areas around the hinges and locks with just the brown tile.

Grout:

For more information, see "Grout" and "How to Mix & Apply Grout" in the Mosaic Materials section.

1. Cover the knobs and mirror frame with painter's tape to protect them.

2. Mix and apply the brown sanded grout.

3. Wipe away the excess and clean with paper towels. Let dry.

4. Remove the tape. Touch up the grout around the knobs, if necessary.

INSTRUCTIONS FOR SIDE TWO

Prepare:

1. Turn over the suitcase. Place it on some old large books so the knobs won't get dislodged as you work on the other side.

2. Draw "ONE WAY" at the center of this side. (My letters are 7" tall and 1/4" wide.)

3. Cut each 1" unglazed yellow tile into fourths.

4. Cut pieces of bronze mirror into 4" squares. (You'll cut these into smaller pieces later as needed.)

5. Break the china plates. Cut into random 1" shapes. (You'll nip these to fit as needed.)

Attach the Tesserae:

1. Using silicone, glue down the yellow tile pieces to form the words.

2. Glue the burgundy china around the letters, nipping the pieces to fit, to cover the side of the suitcase, leaving the 6" edge empty and leaving four 1" circles empty. (You'll place the knobs in these spaces after grouting.)

3. Glue one 1" tile in the center of the "O."

4. On the edge of the suitcase, attach one row of alternating small iridized marbles and 3/4" bronze unglazed tiles.

5. Fill in the rest of the edge with bronze mirror pieces.

Grout:

1. Mix the brown sanded grout and apply to the side and edge of the suitcase, leaving spaces ungrouted for the four knobs.

2. Wipe away the excess and clean up with paper towels. Let dry.

3. Seal with grout sealer.

Finish:

1. Using epoxy adhesive, attach the four knobs in the blank spaces. Touch up the grout around them, if necessary.

2. Glue the travel pin over the tile in the center of the "O."

3. Clean up the hinges, locks, and exposed parts of the luggage, removing stray bits of grout or glue. ❏

Party Animal
Garden Sculpture

Broken pieces of transparent tempered glass give a crackled, translucent appearance when used as tesserae. Paper, paint, and dried flowers – to name but a few – can be placed under the glass to add color and interest.

Here, a sad old concrete turtle I found in an abandoned garden has been reinvigorated with paint, tempered glass, and a party hat.

Pictured on pages 106-107.

SUPPLIES

Surface:
Concrete turtle with 14" shell

Tesserae:
1 sq. ft. panel tempered glass, 1/4" thickness
48 iridescent clear flat-back marbles
2 eyes (either painted clear flat-back marbles or eye cabochons, which are available at bead and craft stores)

Other Supplies:
Acrylic outdoor paints – Teal, pink, orange
Silver glitter dust
Sparkle varnish
Silicone adhesive
Sanded grout – Antique white
Lavender acrylic paint (for tinting the grout)
Grout sealer

For the party hat:
Metal cone, 3" tall with 3" bottom and 1" opening at the top
2-3 cups multi-colored seed beads
1/3 yd. ribbon, 1/4" wide

3 beads (1" blue flat, 1/2" round teal, pink plastic)
16 extra small orange millefiori beads
Wax paper
Epoxy adhesive

Tools:
Old cookie sheet
Hammer
Towel
Disposable brush (for applying epoxy)

INSTRUCTIONS

Prepare:
1. Make sure the turtle is clean. Seal with grout sealer. Let dry.
2. Paint the turtle's head, legs, and tail with two coats of teal paint. Let dry.
3. Using the photo as a guide, paint the shell with teal on the top and a pink band, then an orange band. While the paint is still wet, sprinkle silver glitter dust on the shell. Let dry.
4. Put on safety glasses and gloves. Wrap the tempered glass piece in a towel. Place it on the floor and hit one corner with a sharp whack of the hammer. (It will crackle and shatter.) Some of the glass will break apart as you handle it – that's okay.

Attach the Tesserae:
1. Using silicone, glue the marbles along the bottom edge of the shell.
2. Working from the bottom to the top of the painted shell, attach 1" to 2" pieces of tempered glass. Fully cover the back of each piece of glass with silicone and twist and press

Continued on page 106

continued from page 105

the glass to the surface as you attach it to ensure good adhesion. If your turtle's shell is uneven or patterned, use extra silicone to build up the glass pieces. Mold the pieces to the shape of the shell so there are no sharp, pointy edges sticking out, and keep the pieces fairly close together. Let dry for 24 hours.

Grout:
For more information, see "Grout" and "How to Mix & Apply Grout" in the Mosaic Materials section.
1. Mix the sanded antique white grout with purple paint to get a lavender shade. Make a generous amount – you don't want to have to make a second batch and risk creating a different shade of purple.
2. Apply the grout to the shell, making sure to cover the marble border.
3. Wipe away the excess with a sponge and clean up with paper towels.
4. Let the grout dry 24 hours.

Finish:
1. Seal with two coats of grout sealer. Let dry.
2. Attach the turtle's eyes with silicone adhesive.
3. Touch up the teal paint as needed on the turtle's body. Let dry.
4. Cover with a few coats of sparkle varnish. Let dry.

Make the Party Hat:
1. Cover an old cookie sheet with wax paper. Pour on two to three cups of multi-colored seed beads.
2. Cover the metal cone with a layer of silicone. Roll the cone in the beads until it is completely covered. Let dry 24 hours.
3. For extra protection, cover the beads with a thin layer of liquid epoxy. Mix up a small batch and brush it on the cone. Let dry.
4. Use silicone to adhere the orange millefiori beads along the top edge of the cone.
5. Add embellishments on the top: Glue the 1/2" blue bead on the top of the cone. Run the ribbon up through holes of the cone and the bead. Add two more beads. Loop the ribbon back through the middle bead and back down again through blue bead and cone.
6. Put the party hat on the turtle. Tie the ends of the ribbon under the turtle's chin. ❏

Recycled Bathtub
Garden Planter

Ever wondered what to do with an old plumbing fixture or appliance? Before you haul it off to the dump, consider using it as a surface for a mosaic. I found this old porcelain tub by the side of a country road and lugged it home in the back of my minivan (much to my husband's dismay). After a thorough cleaning and the addition of colored glass and tile, it now sits proudly on my back porch, where I use it as a planter.

I found the black and white tile at a home recycling center, and I used gray grout because it acts as a neutral base for a mosaic with so many colors. Given its size, this project will take longer than a weekend, but the result is well worth the time. Since I planned to use my tub as a planter, the mosaic covers the outside of the tub and the area inside the tub that is visible when plants are in place. If you are going to plant flowers in your tub, it is a good idea to cover the drain with a piece of fiber glass mesh or screen so there will be drainage without all the dirt falling out.

Instructions begin on page 110.

Recycled Bathtub

Pictured on pages 108-109.

SUPPLIES

Surface:
Porcelain tub, 5 ft. x 2-1/2 ft.

Tesserae:
65 black unglazed porcelain tiles, 2"
   square
65 white unglazed porcelain tiles, 2"
   square
6 sheets dark green mirror, 12"
   square
25 golden yellow flat-back marbles
4 sq. ft. opaque canary yellow glass
1 sq. ft. opaque bright red glass
10-12 lbs. of multi-colored scrap
   glass
20 flat-back marbles, 1"

Other Supplies:
Silver and/or gold foil one-sided
   sticky tape
Silicone adhesive
Thinset mortar
Latex admixture
All purpose cleaner and degreaser
Sanded grout – Natural gray
Grout sealer
Sandpaper
Acetone

Tools:
Wheel cutters
4 large glass blocks or decorative
   bricks (if your tub doesn't have
   feet)
Foam pad for the knees
Craft knife *or* single-edge blade

INSTRUCTIONS

Prepare:
1. Thoroughly clean and degrease the inside and the outside of the tub. Dry.
2. Lightly sand the porcelain. Vacuum away the dust.
3. Place the tub where you intend to use (or display) it, elevated on glass blocks or bricks if the tub doesn't have feet. (You don't want to have to move it again – it will be much heavier after you apply the tesserae and grout.)

Pictured above: The inside of the tub.

> TIP: It can quickly become physically uncomfortable to work on a large project low to the ground so it is important to move about and stretch at regular intervals. Protect your knees and backside by kneeling and sitting on garden foam pads.

Attach the Tesserae:

1. Mix a batch of thinset and use it to apply a row of alternating black and white tiles along the outside of the tub just below the rim.

2. Apply another row of black and white tiles on the inside of tub at the same height. Adjust the size of the tiles around the spout to accommodate the black and white alternation. Let the tile dry.

3. Nip and glue randomly shaped pieces of yellow glass above the black and white tile inside of the tub, creating a border about 2" tall. Cut the pieces small enough to follow the curvature of the tub, and intersperse the occasional piece of red glass. NOTE: The top edge of the border does not have a uniform edge, as it will merge with pieces of green mirror.

4. Using silicone adhesive, attach small, randomly cut pieces of green mirror to the rest of the inner rim, up to the edge. Intersperse yellow flat-back marbles.

5. Working one area at a time on the outside of the tub below the row of black and white tiles, use thinset to glue assorted pieces of scrap glass and large flat-back marbles. Cover the backs of transparent pieces of glass with silver or gold foil tape before adhering to hide the adhesive.

Create as much variety as possible. Remember to keep the grout lines consistent in size throughout.

Grout:

For more information, see "Grout" and "How to Mix & Apply Grout" in the Mosaic Materials section. On this project, because of its size, the grout is applied in stages.

1. Mix about one gallon of gray grout. Apply to the inner edge and rim. TIP: Use a grout tool or protect your hands really well to avoid cuts from any sharp edges.

2. Wipe away the excess grout with a damp sponge and clean up with paper towels.

3. Mix another gallon of grout and apply to one side of tub. Follow the same cleaning procedure.

4. Mix a third batch of grout and finish the other side of the tub. Clean up. Let dry.

Finish:

1. After 24 hours, apply two coats of penetrating grout sealer.

2. Remove any excess silicone on the surfaces of the tesserae with acetone and a craft knife or blade. ❏

Pictured below: The edge and side of the tub.

Keys to My Heart
Plaque

This project is a great example of a mosaic using extras and leftovers – old keys, a floor tile, and polished river rocks. This requires a little planning (grouting one project and moving directly to another), but it can be done. If you don't have extra wet black grout handy, simply mix up a fresh batch of thinset and tint with black cement colorant. I jazzed up the design with a pink heart bead and some pieces of gold smalti. I particularly like the contrasts between all the different materials. It can be framed (it's very heavy) or displayed on a sturdy stand. TIP: Apply the tesserae on the back of the base tile (the surface with the ridges). The smooth side will give a finished look to the back of the project.

SUPPLIES

Surface:
Stone or ceramic floor tile, 12" square

Tesserae:
70 (approx.) keys, various shapes and sizes
150 polished black river stones, 1/2" to 1-1/2" in diameter
1 pink glass heart-shaped bead, 1-1/2"
11 pieces gold smalti, 1/4"

Other Supplies:
2 cups dark grout and white PVA glue *or* 2 cups thinset mortar tinted with black colorant
Thinset mortar
PVA adhesive
Black sanded grout
1 bottle stone polish
Optional: Black acrylic paint

Tools:
Dental tool

INSTRUCTIONS

Prepare:
1. Make sure the tile is clean and dry.
2. Mix two tablespoons of white PVA glue into two cups of wet, dark grout. Stir well.
3. Place the ball of grout on the center of the tile. Flatten it with your palm until it is 5" in diameter and 3" thick.

Attach the Tesserae:
1. Beginning at the bottom of the grout disc, insert the head of a key halfway into the grout. Insert another key next to it. Make a complete ring of keys.
2. Begin a second circle of keys on top of the first. TIP: To keep the key heads in place temporarily, set a small flat stone between keys that are laying on top of each other. Continue making circles of keys in the grout, reserving the smallest keys for the innermost circle. Leave a 2" space to place the heart bead.
3. Put some white glue on the back of the heart bead before pressing it into the grout. Let dry.

4. Using thinset mortar, cover the rest of the tile with black river rocks. Place them close together, and leave the occasional space for a piece of gold smalti.
5. Adhere the pieces of gold smalti with PVA adhesive. Let dry 24 hours.

Grout:
For more information, see "Grout" and "How to Mix & Apply Grout" in the Mosaic Materials section.
1. Mix the black sanded grout and apply to the rocks, working the grout around the key base.
2. Wipe away the excess grout from the rocks and clean with paper towels.
3. Use a dental tool to remove any grout on the keys.

Finish:
1. Apply grout sealer to all the grout.
2. *Option:* Paint the edge of the tile with black paint. Let dry.
3. Following the bottle instructions, apply stone polish to the river rocks and the grout for a shiny appearance. ❏

Tempered Glass Collage
Mosaic Table

This glass-on-glass project is semi-transparent –
it looks incredible outside when the light shines
through the glass. Tempered glass tesserae are
placed atop a collage of colored tissue paper.
I found this table at a thrift shop. Since its glass top
sits down in its frame, I didn't have to worry about
the edges. If your tabletop has an exposed edge, you
can cover it with a thin roll of epoxy putty and
paint the putty to match the grout.
Workshops are a marvelous way to expand your
mosaic repertoire. I learned this technique at a
workshop with California artist Ellen Blakeley.

Instructions begin on page 116.

Tempered Glass Collage
Mosaic Table

Pictured on pages 114-115.

SUPPLIES

Surface:
Metal table 20" high with a glass top 17-1/2" square and 3/8" thick

Tesserae:
Panel of tempered glass, 1/4" thick, 18" square

Other Supplies:
4-5 sheets tissue paper, 8" x 10", in different patterns including iridescent
3 bottles glitter dust – 1 blue, 1 gold, 1 silver
Epoxy adhesive
Sanded grout – Natural gray
Grout sealer
White PVA adhesive
Water
Glass cleaner (ammonia-based)

Tools:
Foam brush
Flat-bottomed oblong glass casserole
Towel
Hammer
Craft knife *or* single-edge blade

INSTRUCTIONS

Prepare:
1. Clean the glass tabletop thoroughly with ammonia-based glass cleaner.
2. Wrap the piece of tempered glass in a towel and, wearing your safety gear, smack a corner of the glass piece with a hammer. Set aside the shards.
3. In the glass casserole, mix enough white glue and water (1 part glue to 4 part water) to half fill the dish. The mixture should be the consistency of skim milk.
4. Tear pieces of tissue in 3" to 5" pieces. Working one piece of paper at a time, dip the paper in the glue/water mixture so it's fully wet. Immediately place the wet tissue on the glass tabletop. The tissue may tear when it is wet – that's okay; just make sure it lays completely flat. Keep adding tissue pieces, overlapping them, so the tabletop is completely covered.
5. When the tabletop is covered with tissue and still wet, sprinkle approximately one tablespoon of each color of glitter dust. Let dry 24 hours.

Attach the Tesserae:
Using two-part epoxy, apply adhesive to the backs of 1" to 3" shards of tempered glass. The whole back of the glass piece should be completely covered. Position the glass on the tabletop, working from the edges into the center. Make sure no pieces hang off or have points on the edge. The glass will come apart as you work with it – that's okay once it is laid down – just don't press so hard that the glass continues to break into tiny pieces. Push the smallest pieces together and try to keep the grout lines a consistent size. Let dry for 24 hours.

Adding an Epoxy Coating

If your tabletop has an uneven surface, it can be coated with a layer of liquid epoxy, which will give it more protection and provide a smooth surface. If you use the epoxy coating, the table should not be placed outdoors in direct sunlight.

Here's how:
1. Tape the edges of the tabletop mosaic with several pieces of masking tape to create a stiff border. Cover your work surface with freezer paper and place the tabletop on the freezer paper.
2. Mix the epoxy, following the manufacturer's instructions exactly. Make enough of the mixture to cover the table in one pouring. Stir for at least two full minutes.
3. Pour over the surface. Use a hair dryer to remove the air bubbles. Let dry.
4. Remove the tape. Use fine sandpaper to smooth the edges, if needed. ❑

Grout:

For more information, see "Grout" and "How to Mix & Apply Grout" in the Mosaic Materials section.

1. Mix the sanded gray grout and apply to the tabletop making sure to cover all the edges.
2. Wipe away the excess grout with a sponge and clean up with paper towels. Let dry.

Finish:

1. Seal with grout sealer. Let dry.
2. Scrape away dried epoxy from the surface with a craft knife or blade.
3. *Option:* Apply an epoxy coating. See "Adding an Epoxy Coating." ❑

Glass on Glass
Window Sash

Strips of glass and flat-back marbles in a variety of colors are glued on the glass in an old window sash in a colorful design reminiscent of Art Deco design.
I found this old window sash at the Habitat for Humanity shop. Builders donate leftover materials from construction and demolition sites to the shop, which sells them to the public. The profits, in turn, go toward building new homes for those in need. Shopping is truly guilt-free since the prices are very low and your money goes to a good cause!

Pictured on pages 118-119.

SUPPLIES

Window sash with 6 panes, each
    10" x 13"

Tesserae:
6 sq. ft. translucent glass, various
    colors
18-20 large flat-back marbles, various
    colors

Other Supplies:
Glass cleaner
Brown wood stain (for window sash,
    if needed)
Black sanded grout
Grout sealer
Painter's tape

Clear adhesive for glass
Hooks & chain (for hanging)

Tools:
Glass scorer
Ruler
Running pliers
Wax crayon
Glass scraper
Brush (for stain)
Dental tool *or* toothpicks
Craft knife *or* single-edge blade

INSTRUCTIONS

Prepare:
1. Clean the window sash. (I stripped the paint and scraped the glass, then sanded the window sash.)
2. Stain the window sash and let dry.
3. Cut the glass into approximately 90 strips, varying in height (12" to 2") and width (1/2" to 1").
4. Clean the glass pieces to remove any cutting oil or fingerprints.

continued on page 118

continued from page 117

Attach the Tesserae:

Spread a thin layer of clear adhesive over the back of a piece of glass, covering it completely. Start in the lower left corner, placing the glass strips on the glass pane. Add more strips to cover the window pane, varying the colors and textures of glass. Use three to five glass marbles per pane, interspersing them with the strips of glass in different formations for each pane. If adhesive oozes up between the glass strips, remove it with a toothpick or dental tool. Let dry.

Grout:

For more information, see "Grout" and "How to Mix & Apply Grout" in the Mosaic Materials section.

1. Cover the wood edge with painter's tape.
2. Mix the black sanded grout.
3. Apply to each pane. Wipe away the excess with a sponge and clean up with paper towels. Let dry.
4. Remove any adhesive from the glass surface with a craft knife or window scraper.

Finish:

1. Seal with grout sealer.
2. Attach hooks for hanging. The number and placement depend on the size and weight of the window. ❏

Jungle Rest Stop
Birdfeeder

Some slate pieces left over from a building project were used to cover the roof of this birdfeeder – I hoped it would look like a jungle rest stop. I took apart old costume jewelry to get the various green leaves and added other leaves purchased from a bead store. I prefer to use ceramic birdhouses and feeders for outdoor mosaics. Decorative wooden birdhouses – found in crafts stores – will not survive being outdoors and cannot be cleaned properly. I found this birdfeeder sitting out with the neighbor's trash. I brought it home and gave it a good bleaching and scrubbing, and it was ready to go.

SUPPLIES

Surface:
Ceramic birdfeeder, 14" high

Tesserae:
Slate, 1/4" thick (You'll need enough for about 120 pieces, each 1". Because slate crumbles and the layers separate easily, have enough that you can afford rejects.)
80 pieces small millefiori
20 ceramic leaves, large and small, in two shades of green
14 lime green opaque glass leaves, 2" long (from a bead store)
8 green transparent plastic leaf beads (from a bead store)
5 transparent glass leaves, 1"
3 curly bright green resin leaves, 1"
Dark green mirror glass, 6" square
Opaque green iridescent glass, 8" square
Green rippled glass, 4" square
Light green opaque glass, 8" square

Other Supplies:
Silicone adhesive
80 beads (mostly glass, some plastic) – Red, brown, purple, green
22 gauge copper wire
Sanded grout – Lipstick red, tobacco brown

The birdfeeder as I found it.

Acrylic outdoor paints – Bright red, brown
Grout sealer
Stone sealer (for the slate)
Bleach
White vinegar
Cotton swabs

Tools:
Hammer
Tile nippers
Wheel cutters
Wire cutters
Paint brushes

INSTRUCTIONS

Prepare:
1. Bleach and clean the birdfeeder.
2. Break the slate into small pieces (1" to 1-1/2"), using a hammer and tile nippers.

Attach the Tesserae:
1. With silicone, glue the slate pieces in nine circular rows around the roof, varying the positioning so the pieces don't line up vertically.
2. Below the bottom row of slate, attach one row of millefiori.
3. Cut the green mirror into small pieces and attach with silicone inside the alcove on each side of the birdfeeder.
4. Using the photo as a guide, glue the resin leaves above the opening of the birdfeeder.
5. Glue the glass pieces and bead leaves to suggest leafy branches along the sides of feeder. Fill the empty spaces with green glass, cut in small random shapes.

6. Cut the iridescent green glass into 1/4" wide strips. Glue in a band along the bottom of the feeder. Let dry.

Grout:

1. **Very important!** Seal the slate before grouting – otherwise, it will stain. Follow the package directions, brush the stone sealer on the slate. Let dry.

2. Mix up the red grout. Apply to the slate roof, pushing grout into all the crevices around the stone. For more information, see "Grout" and "How to Mix & Apply Grout" in the Mosaic Materials section.

3. Wipe clean with a sponge and paper towels.

4. Remove any red grout from the slate by wiping off the grout with a cotton swab dipped in white vinegar. Then use a wet (with water) cotton swab to wipe off the vinegar. Let dry.

5. Mix the brown sanded grout. Apply it to the bottom half of the feeder, again pushing the grout into all the crevices.

6. Wipe away the excess with a sponge and clean with paper towels. Let dry.

Finish:

1. Seal the entire birdfeeder with grout sealer.

2. Paint any parts of the birdhouse not covered by the mosaic with bright red outdoor acrylic paint. Let dry.

3. Add two coats of exterior grade varnish. Let dry.

4. String 30" of copper wire through the opening at the top of the bird-feeder.

5. String 12" of beads on each end of the wire. Twist the wire together above the beads.

6. Use the remaining wire to fashion a loop for hanging. ❏

Queen of the Garden
Mosaic Shovel Head

Frying pans and hubcaps have been popular with mosaic artists for making portraits –
here's one using a discarded garden tool! The advantage of a shovel is that it has a built-in nose.
This shovel had a broken handle and was languishing in the corner of a garden shed.
Because the base is metal and it is going to hang outdoors, proper preparation
and using an appropriate adhesive are essential.

SUPPLIES

Surface:
Metal shovel head, 9" x 12"

Tesserae:
8 cups china shards in bright colors and patterns
2 yellow flower metal knobs (for the "cheeks," found at a kitchen decor shop)
1 red lips refrigerator magnet
2 triangular blue beads (for the flower centers)

Other Supplies:
Silicone adhesive
Epoxy adhesive
White marker
Exterior metal primer
Outdoor enamel paint – Black
Black sanded grout
Grout sealer
Steel wool *or* sturdy brush

Tools:
Wheel cutters
Tile nippers
Craft paint brush

INSTRUCTIONS

Prepare:
1. Clean the shovel with steel wool or a sturdy brush to remove any debris.
2. Prime the metal. Let dry.
3. Paint with black paint. Let dry.
4. Use a white marker to draw the outlines of the eyes, using the photo as a guide. Mark where the lips and flower "cheeks" will be placed after grouting. Leave these areas empty until after grouting.
5. Cut the china into shapes:
   3/4" random-sized brightly colored pieces (for the face)
   14 strips, each 1" long, all from the same pattern (for the eyelashes)
   2 dark circles (for the eyeballs)
   4 triangles of white china (for the eyes)
   24 black pieces of various lengths (to outline the eyes)

Attach the Tesserae:
Use the photo as a guide.
1. With silicone, glue the eyes – first the circular eyeballs, then a triangle of either side of each circle.
2. Glue the black china strips to outline the eyes. Cut the pieces so that they angle and flow around the eyes.
3. Glue the eyelash pieces.
4. Adhere china pieces to outline the mouth.
5. Glue down china along the edges of the shovel and along the top above the eyes.
6. Fill in the rest of the face with rows of pieces that follow the same size and shape of the tiles already attached.

Grout:
1. Mix the black sanded grout.
2. Apply to the face, right up to the edge of the mouth and the cheeks.
3. Wipe away the excess with a sponge and clean up with paper towels. Let dry.

Finish:
1. Seal with grout sealer. Let dry.
2. Glue the lips, the cheek flowers, and the beads for the flower centers with epoxy adhesive. Let dry.
3. Touch up the black paint, if necessary. Let dry. ❑

Tropical Pink Flamingo
Garden Ornament

This flamingo, originally a hollow metal form, was a leftover window prop
from a store that was going out of business. I covered it in wire mesh,
concrete, thinset mortar, and glass for a new tropical appearance. It sounds
more complicated than it really is. The key is to work in stages.
Metal animals are available at garden and import shops. (I have seen birds,
ladybugs, turtles, and frogs, to name but a few.) When choosing a metal form as
a base for a mosaic, make sure the points of contact of the metal are securely welded,
and confirm that the base is stable enough to hold the weight of the mosaic.

SUPPLIES

Surface:
Metal flamingo, 6-1/2 feet tall
4 yds. galvanized fine wire mesh *or*
    metal lathe

Tesserae:
10 sq. ft. opaque coral stained glass
2 sq. ft. iridized coral stained glass
3 cups of 3/8" ceramic mixed tiles –
    Coral shades
1 sq. ft. opaque black stained glass
1 sq. ft. opaque white stained glass
40 coral vitreous tiles, 3/4"
6 dark yellow vitreous tiles, 3/4"

Other Supplies:
Acrylic paint – Light orange
Sanded grout – White
Grout sealer
Metal primer
Quick-setting concrete mix
Concrete fortifier
Plastic sheeting
22-gauge tie wire
Silicone adhesive
Painter's masking tape
Thinset mortar

Tools:
Wheel cutters
Glass scorer
Running pliers
Ruler
Long nose pliers
Trowel
5-gallon paint bucket *or* container
Metal shears
Wire cutters
Leather gloves
Sanding tool
Spray bottle
Pencil

INSTRUCTIONS

Prepare:
1. Paint the form with metal primer.
   Let dry.
2. Wearing leather gloves, wrap the
   metal form with the wire mesh and
   mold the wire to its contours. When
   two pieces of mesh meet, tie them
   together with wire. Twist the wire
   tightly with pliers to ensure a firm
   connection. Make sure the entire
   form is covered.

3. Mix the quick-setting concrete with
   fortifier in the 5-gallon container.
   Mix in small batches so it won't set
   up before you can use it all.
4. Working quickly, put some concrete
   mix on the face of the trowel and
   push it across and against the mesh,
   using an upward wiping motion.
   Do not push the concrete inside
   the mesh. In difficult areas (like the
   belly) use your hands to apply and
   compress the concrete. Expect
   pieces to fall off – just reapply them.
5. Cover the body with plastic sheeting and allow the concrete to set up
   according to the package instructions (24 hours).
6. Remove the plastic and spray the
   flamingo form lightly with water.
   Wearing a mask and goggles, use a
   sanding tool to remove any un-
   wanted, excess pieces of concrete.
7. Mix the thinset mortar. Apply a
   thin coating with a trowel over the
   concrete to smooth out the form.
   Cover again with plastic for 24 hours.

Continued on page 126

continued from page 124

8. Remove the plastic and spray lightly with water. Sand away any rough or bumpy spots.
9. Using a pencil, draw the face (nostrils and eyes) directly on the thinset.

Attach the Tesserae:
1. Cut the black glass into small pieces. Using silicone adhesive, attach them to the first 4" of the beak. (See the photo.) Make sure the pieces are small enough to follow the curves without sharp edges.
2. Cut the yellow tesserae into 1/8" pieces. Glue on the nostril outlines.
3. Cut two 1" circles of black glass for the eyes. Glue in place.
4. Cut the white glass into random shapes, making the pieces about the same size as those of the black glass. Glue them on the upper part of the beak and around the nostrils and eyes. (See the photo.)
5. Cut the coral stained glass into rectangles and squares using wheel cutter or glass scorer. Apply to the body of the flamingo, leaving areas for the iridized glass and the vitreous tiles. Using the photo as a guide, try to create flowing lines. TIP: Variety in the size and placement of the glass adds to the overall effect.
6. Cut the iridized glass into small random shapes and fill half the empty areas.

7. Cut the vitreous glass tiles into various shapes. Use them to fill the rest of the empty areas. Let dry.

Grout:
Because this is a big project, it is necessary to grout it in three or four stages. For more information on grouting, see "Grout" and "How to Mix & Apply Grout" in the Mosaic Materials section.
1. Mix the black sanded grout and cover the entire beak and eyes.
2. Wipe away the excess with a sponge and clean up with paper towels. Let dry.
3. Cover the outer edge of the black grouted area with painter's tape.
4. Mix several cups of the white sanded grout with light orange paint until you have a pale peach color. When you mix the colored grout, measure the ingredients carefully and make notes so successive batches will match. **TIP: Cover the flamingo with damp towels to prevent the grout from drying out too fast if you are working outdoors.**
5. Apply the grout to the flamingo, working from the neck down.
6. After applying the first batch, wipe away the excess with a sponge and clean up with paper towels.
7. Mix other batches of grout and apply the same way. Let dry.
8. Remove the tape. Seal with grout sealer. Let dry. ❏

Metric Conversion Chart

Inches to Millimeters and Centimeters

Inches	MM	CM	Inches	MM	CM
1/8	3	.3	2	51	5.1
1/4	6	.6	3	76	7.6
3/8	10	1.0	4	102	10.2
1/2	13	1.3	5	127	12.7
5/8	16	1.6	6	152	15.2
3/4	19	1.9	7	178	17.8
7/8	22	2.2	8	203	20.3
1	25	2.5	9	229	22.9
1-1/4	32	3.2	10	254	25.4
1-1/2	38	3.8	11	279	27.9
1-3/4	44	4.4	12	305	30.5

Yards to Meters

Yards	Meters	Yards	Meters
1/8	.11	3	2.74
1/4	.23	4	3.66
3/8	.34	5	4.57
1/2	.46	6	5.49
5/8	.57	7	6.40
3/4	.69	8	7.32
7/8	.80	9	8.23
1	.91	10	9.14
2	1.83		

Index

Index